POETRY OF
THE PASSION

POETRY OF THE PASSION

Studies in Twelve Centuries of English Verse

J. A. W. BENNETT

CLARENDON PRESS · OXFORD
1982

Oxford University Press, Walton Street, Oxford OX2 6DP
London Glasgow New York Toronto
Delhi Bombay Calcutta Madras Karachi
Kuala Lumpur Singapore Hong Kong Tokyo
Nairobi Dar es Salaam Cape Town
Melbourne Auckland
and associates in
Beirut Berlin Ibadan Mexico City Nicosia

Published in the United States by
Oxford University Press, New York

British Library Cataloguing in Publication Data
Bennett, J. A. W.
    Poetry of Passion.
    1. Jesus Christ in fiction, drama, poetry, etc.
    2. English poetry—History and criticism
    I. Title
    821'.008'0382 PR1195.C48
    ISBN 0-19-812804-5

Library of Congress Cataloging in Publication Data
Bennett, J. A. W. (Jack Arthur Walter)
    Poetry of the Passion.
    Includes index.
    1. English poetry—History and criticism.
    2. Jesus Christ in fiction, drama, poetry, etc.
    3. Devotional literature—History and criticism.
    4. Jesus Christ—Passion.   I. Title.
    PR508.J4B46   1982   821'.009'382   81-18708
    ISBN 0-19-812804-5   AACR2

Filmset in 'Monophoto' Plantin by
Eta Services (Typesetters) Ltd., Beccles, Suffolk
and printed in Great Britain
at the University Press, Oxford
by Eric Buckley
Printer to the University

He is stretched out upon the Cross who by His word stretched out the heavens. He is held fast in bonds who has set the sand a bound for the sea. He is given gall to drink who has given us wells of honey. He is crowned with thorns who has crowned the earth with flowers. . . . That countenance was spat upon at which the Cherubim dare not gaze.

(St. Amphilochius)

A few drops of blood renew the whole world and do for all men what rennet does for milk: joining us and binding us together.

(St. Gregory)

    Recordare sanctae crucis
  qui perfectam vitam ducis
      delectare jugiter.
  Sanctae crucis recordare
  et in ipsa meditare
      insatiabiliter.

(ascribed to St. Bonaventure)

PREFACE

THESE studies make no claim to completeness. They are selective, and the selection is far from systematic. The theme merits the attention of another Abbé Bremond, who could give us a Literary History of Religious Thought in England and could combine the Latin learning of a Louis Gougaud or an André Wilmart with the knowledge of vernacular texts displayed by my friends the late Rosemond Tuve and the late Rosemary Woolf. My prime purpose has been to expose a vein that runs right through those texts, and to indicate how poems cradled in the so-called Ages of Faith can still speak to our condition. I cite cognate prose works only for confirmatory value or when their lyrical tone approaches the condition of poetry. The modern novelists discussed in the closing pages have their place as showing an intuitive awareness of the centrality of the Crucifixion in human experience.

The Cross remains a magnetic *mysterium*. Medieval artists represented *Ecclesia* as a fair and noble lady standing beside that Cross. Modern theology, eager to eschew 'triumphalist' associations, is in danger of reducing its sign-value, and even of misreading its signs: it was a churchman who recently averred that 'in accepting the violence of the Cross God in Jesus Christ sanctified violence into a redemptive instrument for bringing into being a fuller human life'. None of the poets here treated would have understood the meaning of this assertion. The human claims to a portion of divinity, implicit in their verse, as they are in traditional liturgy, rest on far firmer foundations.

J. A. W. B.

Professor Bennett died on 29 January 1981, shortly after delivering this book to his publisher. The Delegates of the Press are grateful to Mrs. Dorothy McCarthy for her work in preparing it for publication, to Mr. Douglas Matthews for the index, and to Professor Norman Davis for a great deal of assistance throughout, including the reading of the proofs.

CONTENTS

I

A VISION OF A ROOD

Dux vitae regnat mortuus.
(Easter liturgy)

THE history of Christian poetry in England begins with a masterpiece. That the poem in question belongs to the early eighth century is suggested by the presence of a long extract from it in runic form carved on the cross that still stands at Ruthwell in Dumfriesshire, and that can reasonably be assigned to that period. The passage cited thereon forms part of a complex programme of lettering and sculpture and was evidently chosen because of its peculiar fitness for a rood-like pillar, making it verily a speaking cross. A monument of such dramatic power, carved with such masterly assurance, set up on the very limits of north-west Europe some fifty years after the Synod of Whitby and probably before Charlemagne was born, must still astonish us. It is rightly called a *beacn*, a beacon, a sign. It casts a strong beam of light in what we are pleased to call the Dark Ages. It should be the first object of English pilgrimage.

The full text of the poem found in part at Ruthwell is preserved in a collection of Anglo-Saxon homilies and verse now at Vercelli in North Italy, once a halting place for English pilgrims to Rome. Like the other poems or parts of poems in the manuscript (including Cynewulf's poem on the discovery, or 'Invention', of the Cross, now known as the *Elene*), it is untitled. To give it a title is to rob it of its enigmatic quality. Modern editors (who needlessly and tendentiously supply modern capitals) call it 'The Dream of the Rood'.[1] But we shall see that this title could be bettered.

Like the stone cross that carries its central lines, the poem is still known to few besides students, so an outline of its main theme will be in order. (Readers unfamiliar with the poem will find it helpful at this point to consult the translation of lines 1–86 appended to this chapter.) A narrator purports to describe a strange dream of a wondrous tree, decked in gold and jewels that illuminate the whole earth whilst stirring in the dreamer a deep consciousness of sin. It changes in aspect, at times revealing marks of a conflict, at times flowing with blood. At length it gives voice; and to this utterance the greater part of the poem is devoted. It tells of a tree cut down to bear a criminal, a tree that a young warrior who is Lord of mankind resolves to climb. Gradually warrior and tree become identified. The dark nails that pierce him pierce the tree. Darkness overwhelms them both.

Though the emotions depicted are complex, the narrative itself is swift and spare. The revelatory climax is quickly reached:

> Rod wæs ic arǽred; ahof ic ricne cyning,
> heofona hlaford, hyldan me ne dorste.

> As a rood was I raised up, bearing aloft a noble King,
> Lord of the heavens. Bend I durst not.

When the tree so names itself again it is in the stark, impersonal half-line: 'Crist wæs on rode' (56).

This rood is not only vocal but sentient. It sees God stretched out in pain (*þearle þenian*, 52). It sees men coming to lift him down, and bends to help them (59). It knows that he rested for a space in a tomb (64). If of its own later history it says merely that it was cut down and buried, to be discovered later and decked with gold and silver, it is because English readers or hearers would take at once this allusion to the Invention of the Cross by Helena the British princess: a legend that was to be annually re-enacted by guilds at Ipswich and Beverley and painted in a Stratford church before it became the theme of Piero della Francesca's masterpiece at Arezzo.

This rood-tree, then, both reflects and shares the sufferings of its human burden, is both obedient to his will and the expression of it. Indeed, we are made more conscious of its pain than of Christ's. It is deeply human, creaturely. When it says, 'Weop eal gesceaft, cwiðdon cyninges fyll'

(55–6: All creation wept; lamenting the death (fall) of the king), it speaks not only for the cosmos but as part of it. This is not simply a literary device but the very *raison d'être* of the poem. And perhaps only poetry can present the ineffable mystery of the two natures of Christ that meets us whenever we survey this wondrous cross on which the Prince of Glory *died*. For in poetry this rood can take on his human voice, his human aspect as a servant obedient unto death ('. . . obediens usque ad mortem, mortem autem crucis': Phil. 2:8), his total *humanitas*, yet at the same time present the warrior-prince who mounts it as God Almighty, intent on redeeming mankind. Creator and created are one; and when the rood utters its griefs it speaks also of its Lord's. That this is how the poet thought is clear from his final posture after he has awoken, and awoken also to the meaning of his vision: 'Gebæd ic me þa to þan beame', he writes (122): 'Then prayed I to that tree'. He prays to the Rood, not to the prince: it has become a symbol, and more than a symbol, for the incarnate Lord, now in heaven. In the figure of the sentient tree the poem brings almost within our grasp the mysterious *communicatio idiomatum* (*una persona, duae naturae*) of the theologians;[2] an achievement that bespeaks both an inventive subtlety and a profound faith, and demonstrates, incidentally, that our earliest poetry was neither primitive nor naïve.

The choice of a dream frame and theme would itself indicate that the poet was steeped in Christian Latin culture. Though every line of the poem is taut with the intensity of personal feeling and experience, we are not required to take it as a literal record, but rather as a fresh and vivid apprehension of the significance of that sign which had in vision appeared to the emperor Constantine with the memorable prophecy, 'In hoc signo vinces'. To that vision Constantine had owed his victory at the Milvian Bridge (AD 312) and the Church its realization of the power of the Cross as image and symbol. But one might say that this poem testifies to a conversion as important as Constantine's: the early conversion of the English poetic mind to the service of the Rood.

The poet's preoccupation with the mysterious identity of

Rood and Ruler (prepared for by the phrase *wealdendes treow*, 17: Ruler's tree) suffices to explain why, unlike later writers, he gives no space at all to the events that lead up to the Crucifixion. There was nothing eccentric in this: they hardly figure in Christian art or literature of the period, though the designer of the Ruthwell cross (for example) devotes large panels to other New Testament scenes. Early Christian art had presented Christ as Pastor, not as a crucified King. To study the poetry of the Passion is to trace the transmutation of *Christus rex* into *Christus miles* and, later, into *vir dolorum*, the Man of Sorrows. Not that early poets ignored his sufferings. In the Anglo-Saxon *Christ* the Saviour himself describes his agonies as he hung on the high rood, and appeals by virtue of them to the men who still hang him on the rood of Sin. Yet throughout that poem Christ is named only as King, Ruler, or Prince of Victory. In the poem before us, earlier than the *Christ* by at least a century, one phrase and one phrase only pertains to suffering: *þearle þenian* (52): he is grievously stretched out—hence he will be described at the Deposition as 'limb-weary' (63): the limbs were stretched to exhaustion. All the other sufferings are associated with the tree. It is the tree that is pierced by the nails (46), drenched with gore (48), acquainted with grief (59). True, in addressing the dreamer the Rood will speak of the sufferings of the Son of God (83–4). Yet it still insists on its own 'sore sorrows' (80).

The rhetorical figure in which inanimate objects are endowed with speech and personality is known as proso-popoeia. Our poet probably knew late Latin examples of it. But for any comparable example of a speaking cross we must go forward five centuries to the rhetorician Geoffrey de Vinsauf (named by Chaucer), who in his textbook in verse, the *Poetria Nova*, happens to give a long complaint by the Cross as an example of this very figure, beginning at the same point as the Rood (cf. 29–30):

Crux ego raptor, vi rapta manu canina . . .

As a cross seized by force, by bestial hands, do I complain . . .

But we can establish no link between the two poets, and

Geoffrey's hexameters are utterly different in tone from the plain, staccato, and intensely human language of the Saxon Rood—the character of which is signalized in its opening words, with the interjected, 'unpoetic' 'ic þæt gyta geman' (28: I still remember it), followed by a rush of kinetic verbs that pile up as if expressing both the agitation of the speaker and the feverish activity of the men: *genaman . . . geworhton . . . heton . . . bæron . . . asetton . . . gefæstnodon* (30–3: the whole operation is over in four lines). This language at once establishes a humility of tone, consonant with the tree's humble obedience to its Lord (35, 45) and in sharp contrast to the measured, formal patterns of the opening lines of the poem, which were equally appropriate in their place, as establishing its serious purpose.

Whatever training in poetics the author had received, it must have included (assuming a monastic framework) some study of Christian Latin verse. Of this verse Alcuin, Aldhelm, Boniface—to cite but three English names—were accomplished practitioners. Their verse is in no sense primitive, but often witty, enigmatic, allusive, and rhetorical. We should not be surprised, therefore, at finding similar features in this early example of vernacular poetry. The profundity and subtlety of its theological meaning are matched by, indeed expressed through, the subtlety and flexibility of its style and metre. At times it moves with the same deliberate dignity that characterizes the young man, the *geong hæleð* whom it celebrates. That a gradual unfolding of meaning, a slow revelation of identity, is not incompatible with what we might call serious wit, early verse-riddles, Latin and English, abundantly testify; and this poem about the ineffable *mysterium crucis* is pre-eminently enigmatic, allusive, concealing its full meaning and significance till the climax at the very mid-point of the central narrative: 'Crist wæs on rode' (56), 'It was Christ who hung there on a cross'. No rendering can express the shock and shame and stark finality of those words. Henryson's 'Bludy Serk', which likewise makes Christ a warrior-prince, was to develop its theme in the same pregnant style; but Henryson's title does not detract from the essential cryptic element in his poem, as the title usually given to the older poem is bound to do. Cryptic allusiveness will remain a characteristic of Passion poetry till the time of Herbert. The careful postponement of the final clue, the consistent transference of the sufferings of the *hæleð* to a *treow*, the veiled allusions to *earmra ærgewin, strange feondas, wergas* (19, 30, 31: the strife of wretched men, strong enemies, criminals)—all these features are formally part of a riddling technique, just as the opening lines of the *narratio* proper (3–6) resemble in their verbal pattern those of one of the finest, and most teasing, of the Old English riddles, that on the Sun and Moon. Lines 4–5: 'þuhte me þæt ic gesawe syllicre treow/on lyft lædan' (It seemed to me I saw a wondrous tree rise aloft) correspond to the first lines of that poem:

> Ic wiht geseah wundorlice
> hornum betweonum huþe lædan,
> lyftfæt leohtlic listum gegierwed:

I saw a creature wondrously bringing booty between her horns, a radiant vessel of the air, skilfully decked.[3]

If the riddling element of the Rood poem is to be preserved, a modern title should be as non-committal as possible.

To adopt the riddling technique as exemplified in either vernacular or Latin verse—and the poet may well have known the riddles of Tatwine or Eusebius—was to ensure that the emotion which the subject calls forth was disciplined and restrained. But there are other reasons why we find here none of what Ruskin in his downright way called 'the horrible images of the Passion by which vulgar Romanism has always striven to excite the languid sympathies of its untaught flock' (a reproach from which he did not exempt Giotto or Fra Angelico and which Dean Stanley was to echo). This poet, like certain poets and artists of a later time, does not apprehend the Passion as Tragedy but as fulfilment of divine purpose, *in plenitudine temporis*. 'Oblatus est quia ipse voluit' (Isa. 53:7) is the unspoken affirmation of the whole work: 'He was sacrificed because he wished it so' (a reading not represented by the Authorized Version, which is closer to the Hebrew). This is why the *treow* is presented as the object of the rapt attention of angels (9), holy souls (*halige gastas*, 11), mankind, the whole creation (12)—and whatever the precise meaning of *forðgesceaft* (10) it must connote the fore-ordained creation of the cosmos. The sentient 'tree' itself not only speaks but perceives the divine purpose of liberating mankind ('he wolde mancyn lysan', 41) and so submits to the divine order and discipline—the *dryhtnes word* (35): 'ne dorste ic hwæðre bugan to eorðan . . . ic sceolde fæste standan' (42–3: Yet I durst not bow down, must needs stand fast). The military undertones here are consonant with an action conceived of in terms of men who are active foes, of soldiery (*hilderincas*) at its appointed tasks (71–2), of a lord who displays great courage (*ellen micel*, 34) in a great battle (*micel gewinn*, 65). And the poet can be selective and terse in his narrative because he can count on such language and imagery to summon up the associations they have in earlier Latin poems on the same theme. If he does not echo the 'triumphalism' of Fortunatus' *Vexilla Regis*, he is none the less writing in the tradition such poems established—a tradition that, as he would be aware, had its origins in a vision resembling the *swefn* he himself describes, the prophetic vision of Constantine. Both dreams would be accepted, to use Macrobius' classic terminology, as *somnia*, visions that bring truth whether allegorically or (as Bede relates of Cædmon: 'adstitit ei quidam per somnium') in the shape of an oracular figure. This one takes place *to midre nihte* (2) when (according to dream-science) the time for *phantasmata* is past. The vision will bring the profoundest of all revelations, an insight into the nature of Deity itself.

Only after the vision of Constantine and his subsequent victory did the Cross become the universal symbol of Christianity; hitherto not only had the image of a crucified Messiah been a *skandalon* but likewise the whole conception of *agape* that it revealed. No certain representations of the Crucifixion are found before those events, the earliest being an ivory plaque of the early fifth century showing a short, firm figure in brief loin-cloth.[4] The story of the shining cross appearing to the emperors in the night sky spread with Christianity. St. Gregory refers to it in one of the first documents of the English Conversion, his letter to Æthelbert (601); and Constantine's adoption of the Cross as symbol of his triumph, 'glittering', as Gibbon says, 'on the helmets, and engraved on the shields of his soldiers', ensured that henceforth the mystery of the Crucifixion would be expressed in terms of conquest over foes. 'The cross which was the justice of thieves (*latronum supplicium*; cf. *fracodes gealga*, 10)', says St. Augustine, in a passage that found its way into the *Golden Legend*, 'is now become the sign of glory on the foreheads of Emperors.' It is in allusion to Constantine's *labarum* that Prudentius writes:

> In quibus effigies crucis aut gemmata refulget
> aut longis solido ex auro praefertur in hastis
> . . .
>
> Christus purpureum gemmanti textus in auro
> signabat labarum . . .
> > (*In Symmachum*, i. 465–6, 486–7)

. . . standards in which the figure of the Cross leads the van, either gleaming with jewels [cf. ll. 16–17 of the English poem] or fashioned of solid gold on the long shafts . . . the mark of Christ [XP] wrought in jewelled gold was on the purple banner.[5]

The prayers for the consecration of a cross in the Lanalet Pontifical of the tenth century (now at Rouen, but of English provenance) reflect the influence of the Constantine story, and allude to the same mode of decoration:

Sanctifica, Domine, istud signaculum passionis tuae, ut sit inimicis tuis obstaculum, et credentibus in te perpetuum perfice vexillum. . . . Radiet hic unigeniti filii tui splendor divinitatis in auro, emicet gloria passionis eius in ligno, in cruore rutilet nostrae mortis redemptio, in splendore christalli nostrae vitae purificatio . . .[6]

Sanctify, O Lord, this sign of thy passion, and make it a hindrance to thy enemies and a perpetual banner for those who trust in thee. May the splendour of the Divinity of thy only-begotten son gleam in its gold, the glory of his passion in its wood, may the redemption of our death glow in blood, the purification of our life in splendour . . .

—a prayer exemplifying the measured cadences that became mandatory for such Invocations.

Everything would favour the early transmission of the Constantine story to Britain; and it may well have been in Oswald's mind when he set up his rood before the victory at Heavenfield (633); the miracles later wrought by that rood or by fragments of it [7] follow the pattern of the legends illustrating the virtues of the true Cross and of relics thereof. Some late manuscripts of Nennius even associate Constantine's motto 'In hoc signo vinces' with Arthur, relating that when he journeyed to Jerusalem he had a cross made of the same size as the life-giving Cross, and asked that by this wood the Lord would grant him victory. In the seventh century Adamnan reported that when at Easter the true Cross was set up on a golden altar in Hagia Sophia it exuded a fragrant liquid, the smallest drop of which would bring health to the sick: a potency of which the Rood speaks in our poem (85–6). Adamnan's narrative was known to Bede, who transcribes his description of the great silver commemorative cross set up on Golgotha, as it was in his day: '. . . argenteam modo pergrandem sustinens crucem, pendente magna desuper aerea rota cum lampadibus' (now bearing a very large silver cross with a great bronze wheel with lamps hanging above it). Of the predecessor of this commemorative cross we can gain some idea from the presumed picture of it in the late fourth-century apsidal mosaic of Santa Pudenziana in Rome. This has been fairly heavily restored, but the towering cross showing five red stones (symbolizing the five wounds) at the intersection (cf. 'fife wæron/uppe on þam eaxlegespanne', 8–9), is probably genuine; it seemingly illuminates the whole sky, and originally must have been even more impressive than it is now. Nothing could be in stronger contrast to the earlier conception of the Crucifixion as a scandal and an indecency. Heraclius' return of the Cross to Jerusalem after its removal by Chosroes (629) marked the final stage in the development of the cultus. To it we owe the institution of the Feast of the Exaltation of the Cross by Sergius, the pope who baptized Cædwalla (on Holy Saturday, 689), who was in correspondence with Wearmouth and Jarrow, and who consecrated St. Willibrord, English missionary to the Germans.

Meanwhile the honour accorded to the Cross as object and as symbol bore fruit in literature and in liturgy, and first, naturally, at Jerusalem: the prayers for catechumens there in the Liturgy of St. James (*c.* 400?) include the petition, 'Lift up the horn of the Christians by the power of the venerable and life-giving Cross'. How, and how quickly, the devotion spread to England we cannot yet say; prayers belonging to it appear in the tenth century in the *Regularis Concordia* and may well have had earlier English equivalents. At the Feast of the Exaltation Fortunatus' two great hymns, *Vexilla Regis* and *Pange, lingua*, were sung—appropriately enough, since they were written for the reception of a fragment of the true Cross which had been sent to Queen Radegunde (whose feast, for local reasons, still figures in the Cambridge Calendar). But inevitably the hymns came to be used on Good Friday as well (the latter from as early as the sixth century in some places). And devotions to the Cross, both public and private, were to become a central feature of worship on that day. The dreamer in our poem (as distinct from the men who *reste wunedon*, 3) is evidently prostrate before the Cross (*þær licgende*, 24) at the beginning of his dream. 'Exaudi me prostratum [ac] adorantem tuam gloriosissimam crucem', runs an early prayer; and the sleep that brings the vision would be such as the rigours of Lent induced—even if they had been modified since the fifth and sixth centuries, when the Maundy Thursday vigil at Jerusalem lasted all night, and the Friday vigil was kept all night without a light. We are justified in inferring that the English poet, like Dunbar seven centuries later, would have us associate his dream firmly with Good Friday.

In the eighth century the liturgy for Holy Week had not taken its present form. But some of the practices and scriptural passages that it ultimately embodied were probably already associated with this season, and the present services are pertinent at least insofar as they include texts that correspond in thought and language with the poem, if they did not suggest them. Of these perhaps the most notable is the prophecy from Isaiah 63:1—

Iste formosus in stola sua, gradiens in multitudine fortitudinis
suae. Ego qui loquar justitiam et propugnator sum ad
salvandum . . .

One glorious in his apparel, travelling in the greatness of his
strength. I who speak righteousness and am a warrior come to
save . . .

—which might serve almost as an epitome of the central
part of the poem; it became the first lesson for the
Wednesday of Holy Week and the inspiration for
Langland's depiction of the Passion in scenes which he too
sets in an Easter dream. The martial language recurs in the
Introit for Monday in Holy Week, Psalm 35:1–2: 'Judica,
Domine, nocentes me, expugna impugnantes me: ap-
prehende arma et scutum'. (Plead my cause, O Lord, with
them that strive with me: fight against them that fight
against me. Take hold of shield and buckler.) In counter-
point to such verses run the Pauline texts on the mystery of
the Cross, which became the Introits for Tuesday and
Wednesday: Gal. 6:14: 'Nos autem gloriari oportet in cruce
Domini' (But we ought to glory in the Cross of the Lord);
Phil. 2:8: 'Dominus factus est obediens usque ad mortem,
mortem autem crucis' (The Lord became obedient even to
death, death on the Cross)—the latter the only text that, like
the poem, associates the Cross with obedience. On Good
Friday itself (disregarding the comparatively late
Improperia) comes the ninth-century antiphonal: 'Crucem
tuam adoramus, Domine; et sanctam resurrectionem tuam
laudamus . . . ecce enim propter lignum venit gaudium in
universo mundo' (We worship thy Cross, O Lord; and we
praise thy holy resurrection . . . for behold, through the tree
came joy in all the world), followed by the chanting of the
verse from *Pange, lingua*:

> Crux fidelis, inter omnes
> Arbor una nobilis
> Nulla silva talem profert
> Fronde flore germine
> Dulce lignum, dulces clavos
> Dulce pondus sustinet;

which a later poet was to render:

> Steddefast crosse, inmong alle other,
> thow art a tre mykel of prise,
> in brawnche and flore swylk[a] another
> I ne wot in wode no rys[b],
> swete be the nalys
> and swete be the tre
> and sweter be the birdyn that hangis uppon the![8]

[a] such [b] nor branch.

Whether or not the Anglo-Saxon poet had assisted at services in which this verse was sung, it can hardly be doubted that the verse was in mind when he had the Rood say: 'me þa geweorþode wuldres ealdor ofer holtwudu' (90–1: the king of glory exalted me above other trees in the wood), and *crux fidelis* asserts the tree's constancy just as the Rood does: 'ic fæste stod' (38): 'I stood firm and faithful'; the tree, like the *geong hæleð* who is the 'Redemptor sponte libera/Passioni deditus' of the hymn, is fulfilling an appointed task. 'Ipse [deus] lignum hunc notavit' (God himself marked out the tree), says Fortunatus, who likewise refers explicitly to the *plenitudo temporis* (st. 4), the *forðgesceaft* of l. 10 (imperfectly rendered by 'eternity').

But the foremost theme of his hymn is of battle won and warfare ended:

> Pange, lingua, gloriosi
> Proelium certaminis
> Et super Crucis trophaeo
> Dic triumphum nobilem.
>
> Tell, my tongue, of warfare ended,
> Battle gloriously won,
> Speak the noble triumph shown
> In the trophy of the Cross.

Fortunatus was born near Ravenna when it was a seat of empire, and may well have seen there the mosaic showing a man in military dress (Kantorowicz thought that of an emperor) who bears a long-staffed cross on his shoulders and tramples underfoot the lion and the basilisk. Fortunatus' imagery takes us closer to secular imperial triumphs and Constantine's purple banner than any Pauline figure does; and the English poet—when describing the Harrowing of Hell—wisely employs less precise, less limiting terms: 'sigorfæst on þam siðfate, mihtig and spedig' (150–1: victorious in that enterprise, mighty and successful). But both poets were writing for audiences familiar with the Messianic application of such verses as 'Dominus regnavit, decorem indutus est: indutus est Dominus fortitudinem, et praecinxit se' (Ps. 93:1: The Lord is King, he is clothed in majesty; the Lord is clothed in strength, and has girded himself). That such language had a special appeal to the faithful who thought of themselves as *milites Christi* is shown in a hymn ascribed to the ex-barbarian king Chilperic (d. 548), one line at least of which—'sacrata crucis vexilla coruscant'—recalls the *Vexilla Regis*. 'Regnavit a ligno Deus', God has reigned from a tree, the Messianic text round which *Vexilla Regis* is built, might be called the key to the riddling paradox of the *Vision*. Moreover, in such phrases as Fortunatus' 'plaudis triumpho nobili' (thou dost clap hands in triumph), we have a hint of the prosopopoeia that the English poet was to develop so brilliantly; whilst all the other attributes that he ascribes to the *syllicre treow* (4: a most wondrous tree) are implicit in this hymn in praise of the

> Arbor decora et fulgida
> Ornata regis purpura
> Electa digno stipite.

> Tree of dazzling beauty
> adorned with royal purple
> chosen from worthy stock.

The English and the Latin poets are alike in their gifts of conciseness and of endowing natural objects with sentience. In yet another hymn written in honour of the true Cross, *Crux benedicta nitet* (the blessed Cross shines), Fortunatus combines the conception of a gleaming cross with that of a tree to which the True Vine clings: 'tu plantata micas' (thou, vineyard, gleamest)—a figure that the Middle Ages will seize on.[9]

The martial effect of *Pange, lingua* is due as much to its

metre as to its language. Its imagery complements rather
than repeats that of *Vexilla Regis*. The Cross is not only
king of all the forest trees, it is the source of a cleansing
flood that pours over *terra, pontus, astra, mundus* (earth, sea,
stars, world)—*eall þeos mære gesceaft*, 'all this wondrous
creation', as the Anglo-Saxon poet puts it (12). The
conception of a cosmic redemption has largely disappeared
from our theology, but has good patristic warrant and is of a
piece with the universal mourning tersely summarized in
'Weop eal gesceaft' (55) (which half-echoes the groaning of
omnis creatura in Rom. 8:22). 'It was fitting', says Gregory,
'that creation should mourn with its creator.' 'The darkened
sun, the trembling earth', says Jerome, 'show that he was
the son of God.'[10] The poet of the Old English *Christ* (III)
expresses a similar belief. *Pace* Curtius, one may also
suppose that Christian poets were not uninfluenced by the
tradition in classical pastoral that Nature showed sympathy
for human loss (as in Virgil, *Eclogues*, x. 13–16).[11] On the
face of it this is a prime example of the pathetic fallacy. But,
as Northrop Frye remarks, it can hardly be a fallacy when
God is the hero of the action. Editors of our poem have seen
a 'striking similarity' in the Prose Edda's account of the
lament at the death of the Norse god Balder, when all
things wept save only the giantess Thǫkk—the theme of one
of Arnold's longer and more tedious poems. But that lament
is not spontaneous and the tears are rationalistically
identified with the moisture produced by natural objects
when they 'come out of cold and into heat'. There is no
reason to suppose that the English poet was familiar with
the Norse story; on the other hand he would certainly know
the patristic interpretation of the eclipse and earthquake.
The climactic 'Weop eal gesceaft' consciously echoes and
resumes the phrases of ll. 11–12, where 'eal gesceaft'
embraces not only the cosmos but men and angels (*engeldryhta*, 9). It thus recalls another Easter hymn, that by
St. Ambrose, which says: 'Opus stupent et angeli/poenam
videntes corporis' (Creation and angels are stunned at the
sight of the body's suffering)[12]—a vivid yet legitimate
application of the reference to the Paschal mystery in 1 Pet.
1:12: 'in quem desiderant angeli prospicere' (which things

the angels desire to look into). Presumably it was this verse and similar extensions of it that led to the introduction of angels into representations of the Crucifixion: the two angels now somewhat awkwardly placed on the east wall of St. Aldhelm's church at Bradford-on-Avon were perhaps part of such a scene, hovering above the cross-piece of a stone rood; so they are shown on many a later miniature.

In yet another Easter hymn St. Ambrose, like the English poet, describes Christ as climbing the Cross: 'Iam surgit hora tertia/qua Christus ascendit crucem'. 'He me wolde on gestigan', says the Rood (34: he purposed to climb up on me); 'gestah he on gealgan heanne/modig on manigra gesyhðe' (40–1: he climbed the high gallows unafraid in the sight of the multitude). The use of the verb 'to climb' in this context was not in itself unusual. St. Hilary too writes: 'scandere crucem jubetur'. But in St. Ambrose the verb is colourless and in St. Hilary the emphasis is upon the compulsion. So Herbert, in 'The Sacrifice', will say, 'Man stole the fruit, but I must climb the tree'—glancing at the identity indicated by Bede: 'About the same hour in which the first man touched the tree of Paradise, the second man ascended the Tree of Redemption' (*De Gen. in litteram*, iii. 18). The use of *ascendere* to express deliberate purpose springs from still another prophetic passage, which Bede doubtless had in mind: 'Ascendam in palmam et apprehendam fructus eius' (S. of S. 7:8: I shall go up the palm tree and take hold of the fruits thereof). That this was an acceptable conjunction one of the greatest and most intricate English representations of the Cross assures us. Amongst the 108 figures and 60 inscriptions on a tree-like ivory crucifix of the twelfth century associated with Bury St. Edmunds[13] appears the figure of Solomon bearing a label with this very verse. Below it are carved other prophetic texts equally pertinent: Hosea proclaims, 'Ero mors tua, O mors' (Hos. 13:14: O death, I shall be thy death), and Isaiah announces, 'Oblatus est quia ipse voluit'—which is the quintessence of our poet's paschal theology and the warrant for the line 'he me wolde on gestigan'.

A hint for this figure, and this emphasis, the poet may

have taken from the *Passio Sancti Andreae*. St. Andrew was pre-eminently the preacher of the Cross, and churches were dedicated to him in the sixth and seventh centuries at Rochester, Medeshamstede (Peterborough), and (notably) at Hexham. The office for his Feast Day in the York and Sarum Use quotes his *Passio* as follows:

Ego crucis Christi servus sum, et crucis trophaeum optare potius debeo quam timere: Col. VIII. Ego si patibulum crucis ex-paverescem, crucis gloriam non praedicarem.

I am a servant of the Cross of Christ and ought rather to desire than fear the trophy of the Cross: Col. VII. Were I to dread the footrest of the Cross I could not preach the glory thereof.

And the sections in the modern Breviary are based on the following passage in St. Andrew's Legend: 'When the saint approached the place where the cross had been prepared for him and saw it from afar he cried out: Hail, cross, thou which art dedicated in the body of Christ, and hast been ornamented with his limbs *as with pearls*. Before our Lord climbed up on thee thou didst show mortal fear [cf. 'Bifode ic þa mc se beorn ymbclypte', 42: 'I trembled when the man embraced me'] but now thou showest heavenly love. Glad and untroubled do I come to thee. Long have I been thy lover and desired to embrace thee'—an invocation that in the Breviary concludes as follows:

O crux admirabilis, o crux desiderabilis, o crux quae per totum mundum rutilas, suscipe discipulum Christi ac per te me recipiat qui per te moriens redemit. O bona crux, quae decorem et pulchritudinem de membris Domini suscepisti, suscipe discipulum.
                                                              (30 Nov., lectio viii)

O cross to be wondered at and longed for, glowing throughout the whole world, take up the disciple of Christ and let him who in dying by thy means redeemed me by thy means receive me. O good cross, who assumed grace and beauty from the Lord's limbs, take up the disciple.

St. Ambrose's hymn and St. Andrew's legend, however, may themselves be adaptations of a much earlier hymn and story associated with Christ himself. There was recently discovered in the ruins of a monastery near Abu Simbel an ancient Coptic prayer book that includes the text of a hymn which Christ is said to have recited to his disciples:

Rise up, O holy Cross, and lift me, O Cross. I shall mount upon you, O Cross. They shall hang me upon you as a witness to them. Receive me to yourself, O Cross, Amen. But be joyful, O Cross. Amen. I have put on the crown of the kingdom.

(*The Times*, 24 Dec. 1965)

The English poet's boldness, it is clear, has venerable precedent. In the thirteenth century the *Meditationes Vitae Christi* will present Christ actually ascending the Cross by 'a short ladder', as does a Romanesque painting in the Accademia at Florence, and the painting in Cell 36 in San Marco, formerly considered to be by Fra Angelico.[14]

Besides being the source of the conception of the Crucified *embracing* the Cross which is developed in the hymn *Salve tropaeum gloriae* attributed to Bede, the St. Andrew Passion is notable for its attribution of sentience to the Cross, and for the image of limbs gleaming like pearls that shine over the whole world. Fortunatus probably knew St. Andrew's prayer and adapted phrases from it.[15]

Persistent and pervasive as the echoes of the Church's hymnody and liturgy are throughout the English poem, it also includes several allusions—so brief and veiled that they may be overlooked—which depend solely or primarily on Scripture. The central narrative needs no documentation, though one may suggest that the emphasis on Christ as *rice cyning* (44) and *wealdend* (115: Lord) points especially to St. John's Gospel, which refers only briefly to Christ's sufferings and frailty, uses the title *rex* some dozen times, speaks of Christ as overcoming the world (John 16:33), and like the closing lines of the poem links his kingship with his relation to the Father.[16] The figure in 'Deað he þær byrigde' (101: There he tasted death) evidently derives from Heb. 2:9: 'pro omnibus gustaret mortem'. Yet some phrases remain cryptic despite the commentators, and despite scriptural parallels. Thus *halige gastas* (11) can scarcely be angels, though the same words are used of angels in the Old English *Daniel*; they are more probably the souls in limbo, the spirits of the just who are awaiting

the climactic moment of their redemption and who will
make up the *gasta weorod* of l. 152 (an interpretation
supported by *Phoenix*, 539, where the phrase is a variation
upon *sawla soþfæste*). 'Geworhton him þær to wæfersyne'
(31: Then they made a spectacle of me) is evidently a
reminiscence of the verse in which St. Paul speaks of the
death (by crucifixion) appointed for Christian martyrs:
'quia *spectaculum* facti sumus mundo et angelis et hominibus' (1 Cor. 4:9: for we are made a spectacle to the world
and to angels and to men)—where the last words hold a
suggestion of 'engeldryhta feala . . . men . . . gesceaft' (9–
12).[17] The deliberately imprecise *beornas* (men) in 'bæron
me þær beornas on eaxlum' (32: men bore me there on their
shoulders) is not simply part of the riddling mode (like
æþele in the carved Ruthwell Cross version of l. 158, with
the same reference): it represents a poet's conflation of the
accounts in the Synoptic Gospels, which say that Simon of
Cyrene carried the Cross, and the statement by St. John
that Christ himself bore it.

The dramatic lines 'Ongyrede hine þa geong hæleð—þæt
wæs god ælmihtig/strang and stiðmod' (39–40: Then the
young hero—it was God almighty—strong and resolute,
stripped himself) at first suggest no more than the forcible
disrobing of the Gospel narrative, or the undraped upright
figure of the so-called 'Antioch' type of painting in contrast
to the bent and drooping body that begins to appear in the
art of the late ninth century, introducing a new note of pathos.
But behind the simple lines (which continue the purposeful
action of l. 33, where the *frea mancynnes* hastens with great
zeal to climb the tree) lies a wealth of scriptural association,
beginning with the patristic exposition of Ps. 19:5: 'et ipse
tanquam sponsus procedens de thalamo suo. Exultavit ut
gigas ad currendum viam': 'he is as a bridegroom coming
out of his chamber and rejoiceth as a strong man to run a
race'. A hymn of St. Ambrose provides the standard gloss,
in which the *thalamus* is the Blessed Virgin:

> procedit a thalamo suo
> pudoris aula regia
> geminae gigans substantiae
> alacris occurrat viam

egressus eius a Patre
regressus eius ad Patrem
excursus usque ad inferos
recursus ad sedem dei

aequalis aeterno patri
carnis tropaeo cingere.[18]

He proceeds from his chamber, the royal hall of chastity [viz. the Virgin's womb], a giant of twin substance, and eagerly runs his course, having gone out from his Father, and returned to his Father, gone forth even to hell and returned to the throne of God. Equal with the eternal Father, thou girdest thyself with the trophy of flesh.

Here *tropaeum* anticipates the victory of the Cross and *recursus ad sedem dei* announces the return to the Father and *godes rice* (152).

Ongyrede (39) however, if we keep to the older rendering 'stripped himself' rather than 'made ready', will perhaps take us beyond the figure of the warrior-athlete to the profounder implications of the action—to the *kenosis* of Phil. 2:6–8: 'Sed semetipsum exinanivit [emptied himself], formam servi accipiens ... et habitu inventus ut homo. Humiliavit semetipsum factus obediens usque ad mortem, mortem autem crucis.' That text was part of the Proper for Palm Sunday from at least the eighth century, when it would be read in the light of the controversy over the two natures of Christ and their hypostatic union. But the force of the English alliterative lines is such as to dispel all thought of theological debate, and almost to resolve the paradox. They epitomize the perfect balance between 'dolourism' and 'triumphalism' that characterizes the whole poem. Further, they alert us to the even more pregnant juxtaposition in *eaðmod, elne mycle* (60: humble, with great zeal). There, as we have seen, the rood is enacting Christ's own role: as Christ had hastened *elne micle* (34), the rood can say that with the same zeal it humbled itself and became *obediens*. That the verbal identity of ll. 34 and 60 is not fortuitous is shown by the third occurrence of the phrase *elne mycle* at l. 123 in a context indicating that the dreamer is now identifying himself with the Cross.

The mortal fear and sorrow of the rood are linked in the poem with the embrace of the crucified, but both take on a new profundity: 'Bifode ic þa me se beorn ymbclypte'. Here the tree is so closely identified with Christ that its trembling suggests his agony in Gethsemane whilst the embrace symbolizes complete acceptance of the Divine Will. Thus in a few bare words the apposition of *geong hæleð* and *god ælmihtig* (39) is given a new aspect. The tree's ultimate and decisive firmness may even be said to figure succinctly the mysterious harmony of the two natures as St. Leo had formulated it: 'His body did not become impassible because of his divinity, nor could his divinity come to suffer through his body.'[19] The rood's conscious participation is further implied by the emphasis in 'ahof ic ricne cyning' (44: It was I who bore aloft the mighty king) and in 'hnag ic hwæðre þam secgum to handa' (59: yet I bent to the hands of men). In the latter line the conceit of an almost untranslatable stanza in *Pange, lingua* is given a fresh dynamic force, possible only because the tree identifies with the Man who humbled himself.

> Flecte ramos, arbor alta,
> tensa laxa viscera
> et rigor lentescat ille
> quem dedit nativitas
> et superni membra regis
> tende miti stipite.

Bend your branches, noble tree, relax your taut fibres, let your natural hardness yield to suppleness and offer yourself as gentle support for the limbs of the supernal king.

H. R. Patch long ago noted that the last two lines of this Latin stanza correspond to 'Geseah ic weruda God/þearle þenian' (51–2: I saw the God of Hosts grievously stretched out), but we may also note how much the addition of *þearle* (grievously) intensifies the picture, and strengthens the antithesis of omnipotent God and suffering man.

In the central *sermocinatio*, the address of the tree, scarcely a line is without specific scriptural undertones. Thus *bysmeredon* (48: mocked) is the verb used in the Anglo-Saxon Gospels to render *inludentes* (in mockery) in (for example) Matt. 27:41; and 'siððan he hæfde his gast onsended' (49) is more than a calque on 'emisit/tradidit spiritum': it recalls the seven last words as St. Luke records them: 'Pater in manus tuas commendo spiritum meum' (Father, into thy hands I commend my spirit). In a poem sparing of pronouns, *his gast* strengthens the impression of the *hæleð*'s considered acceptance of his role. In l. 54 'scirne sciman sceadu forðeode' (a shadow covered the bright radiance) still offers difficulties, but they are not avoided by appealing to the Prosa Edda's description of the god Balder as 'radiant'. Interpretation must be controlled by patristic exegesis of the Vulgate's 'tenebrae factae sunt'; this indicates that *scima* is a trope for the sun, 'which woeful darkness overshadowed as Christ was dying'—so said St. Maximus in his sermon for Easter Day.[20] 'Eall ic wæs mid strælum forwundod' (62: I was sore wounded with arrows), which appears to have retrospective force, is strictly speaking without warrant in the Gospels. Whether or not it refers to the side-piercing spear, it probably reflects such Messianic passages as 'sed exasperaverunt eum et jurgati sunt. Inviderunt illi habentes jacula' (the archers have sorely grieved him and shot at him).[21]

In describing Christ's death as *cyninges fyll* (56: the fall of a king) the poet uses a native phrase, once applied to Beowulf himself (*Beowulf*, 2812); but whereas in the epic it has a precise and literal meaning, here the decorum of a riddling poem only requires us to apprehend it as the climax of the action; and it allows the poet to say later without incongruity that he is *limwerigne* (63) and that 'he hine ðær hwile reste/meðe æfter ðam miclan gewinne' (64-5: he rested there a while, exhausted after the mighty battle). These phrases do not necessarily connote sleep, yet the poet doubtless had in mind such expressions as St. Leo's: 'So swift was the revivifying of his uncorrupted body, that we have here the appearance of sleep rather than of death: for the Divinity which departed not from either substance of his assumed humanity, joined together by its power what by its power it had sundered.'[22] And the picture of a weary Christ at rest is no poetical embellishment: witness St. Augustine's comment on 'Et inclinato capite, tradidit spiritum' (John 19:30): 'The first woman was made out of man as he slept, the second Adam with bowed head slept upon the Cross, that thence might be formed from him a wife [the Church].' 'He that reste him on the rode' was to become a Middle English formula:

> I have laborede sore and suffered deyth
> and now I rest and draw my breyth,

says Christ in a fifteenth-century verse.[23] The carefully chosen nonce-word *limwerigne* in our poem has its particular force as recalling the limbs painfully stretched on the Cross, but it also suggests the exhaustion of a single combat. That combat is, essentially, with Death and Satan, as will be made explicit in *Piers Plowman*. It is to be resumed in the period between the Deposition and the Resurrection—hence the appositeness of *sigora wealdend* (67: lord of victories), unexpected as that anticipatory phrase is in its context.

The picture of the disciples after the Deposition standing 'æt his lices heafdum' (63) has been read as reflecting the Germanic idea of *comitatus* loyalty, and it does indeed recall the scene where Wiglaf sits by the dead Beowulf, keeping watch in distress of soul: 'Healdeð higemæðum heofodwearde' (*Beowulf*, 2909). But the verbal similarity is misleading, for *heofodweard* has the quite general sense of 'guard over the king's person'. The picture of the faithful few who 'ongunnon him þa sorhleoð galan' (67: sang a dirge over the dead body), has similarly been taken as preserving 'an archaic feature of Old English burial rite', and *Beowulf* 2460 has been adduced in support. But *Beowulf* 2460–1 is not about a burial, and the lament there is a private one—a father's for his son. Keenings in the presence of the dead do find a place in *Beowulf*, but in both instances (1117, 3160 ff.) we have a solitary woman mourning for her son or for her king—a figure, to be sure, that our poet could easily and warrantably have introduced (in the light of scriptural references to the Virgin) at this point. But he does not do so; lines 68–9 are in fact suggested by 'percutientes pectora sua revertebantur' (Luke 23:48: the people smote their breasts and returned). Compare 'þa hie woldon eft siðian' (68: they resolved to depart).

To question Beowulfian correspondences is not to say that supposed reminiscences of native 'heroic' life and poetry in the earlier poem are illusory. Insofar as the poet assimilates the military images and attitudes of Christian-Latin poetry he does so precisely because it was at these points that two poetic traditions touched, and could be fused. He can thus easily adapt certain native conceptions to his own purposes. If there is anything 'Teutonic' in his thought it is to be found in the value assumed to attach to steadfastness and loyalty; but this is more consistently manifest in the characterization of the faithful rood than in the presentation of Christ as a *hlaford* with a troop of thegns. And the martial metaphor does not connote—any more than it does in St. Paul—a vestigial fondness for the battlefield: it is the only trope that adequately expresses commitment to a king or a credo, even unto death.

Since the cross is sentient, the three crosses can be duly identified with the mourners of Luke 23:49: 'Stabant autem omnes noti cius a longe' (all his acquaintances stood afar off). Hence lines 70–1, 'Hwæðere we ðær greotende gode hwile/stodon on staðole' (Yet stood we there in our sockets a great while weeping), where *greotende* embraces not only the grief of the crosses (and so calls up the figure of the penitent thief) but by a masterly prolepsis the later grief, at the open tomb, of the Magdalene (named by Matthew as one of the bystanders at Calvary): 'Maria autem stabat monumentum foris plorans' (John 20:11). In some medieval representations she clutches the foot of the Cross, weeping below the dead body. In the next few lines the Resurrection and the Invention of the Cross centuries later are similarly telescoped. Like the Lord, the Rood is buried, like him, it is found by his disciples, and rises again to life and glory. Thus Helena's band of Christian warriors (*Dryhtnes þegnas*, 75) who accompany her on her voyage of discovery can be juxtaposed with the Roman soldiers (*hilderincas*) who had guarded Cross and Tomb. 'Stefn up gewat/hilderinca' (71:2: the noise of soldiers' voices died away) glances at the role of the legionaries who broke the

bones of the two thieves, as described in John 19:32, the
last reading for Good Friday, and as shown in later
medieval art.

With the expository stage of the poem (78–121) we return
to the formal language of the Introduction. The final
Gospel allusion comes in this passage (83–4), where *bearn
godes* translates *filius dei*, Matt. 27:54, the only instance of
the phrase in the Passion narratives. But with the identity of
the Rood fully established new attributes can be introduced.
The Rood that men honour far and wide (81) is not only the
true Cross (the fragments of which could still be described
as 'decked with gold and silver' in the poet's time) but the
Cross as symbol of salvation and (113–14) of martyrdom,
such as St. Andrew's. So the poet can apply to it (81) the
terms used in Scripture of Christ: 'videmus Jesum, propter
passionem mortis, gloria et honore coronatum, ut gratia Dei
pro omnibus gustaret mortem' (Heb. 2:9: we see Jesus
[made a little lower than the angels] for the suffering of
death crowned with glory and honour, that he by the grace
of God might taste death for every man)—a passage that
proceeds to speak of the *auctor salutis* 'qui multos filios in
gloriam adduxerat' (the captain of their salvation who
brought many sons into glory); which provides the *conclusio*
of 152–3: 'he mid manigeo com, gasta weorode, on Godes
rice' (he entered with a multitude, a host of souls, into
God's kingdom). Again, the Rood's claim to powers of
general healing (85–6) suggests an identity with the Tree of
Life, the leaves of which were for the healing of the nations
(Rev. 22:2), as well as with the true Cross which had
brought the dead to life at the Invention, and in every
fragment of which physical and spiritual virtue inhered.
The Anglo-Saxon reliquary cross once in the church at
Arnhem and now at Brussels evidently enclosed such a
fragment, and appropriately carries a version of ll. 44–8 of
our poem, which there retain some of their riddling force:

> Rod is min nama. Geo ic ricne cyning
> bær byfigende blode bestemed.

Rood is my name. Aforetime I bore a mighty king, and trembled,
bedewed with blood.

And the antepenultimate lines of Rood's speech (117–18) proclaim yet another potency:

Ne þearf ðær þonne ænig anforht wesan
þe him ær in breostum bereð beacna selest.

None need be fearful who bears in his breast this best of emblems.

If we have understood the poet's types of ambiguity aright, we shall read this as a promise of saving power to the faithful who carry the message of the Cross imprinted in their hearts, no less than to those who signalize their devotion by making the sign of the Cross as Bede had enjoined or by wearing crucifix or pectoral cross—such as the one (with five gems) at Durham, which used to be called St. Cuthbert's. It was with the affirmation of this salvific virtue that Langland was to end *his* Easter vision, when he called on his wife and daughter:

'Ariseth and reverenceth Goddes resurrexioun
And crepeth to the crosse on knees and kisseth it for a jewel
For Goddes blissed body it bar for oure bote
And it afereth the fend, for such is the mighte
May no grisly gost glide there it shadweth!'
                              (*Piers Plowman*, B xviii. 427–31)

To the term *jewel* as used of the Cross there had accrued, by Langland's time, a weight of meaning that we are hardly conscious of when we read the Anglo-Saxon poem. Langland's greatest contemporary bears like witness to the continuity of this devotion. For Chaucer inserts into Nicholas Trivet's tale of the falsely accused Constance, about to be launched in a rudderless boat, a prayer that is not only appropriate to the occasion (for the Cross was invoked in votive masses of travellers by sea) but also, being derived from antiphons sung on the Feast of the Exaltation of the Cross (14 September), indicative of the direction taken by later medieval piety. The rood is still hailed as a *sigebeam*, a 'victorious tree'; but it is also seen as an altar, on which stands a Lamb as it had been slain.[24]

After Chaucer's time we hear strangely little of this tree of victory or of Christ the young hero. St. Bonaventure had affirmed that Christ's willingness to die was 'a more heroic

act of perfection and charity' than was willingness to live
'for the honour of God'. But when, centuries later, Ibsen's
Brand proclaimed, 'My God is young, like Hercules', the
intent, and result, was to shock. Christianity had by then
become synonymous for many with a passive rather than a
passible God; a confusion reflected in the arguments of

A Vision of a Rood (lines 1–86)

Hwæt, ic swefna cyst secgan wylle,
hwæt mē gemǣtte tō midre nihte,
syðþan reordberend reste wunedon.
Þūhte mē þæt ic gesāwe syllicre trēow
5   on lyft lǣdan lēohte bewunden,
bēama beorhtost. Eall þæt bēacen wæs
begoten mid golde; gimmas stōdon
fægere æt foldan scēatum, swylce þær fīfe wǣron
uppe on þām eaxlegespanne. Behēoldon þær engeldryhta feala,
10   fægere þurh forðgesceaft; ne wæs ðǣr hūru fracodes gealga,
ac hine þǣr behēoldon hālige gāstas,
men ofer moldan, and eall þēos mǣre gesceaft.
Syllic wæs se sigebēam and ic synnum fāh,
forwunded mid wommum. Geseah ic wuldres trēow
15   wǣdum geweorðod wynnum scīnan,
gegyred mid golde; gimmas hæfdon
bewrigen weorðlīce wealdendes trēow.
Hwæðre ic þurh þæt gold ongytan meahte
earmra ǣrgewin, þæt hit ǣrest ongan
20   swǣtan on þa swīðran healfe. Eall ic wæs mid sorgum
      gedrēfed;
forht ic wæs for þǣre fægran gesyhðe. Geseah ic þæt fūse
      bēacen
wendan wǣdum and blēom; hwīlum hit wæs mid wǣtan
      bestēmed,
beswyled mid swātes gange, hwīlum mid since gegyrwed.
Hwæðre ic þǣr licgende lange hwīle
25   behēold hrēowcearig hǣlendes trēow
oð ðæt ic gehȳrde þæt hit hlēoðrode.
Ongan þā word sprecan wudu sēlesta.
  'Þæt wæs gēara iū, ic þæt gȳta geman,
þæt ic wæs āhēawen holtes on ende,

those who today countenance violent action against oppression. One cannot account for this confusion without tracing the development of a medieval devotion, closely associated with the name of St. Bonaventure himself, a devotion that focused not on the warrior-prince but on his sufferings and his wounds.

Hearken, the rarest of dreams I purpose to tell
Which I dreamed one midnight
When men with their voices were at rest.
It seemed to me that I saw a most wondrous tree
Rising in the sky and encircled with light,   5
Brightest of beams. The whole of the beacon
Was decked in gold. Gems gleamed
Fair at the earth's four corners, and five there were
High up on the cross-beam. Hosts of angels beheld it,
Timeless in their beauty. It was no felon's gibbet,   10
Rather, it held the gaze of holy souls,
Of men on the earth and the whole glorious creation.
Wondrous, this triumphant tree, and I stained with vice,
Sore wounded with sins. I gazed on the tree of glory,
Royally decked as it was, gleaming brightly,   15
Attired in gold: gems had covered
Befittingly the tree of a Ruler.
Yet beneath that gold I could make out agony
Once suffered at the hands of wretched men.
Soon it ran sweat on its right side. Afflicted with griefs,   20

I was terrified by that wondrous sight. I saw this ardent
    beacon
Alter in vesture and colour; now it was bedewed with
    moisture,
Drenched in flowing sweat, now gleaming with treasure.
So lay I there for a long time,
Gazing sad at heart on a healer's tree   25
Till I heard it give voice,
Uttering words, this most precious wood:
'It was long since—yet I well remember—
That I was hewn down at wood-edge,

30   āstyred of stefne mīnum. Genāman mē ðǣr strange fēondas,
      geworhton him þǣr tō wǣfersȳne, hēton mē heora wergas
        hebban.
      Bǣron mē þǣr beornas on eaxlum oð ðæt hīe mē on beorg
        āsetton,
      gefæstnodon mē þǣr fēondas genōge. Geseah ic þā frēan
        mancynnes
      efstan elne micle þæt hē mē wolde on gestīgan.
35   Þǣr ic þā ne dorste ofer Dryhtnes word
      būgan oððe berstan þā ic bifian geseah
      eorðan scēatas. Ealle ic mihte
      fēondas gefyllan, hwæðre ic fæste stōd.
      Ongyrede hine þā geong hæleð—þæt wæs God ælmihtig,
40   strang and stīðmōd; gestāh hē on gealgan hēanne,
      mōdig on manigra gesyhðe, þā hē wolde mancyn lȳsan.
      Bifode ic þā mē beorn ymbclypte; ne dorste ic hwæðre būgan
        tō eorðan,
      feallan tō foldan scēatum, ac ic sceolde fæste standan.
      Rōd wæs ic ārǣred; āhōf ic rīcne cyning,
45   heofona hlāford, hyldan mē ne dorste.
      Þurhdrifan hī mē mid deorcan næglum, on mē syndon þā dolg
        gesīene,
      opene inwidhlemmas. Ne dorste ic hira ænigum sceððan.
      Bysmeredon hīe unc būtu ætgædere. Eall ic wæs mid blōde
        bestēmed,
      begoten of þæs guman sīdan siððan hē hæfde his gāst
        onsended.
50   Feala ic on þām beorge gebiden hæbbe
      wrāðra wyrda. Geseah ic weruda God
      þearle þenian; þȳstro hæfdon
      bewrigen mid wolcnum wealdendes hrǣw,
      scīrne scīman sceadu forðēode,
55   wann under wolcnum. Wēop eal gesceaft,
      cwīðdon cyninges fyll. Crīst wæs on rōde.

       Hwæðere þǣr fūse feorran cwōman
      tō þām æðelinge; ic þæt eall behēold.
      Sāre ic wæs mid sorgum gedrēfed, hnāg ic hwæðre þām
        secgum tō handa,
60   ēaðmōd elne mycle. Genāmon hīe þǣr ælmihtigne God,
      āhōfon hine of ðām hefian wīte, forlēton mē þā hilderincas

      standan stēame bedrifenne; eall ic wæs mid strǣlum
        forwundod.

Struck off from my stem. Strong foes seized me,   30
Set me up for spectacle, bade me raise their felons.

Men bore me on their shoulders, setting me on a hill

Where foes aplenty fastened me. Then I saw Man's Lord

Hasten with great courage, intent on climbing me.
Durst I not then oppose the word of the Lord   35
And bend or break, though I saw tremble
The surface of earth. All those foes
I could have felled, yet I stood firm.
Then the young warrior—it was God Almighty—
Stalwart, resolute, stripped himself; climbed the high gallows,   40
Gallantly before the throng, resolved to loose Man's bonds.
Trembled I when this warrior embraced me

Yet durst I neither bow nor fall. I must needs stand fast.
As a rood I was raised up, bearing a noble king,
The heavens' lord; waver I durst not.   45
With dark nails they pierced me, leaving scars yet visible,

Open strokes of malice. Yet harm them I might not.
Each of us two they reviled at once. I stood drenched with
     blood
Poured forth from his side when he yielded up his spirit.

Many the despitous wrongs   50
I have endured on that hill, where I saw the Lord of hosts
Grievously suffer. Clouds had masked
The ruler's corpse,
The bright radiance a shadow covered,
Wan 'neath the welkin. All creation wept,   55
Lamenting a king's fall. It was Christ who hung there on a
     cross.
Yet to this prince I saw men from afar come hastening.
Oppressed as I was by sorrows, I yet bowed humbly,
Gave myself eagerly into these men's hands.

It was God Almighty they there were handling,   60
Removing him from the instrument of torture; whilst the
     soldiery left me
Drenched in moisture, sore wounded with their
     weapon-points.

Ālēdon hine ðǣr limwērigne, gestōdon him æt his līces
    hēafdum,
behēoldon hīe ðǣr heofenes Dryhten, and he hine ðǣr hwīle
    reste,
65   mēðe æfter ðām miclan gewinne. Ongunnon him þā moldern
    wyrcan
beornas on banan gesyhðe, curfon hīe ðæt of beorhtan stāne,
gesetton hīe ðǣron sigora Wealdend. Ongunnon him þā
    sorhlēoð galan
earme on þā ǣfentīde. Þā hīe woldon eft sīðian
mēðe fram þām mǣran Þēodne, reste hē ðǣr mǣte weorode.
70   Hwæðere wē ðǣr grēotende gōde hwīle
stōdon on staðole, stefn up gewāt
hilderinca; hrǣw cōlode,
fæger feorgbold. Þā ūs man fyllan ongan
ealle tō eorðan; þæt wæs egeslic wyrd.
75   Bedealf ūs man on dēopan sēaþe; hwæðre mē þǣr Dryhtnes
    þegnas,
frēondas gefrūnon,
gyredon mē golde and seolfre.
    Nū ðū miht gehȳran, hæleð mīn se lēofa,
þæt ic bealuwara weorc gebiden hæbbe,
80   sārra sorga. Is nū sǣl cumen
þæt mē weorðiað wīde and sīde
menn ofer moldan and eall þēos mǣre gesceaft,
gebiddaþ him tō þyssum bēacne. On mē bearn Godes
þrōwode hwīle; for þan ic þrymfæst nū
85   hlīfige under heofenum, and ic hǣlan mæg
æghwylcne ānra þāra þe him bið egesa tō mē . . .

Limb-weary as he was, the men put him down, taking their
    posts at the corpse's head,
Keeping guard over the Lord of heaven. And he rested there a
    while,
Exhausted by his great battle. They prepared him a tomb   65

In his slayers' sight, cut it out of gleaming stone,
And there they laid down the victorious lord, singing in their
    woe an evening dirge.
Then wearily went away from that mighty prince:
Small indeed was the band that watched as he rested.
Yet we three stood for a long time weeping   70
When the shouts of the soldiers
Died away. The corpse grew cold,
Fair house of life. Then were we all
Levelled to the ground—a fearful fate—
In deep pit buried.   75

Yet thegns and friends of the Lord found me there
And richly adorned me in gold and silver.
So now it is given thee to hear, O man beloved,
What woes I suffered from wicked men,
What sorrows sore. Now is the time come   80
That I am honoured far and wide
By men on earth and the whole creation in its glory,
As they offer prayers to this beacon.
On me the Son of God once suffered. So now I tower
High and mighty beneath the skies, having power to heal   85
Whosoever shall bow to me . . .

II

THE MEDITATIVE MOVEMENT

i

Nou goth sonne under wod,
Me reweth, Marie, thi faire rode[a].
Nou goth sonne under tre,
Me reweth, Marie, thi sone and the.
[a] countenance.

ii

Whyt was hys nakede brest and red of blode hys syde,
Bleyc was his fair andled[a], his wnde dop ant wide,
And hys armes ystreit hey upon the rode;
On fif studes[b] on his body the stremes ran o blode.[1]
[a] pale was his beautiful face   [b] five places.

THESE two simple thirteenth-century quatrains, wholly
English in idiom and vocabulary, illustrate one of the
greatest revolutions in feeling that Europe has ever witnessed, and each line holds in embryo seeds that will
burgeon richly in devotional verse for four hundred years
and more. Beside this phenomenon the emergence of
'courtly love', so called, is a mere ripple on the surface of
literature, though, as the setting of the first stanza will
show, the two developments are not entirely unrelated.
Nothing in Anglo-Saxon verse and little in Latin hymnody
prepares us for such presentations of sacred scenes and
emotions as these. True, from an iconographic aspect they
may be referred to movements that had begun centuries
before in the Eastern Church. Émile Mâle has traced the
migration of Eastern Crucifixion motifs to Northern Italy,
where Peter Damian among others was moved to a new
apprehension of the sufferings of Christ—though Mâle
perhaps post-dates the appearance of features that are to be
associated with postures of pain, dejection, and defeat: a
Crucifixion panel at St. Catherine's Monastery, Mount

Sinai, probably as old as the eighth century, already shows the Saviour with eyes closed in death;[2] and the Byzantine origin of the drooped and dying posture has been questioned more than once since Mâle wrote, Kunstle seeing in it the influence of early scholastic 'satisfaction theories' of sacrifice.[3] The ultimate causes of these changes are complex and mysterious; at present one can only sketch the major phases.

Like many other French art-historians, Mâle was curiously indifferent to late Anglo-Saxon art. In at least two pre-Conquest English psalters the body is shown in such a posture, and the sense of defeat and dejection that it conveys is reflected in the attitude and countenance of the two bystanders, the Blessed Virgin and St. John, who now appear for the first time.[4] They figured also on the great rood that Lanfranc set up at the east end of his new cathedral at Canterbury towards the close of the eleventh century; an example followed at once by the Archbishop of York and the Bishop of Winchester. But we know nothing of the iconography of these figures.[5] The feelings represented in the psalter miniatures may well have been called forth by such native poems as the Old English *Christ*, which already emphasizes the pain of the scourging and of the thorns cruelly pressed down on the head.[6] Certainly there is a great gulf in time between these miniatures and the first Continental Crucifixion-paintings that show the figure (no longer wearing a regal crown, but thorns) with eyes closed, head fallen, and the feet nailed, as a refinement of torture, with a single nail. Midway between these presentations comes the psalter from St. Albans (now at Hildesheim), which is probably to be dated 1123.[7] The miniatures in this psalter are full of Anglo-Saxon reminiscences, and include a striking series of incidents of the Passion, in which a tall and regal Christ still retains his dignity. The scene of the Mocking recalls a mosaic in St. Mark's, Venice, and the Flagellation has Carolingian antecedents.[8] Christ, bare-backed, carries the Cross. There is no piercing with the spear, and, what is more surprising, no Crucifixion at all; the Deposition appears to do duty for it. A century later the Latin prayer to the salvific Cross prescribed in the English guide for anchoresses still uses the language of Carolingian devotion and even of Fortunatus' hymns. [9]

With the earlier conceptions the first stanza printed at the head of this chapter marks a clear break. Probably composed shortly after *Ancrene Wisse*, it is attributed to 'unus Anglicus, pietate motus' in the *Speculum Ecclesie*, which was composed by the learned and sainted Edmund of Abingdon (Archbishop of Canterbury, 1234–40), one of the first English writers to urge meditation on the Passion— though he probably had religious primarily in mind, the events of Christ's life and death being keyed throughout to the liturgical hours, as they were to be in many similar works. [10] The stanza is the earliest expression in vernacular poetry of a new feeling for the Cross and its burden that had been generated, in different ways, by the writings of St. Anselm, St. Bernard, and St. Bonaventure, or works ascribed to them. To expatiate on this phenomenon would be to rewrite the history of medieval spirituality. Enough here to note that though these saintly teachers wrote chiefly in prose, it was prose often lyrical in tone; and that tone was preserved in the vernacular writings modelled on or prompted by the devotional works in question. The three names are sufficient indication that these works were firmly rooted in orthodox theology; nor were they fundamentally different in spirit from scholasticism in its earliest flowering. John Pecham, whose *Philomena* has been described as the loveliest of all the Latin poems on the Passion, was a lecturer in theology at Paris and Oxford before he became Archbishop of Canterbury (1279–92); at Paris, as a Friar Minor, he had sat at Bonaventure's feet. True, by far the most influential book with which we are concerned, the *Meditationes Vitae Christi*, though it owed part of its prestige to being attributed to St. Bonaventure, was probably not compiled by him; yet there was probably some reason for the ascription, and it is not improper to speak of the new mode of feeling as Bonaventuran. [11]

The novelty of this mode will be evident if we compare the two stanzas cited with the Old English poem that was the theme of the opening chapter. Three differences at once emerge:

1. A new figure, the Virgin, has appeared on the scene. Indeed it is to her, in the first quatrain, that compassion is chiefly directed.

2. In the second quatrain the attention is on the marred beauty of the body—the white skin reddened with gore, the comely countenance grown pale.

3. The writer of the first stanza is not simply a narrator or spectator. He is emotionally involved in the scene, and so closely involved as to feel impelled to address the mother of God herself, here identified with her son in that her 'faire rode', her lovely face, has (it is implied) been marred like his. Distance of time and space is here annihilated.

It is this emotional identification with the Divine Mother at the foot of the Cross that gave impetus to the devotional tide which swept through Europe for two centuries. Not that the spare and restrained Gospel narratives were ignored or slighted. Rather, the least detail that they offer was seized on, lovingly scrutinized, and developed, sometimes according to the precedent of the Apocryphal Gospels, which themselves occasionally contributed new incidents. The intensifying of feeling takes place at the very time that Christian drama, as distinct from liturgical drama, is being born. As a few verses of Genesis grew into the Anglo-Norman play *Le Jeu d'Adam*, so the Gospel narrative of the Passion was extended early in the twelfth century into the Montecassino Passion Play, in the thirteenth into the Benedictbeuern *Ludus de Passione*, and later into the St. Gallen *Passionsspiel*; whilst in France a poem on the Passion, evidently widely circulated by jongleurs at the beginning of the thirteenth century (and, later, translated into English), was made the basis for the earliest vernacular Passion plays.[12] Already in the Montecassino play the *humanitas* of Christ is evident in his sufferings; and, following the example of St. Bernard, who himself followed St. Chrysostom in imagining a dialogue between the Virgin and her son, the playwrights greatly expanded the brief address to her recorded in the Gospels. In the Montecassino Passion she laments (significantly, in the vernacular), 'Why did I bear you in my womb?' A *Dialogus Beatae Mariae et Anselmi*—not an authentic work of that saint but like the

Bonaventuran *Meditationes* deriving some of its status from
the name attributed to it—which presented the Virgin as a
suffering mother and the Crucifixion as the more painful
because Christ was imagined as nailed and stretched to a
recumbent cross, had a marked influence on later plays and
poetry, French and English. The Passion thus becomes a
contemporary, a recurrent event, the action a continuous
present. And the regular use of the dramatic present early
distinguishes the treatment of the tragic sequence even in
prose works, as in the alliterative *Wooing of Our Lord*: 'Ah,
now they have brought him hither. Ah, now raise they up
the rood, set up the outlaw's tree [*warhtreo*: cf. *wergas* in *A
Vision of a Rood*, 31]. Ah, now my dear one is stripped. Ah,
now drive they him up with whips and with scourges.'[13]

The seeds of a dramatic role for 'la douce Marie' are
already present in St. Edmund's *Speculum*, where she is
given the words 'Call me not fair henceforth, for the
Almighty has filled me with bitterness and grief'. They are
adapted, as St. Edmund notes, from the Canticum
Canticorum: 'Marvel not that I am dark for the sun has
discoloured me' (1:6). But the saint calls it 'le chaunson de
amor', and that is the thirteenth century's distinctive and
revealing title for the Canticles: it was read as a love-song of
the Virgin and of Christ (and drawn on as much as Ovid for
the images of courtly love-lyric). Hence it is that the
English quatrain dwells on Mary's 'faire rode' and the
declining sun. 'Nolite considerare quod fusca sim, quia
decoloravit me sol.' She had borne the heat of the sun (even
though it had been darkened that Good Friday), standing
all day in front of the Rood tree, in this verse silhouetted
against the sky at sunset. But the stanza carries a deeper
poignancy. Not every reader or listener would think at once
of Mary as discoloured by the scorching sun; all would
imagine her as ravaged by grief. The weeping Mary was at
this very time taking her place at the foot of the Cross in
Latin hymns as in manuscript illuminations (and most of all
in psalters).[14] Alongside the plangent *Stabat Mater* is the
crisply dogmatic *Stabat iuxta Christi crucem*; both were
soon to be given English versions notable for their tenderness of feeling.[15]

The simple English verses are eloquent in their stark economy. But the submerged allusion to the Canticles signifies that the poet had been touched by the fecund stream of fervent devotion that flowed from St. Bernard's allegorical exposition of that book. The second quatrain of our headpiece, markedly ampler in description, likewise has a Latin antecedent. It is one of several translations or adaptations of a passage from the *Liber Meditacionis* of John of Fécamp (attributed also to Augustine), in carefully balanced Latin prose that is already half-way to verse:

Candet nudatum pectus. Rubet cruentum latus. Tensa arent viscera. Decora languent lumina. Regia pallent ora. Procera rigent brachia. Crura dependent marmorea. Et rigat tenebratos pedes beati sanguinis unda.

In the *Liber* this forms part of a prayer to God the Father, beseeching him to look on the sufferings of Christ and be merciful to man. The English lines, which were copied repeatedly, eventually become absorbed in longer meditations on the Passion, and in the fourteenth century Richard Rolle, the Yorkshire mystic, will have no qualms about inserting a version in a prayer addressed to Christ:

Meditacio de passione Christi

My keyng, that water grette and blode swette;
Sythen ful sare bette, so that hys blode hym wette,
When thair scowrges mette.
Ful fast thai gan hym dyng and at the pyler swyng,
And his fayre face defowlyng with spittyng.

The thorne crownes the keyng; ful sare es that prickyng.
Alas! my joy and my swetyng es demed to hyng,
Nayled was his handes, nayled was hys fete,
And thyrled was hys syde, so semely and so swete.

Naked es his whit breste, and rede es his blody syde;
Wan was his fayre hew, his wowndes depe and wyde.
In fyve stedes of his flesch the blode gan downe glyde
Als stremes of the strande; hys pyne es noght to hyde.

This to see es grete pyté, how he es demed to the dede
And nayled on the rode tre, the bryght aungels brede.
Dryven he was to dole, that es owre gastly gude,
And alsso in the blys of heven es al the aungels fude.

A wonder it es to se, wha sa understude,
How God of magesté was dyand on the rude.
Bot suth than es it sayde that lufe ledes the ryng;
That hym sa law hase layde bot lufe it was na thyng.

Jhesu, receyve my hert, and to thi lufe me bryng;
Al my desyre thou ert, I covete thi comyng.
Thow make me clene of synne, and lat us never twyn.
Kyndel me fire within, that I thi lufe may wyn,
And se thi face, Jhesu, in joy that never sal blyn.

Jhesu, my saule thou mend; thi lufe into me send,
That I may with the lend in joy withowten end.
In lufe thow wownde my thoght, and lyft my hert to the.
My sawle thou dere hase boght; thi lufer make it to be.

The I covete, this worlde noght, and for it I fle.
Tho ert that I have soght, thi face when may I see?
Thow make my sawle clere, for lufe chawnges my chere.
How lang sal I be here?[16]

The unexpected secular allusion in the very centre of these verses:

But sooth then is it said that love leads the ring;
That him so low has laid but Love it was no thing
[That which has laid him so low was nothing but Love]

is intelligible only if we consult Rolle's *Incendium Amoris*, which retains the ancient conception that Christ hastened to embrace the Cross ('ad crucem festinavit'): 'sed verum dicitur quia amor preit in tripudio, et coream ducit'. Love leads the ring-dance, the carole.

Rolle, like the Old English poet, sees the crucified figure as a King and Lord of majesty. But now pity is the prime emotion, and the paradox of the Incarnation is expressed in a typical medieval image, consonant with the frequent presence in painting of angels on either side of the upright beam of the Cross: 'nayled on the rode tre, the bryght aungels brede'—a phrase translating *panis angelorum* in the Easter liturgy, twice repeated by Rolle in another song of love-longing adapted into a different context by another poet ('Preye we to god that dyed on rode ... That Cristes face may ben *ur* fode'), and to be given a new intensity by Dunbar.

The passage from John of Fécamp that Rolle has adapted to his purpose is notable for its insistence on the whiteness of the body, the pallor of the face. Colour, and changes in colour, were one of the earliest additions to the Gospel narrative: 'The pallor of death had spread over his face; but Christ's cheeks and mouth were red with blood' is a rhetorical description attributed to Augustine; and when the Cistercian Ailred of Rievaulx composed the first English meditative exercise in the form of a letter to his sister he adjured her not to remain with those who stood afar off, but with the Virgin to approach the Cross and behold the face that was *perfusum pallore*. Later 'blody' and 'blo' (livid) became the characteristic epithets for the rent body on the Rood. Such emphases grew more marked as painted rood-screens or crucifixes became the focus of vision in every monastery and church, and the Crucifixion became a fixed part of the iconographic programme of psalters, Books of Hours, and missals (where it stood, as in later printed texts, before the Canon of the Mass). In all such figures the crown of thorns takes the place of the earlier regal crown, as the Man of Sorrows replaces the *Rex gloriae*. The familiarity of the image, in wood or stone, paper or vellum, meant that a writer or preacher could always appeal to it. So Friar John of Grimestone, when rendering 'Candet nudatum pectus', can add, 'the body stark, *as well thou seest*'. And a later rendering of a similar Latin text, 'Respice in faciem Christi' (sometimes ascribed to St. Bernard, and quoted in the *Golden Legend*), will begin, 'Loke to thi Lord, man, ther hangeth he on rode', and finish with the same direction to the tortured body:

> Bigin at his molde[a], and loke to his to[b]
> Ne saltu no wit vinde but angwisce and wo[c].[17]

[a] head   [b] toes   [c] You will find no sense but anguish and pain.

Such images and such simple, indeed archaic, diction brought the agony of the Passion within the awareness of the simplest peasant. Suffering is a universal language. A recurrent figure, present in the early *Ancrene Wisse*, is that of the dovecote that stood in the vicinity of every manor: 'For as a dovehouse is full of holes,' says Rolle in his

Meditations, so is thy body full of wounds'[18] (it is also 'like a book written with red ink'). In the Holkham Bible Picture Book the completely naked body of the Crucified is pierced with scores of such gaping, dripping wounds.

Pity and love are the persistent terms of the new poetry. Rolle's whole purpose was to induce tears. 'If thou wilt think this ilk day,' says a headnote to his prose *Meditations on the Passion*, 'thou shalt find sweetness that shall draw thy heart up, that shall cause thee to fall into greeting [weeping].' 'Weep, if thou mightest, tears all of blood', runs the English rendering of the *Respice*. The poems in Friar Grimestone's collection, made later in the fourteenth century (1372), are so many extensions of or variations on the refrain

> Luveli ter of loveli eye, whi dostu me so wo?
> Sorful ter of sorful eye, thu brekst myn herte ato[a].[19]

> [a] in two.

'Jesu', pleads another poet, who (like Crashaw later) did not disdain to use an image of secular love-song, in which Cupid figured as love's agent,

> Jhesu let me fele what joy hit be
> To suffyre wo for love of the,
> How myry hit is for to wepe,
> How softe in harde clothes to slepe.
> Lat now Love his bow bende
> And love-arowes to my hert send,
> That hit mowe percen to the roote
> For suche woundes shold be my bote.[20]

This is the climax of a verse-meditation on every step of Christ's journey to the 'hard knotty rode tree' that made him 'shiver and quake' and that he bore 'with reuthly chere—the teres ran down by thy lere'. 'In seiynge of this orisoun,' says the rubric, 'stynteth and bydeth at every cros and thynketh whate ye have seide.' 'Wel owe I to wepe that stounde [at that hour]' is the poet's application of the sufferings:

> Write upon my hert boke
> Thy faire and swete lovely loke.

It will by now be apparent why in the Middle Ages tears were accounted a grace rather than a disgrace. It was said of Marie of Oignies that after meditating on or reading of the Passion she wept till she was so feeble that she could not bear to behold the Cross. Margery Kempe's unrestrained and embarrassing sobbings were of the same origin and order. Christ, she averred, assured her that her tears were 'angels' drink and very piment [sweetened wine] unto them'.[21] The phrase reveals that the voice she heard was not Christ's but St. Bernard's: it is to Bernard that the *Speculum Christiani*[22] attributes the phrase 'tears of penance be wine of angels'. Margery's manifestations of grief were undoubtedly extreme, if not psychopathic. Yet masculine intellects before and after her time exhibited similar grief. Donne will pour forth tears to the Cross as naturally as to his mistress.

When in the fourteenth and the fifteenth centuries the books of devotion multiply, so do the elements of mourning and complaint; and so do depictions of the sufferings. Just about the time that Rolle[23] was writing his poem, a Dominican friar (it appears) commissioned for a new kind of public a series of miniatures depicting the Life, Death, and Resurrection of Christ that included no less than thirty scenes of the Passion.[24] In them the crown of thorns is reduced to a fillet. But the artist pays special attention to the colour of the Rood. At first it is green (as in some other paintings, including Duccio's *Maestà*); but it appears to die with Christ, becoming brown—perhaps an idiosyncratic allusion to Christ's words as he was led away to be crucified (Luke 23:31).

Nowhere are the effects of the new and intense devotion to the Passion more marked than in the *Revelations* of Julian of Norwich. It is to this devotion that the *Revelations* owe the particularity which now strikes us as so novel.

... the great drops of blood fell down from under the garland [of thorn] like pellets, seeming as it had come out of the veins. . . . the plenteoushead is like to the drops of water that fall off the eaves of a house after a great shower of rain . . . and for the roundness they were like to the scale of herring . . . And one time I saw how half the face, beginning at the ear, over-rede with dry blood, till it closed in to the mid face, and after that the other half beclosed on the same wise.[25]

What marks out her descriptions of the sufferings is the series of vivid similes—sagging cloths, herring scales, raindrops dripping from eaves—and the unchronological sequence: the scourging comes after the bleeding, the vision shifts back and forth. But it is all occasioned by the sight of the crucifix held up before Julian when she was on the point, it seemed, of death; and as a woman she sees it all through the eyes of the Virgin Mother: 'Our Lord God showed our Lady saint Mary [to me] *in that same time*: that is to mean the high wisdom and truth she had in beholding of her maker . . . and with this she saw herself so little and so low, so simple and so poor, in regard [respect] of her Lord God . . . and thus she was fulfilled of grace [*plena gratiae*] and of all manner virtues.' This is not mystical experience in the strictest sense: it is the result of constant absorption in the *humanitas* of Christ, as enjoined in the books of meditation. So too, when Margery Kempe presents herself as telling Our Lady to cease sorrowing, for her son is out of pain, and as taking her home, where she 'made a good caudle of broth to comfort her', she is following literally the prescription of the Bonaventuran *Meditationes*, which, in the rendering made by Nicholas Love about the time of Margery's visions, enjoins: 'And then also *by devout imagination as though thou were bodily present*, comfort Our Lady and that other fellowship, praying them to eat somewhat for yet they be fasting.'[26] When St. Louis, roused from contemplation at Mass, had said he thought that he was in the desert, walking with Jesus, he was really testifying to the effects of prescribed meditative practice. We know that Margery read Bonaventuran books; and her travels on the Continent would bring her in touch with the cultus of the suffering Son that was so powerful in Northern Europe in her day—especially amongst women[27]—and that Ludolf of Saxony had set forth in his *Vita Christi* with Germanic thoroughness.

But all the divine dolours described in such harrowing

detail[28] were read as demonstrations of Christ's love. Says Julian:

The Union (one-head) of the godhead gave strength to the manhood *for love* to suffer more than all men might suffer . . . Our Lord looked unto his side and led forth the understanding of his creature by the same wound into his side within. And then he showed a fair delectable place and large enough for all mankind that shall be saved to rest in peace and in love. And with the sweet beholding he showed his blissful heart even cloven in two . . . stirring the pure soul to understand . . . the endless love that is and shall be ever.

The cloven heart is a feature of the *imago pietatis*, the figure of the wounded Christ, now detached from the Cross, who presents his pierced heart and his five wounds to the beholder.[29] So when a fifteenth-century verse addressed to 'Man unkind [unnatural]' concludes 'Lo here myn herte', the appeal is visual; it is to be taken literally. But the most poignant of all the utterances from the Cross, the cry of *Sitio*, 'I thirst', is now regularly read as having a deeper meaning than the literal: it too is transformed into a cry of love. The figurative interpretation in fact is found as early as Bede, who wrote: 'tu dixisti *sitio*, sc. salutem animarum sanctorum quae in limbo erant' (thou saidest 'I thirst', that is for the salvation of the souls of the saints which were in limbo); *Ancrene Wisse* follows this gloss, when saying that Christ thirsted for man's 'heal', and it was the basis of a Latin prayer often attributed to Bede and included in Books of Hours, as well as in a late Scottish collection, where it runs: 'I thrist, that wes the heill of the haly fatheris and saulis bidand my cuming to the Limbe.'[30] 'Amore sitio, sitiendo pereo' (I thirst for love, thirsting I perish) runs another pregnant formulation.[31] Langland will give the figure new force and content.

The Dominical words on the Cross were thought to provide warrant for putting into Christ's mouth, first, the prophetic utterance in Jeremiah's Lamentations over Jerusalem: 'Is it nothing to you, all ye that pass by? Behold and see if there is any sorrow like unto my sorrow . . .' (which the English writer of the longest of all Passion poems inserts into his version of a far older French text);[32] and secondly an appeal to his tormentors, who stand for all sinful men. For every act of sin is a torture to Christ, hence a cause of his suffering.[33] This address from the Cross can be of love, or reproach, or both. When of love it may be in the phrase of secular lyric, with man's soul figuring as a wooed mistress:

> Swete lemman[a], y deye for thi love:
> Yf I deye for the
> Wy ne wiltu lenden me thin ore[b]?
> Thi love bindes me so sore.
> Think wat I tholie, lef[c], for the,
> Bilef[d] thi sinne and toren[e] to me.

[a] lover   [b] show me thy mercy   [c] what I endure, dear   [d] leave   [e] turn.

And man replies:

> Whan I have done al my folie
> Than wil I 'Iesu, mercy' the crye,
> 'Thin ore, thin ore, mi swete lemman.'

Here *ore* is not only favour shown to a suppliant lover but the divine mercy shown to a sinner. (The first line of the reply is somewhat out of key.) In the light of such verses it is not so surprising that a West Country priest (as Giraldus Cambrensis tells the tale), after he had sung and danced the night away, should have begun his morning mass with the refrain from a love-song: 'Swete lemman, thin ore'. After which his bishop had good grounds for interdicting the song.[34]

The addresses of reproach have a longer and more intricate history. In the Old English *Christ* the Saviour bids man behold his wounds, in a passage with no liturgical origin. But he is there speaking on Judgement Day. The medieval Reproaches derive ultimately from the ancient *Improperia* of the liturgy for Good Friday, a moving catena of verses from Lamentations, Micah, and Isaiah, of which George Herbert will provide the finest English rendering; earlier versions are therefore best considered in relation to his.[35] In our own day a phrase in Eliot's 'Ash Wednesday' harks back to the same lament: 'O my people'.

It will be timely to pay some attention at this point to the chief prose sources of medieval accounts of the Passion whence came the ore that the fervour of preachers and poets refined into precious metal. The chief quarry of all such materials, the *Golden Legend*, Jacobus de Voragine had compiled about 1270, at the very time that devotion to the humanity of Christ was reaching its culmination in the Cistercian and Franciscan orders that did so much to disseminate it. The *Legend* was not accessible in English before the fifteenth century, when Caxton made a fine rendering of a French version that William Morris re-printed in three noble folios.[36] The section on the Passion comes early in the book, bringing together the patristic teachings under a sequence of Latin rubrics, as thus:

Popule meus [Micah] is an excusation we say on Good Friday like as Jesus Christ would say: 'Thou accusest me because that I defend[a] to pay my trewage and thou oughtest rather to thank me of that I have delivered thee from trewage ... thou accusest me that I say me to be the son of God, and mightest more to thank me that I have chosen thee to be in my vineyard.

[a] refuse.

The image of the vineyard derives from Isa. 5:2, a tract for Holy Saturday. In the Canticles the Vineyard figures with the Orchard as an abode of the beloved; and in the most haunting and mysterious of all medieval poems, *Quia Amore Langueo* (which takes it name and refrain from Cant. 2:5, a verse that gives a new verb to the English language),[37] the vineyard motif from the *Improperia* is decorously translated into English thus:

> Fair love, lete us go playe,
> Apples be ripe in my gardyne.

The pattern of contrast that controls the *Improperia* likewise appears in the English poem:

> My faire spouse and my love bright
> I saved her from beting and she hath me bet:
> I clothed her in grace and hevenly light
> This blody sherte she hath on me set.

'This blody sherte' is the *vesta purpurea* of John 19:2, 5. In poems that we have yet to consider it will be given a specifically knightly cut.

In the *Golden Legend* almost all the Messianic scriptures find a place and are duly interpreted. So Job's complaint, 'Noti me quasi alieni recesserunt' (My familiar friends have forgotten me: Job 19:14), is counterbalanced by a sentence from Augustine: 'What shall he now do when he shall reign that hath done this when he should die?' Interspersed are passages from the Synoptic Gospels (and, from St. John, Pilate's question, 'What is Truth?'; on which de Voragine anticipates Bacon's comment: 'He abode not the answer, nor was he worthy to hear it'). There is much, however, in the *Legend* that is not in the Gospels: like the unspeakable stench of Calvary, from the rotting corpses, and the explanation of the vinegar mingled with gall: given so that the crucified victim might have more pain and die the sooner, enabling the soldiers to go off duty earlier.

For the account of the physical sufferings St. Bernard is cited, not implausibly. For St. Bernard, austere in so many ways, was at the same time a skilled rhetorician, who would lavish all his powers on the spectacle of the dying Lord: 'The eyes more shining than the sun be extinct in death. The ears hear not the song of the angels but the assaults of sinners. The hands that formed the heavens be stretched on the Cross.' In a passage beginning 'Tu es Homo', the saint, or someone of the Cistercian school, had supplied his own version of the Reproaches, seizing on the *vestis alba* of Luke 23:11 (the Authorized Version is closer to the Greek)[38] to make a rhetorical point. In Caxton's rendering of the *Legend* the passage runs:

Thou art a man and hast a chaplet of flowers, and I am God and have a chaplet of thorns. Thou hast gloves on thy hands, and I have nails fixed in my hands. Thou dancest in white vestures, and I God am mocked and vilipended, and in the house of Herod had received a *white garment*. Thou dancest and playest with thy feet; and I with my feet have laboured in great pain. Thou stretchest out thy arms across in carolling and gladness, and I stretch mine on the Cross in great opprobrium and villainy. Thou hast thy side and thy breast open in sign of vain-glory, and I have mine opened with a spear. Nevertheless return to me and I shall receive thee . . .

It is these Bernardine reproaches that yield almost all the images in Middle English poems of the Passion that on a first reading seem so bold and new. From this source also comes the special attention to the crown of thorns (made of 'jonkes' of the sea)[39] that was pressed into the 'brains of the soul', as Julian saw, so that blood sprang out. It is 'St. Bernard', to take a final instance, who interprets the four corners of the Cross (adorned, much as in the Anglo-Saxon poet's vision, with gems and precious stones) as the four virtues that Christ embodied: Patience, Humility, Obedience, Charity. To the Bernardine exegesis the *Legend* adds St. Anselm's doctrine on the sufferings and St. Augustine's on the sacrifice of Christ as the second Adam, who suffered death at midday on a Friday in March in the very place ('some say') where Adam was buried, and naked as Adam was naked. In the *Legend* too is the bizarre motif of the hook of divinity hidden in the flesh of humanity. For had not Job said (41:1): 'May ye not take the fiend with an hook?' In fact Job had not said that, but 'Canst thou draw out Leviathan with an hook?'; Bernard (or his imitator) is following the gloss in Gregory's *Moralia*.[40] Even the Payment theory of Redemption is touched on in the *Legend*: Christ, being 'departed from the debtors', could not shed his blood as a debtor, but with it could cancel the chirograph, or bill of indictment,[41] and the debt that had been mounting with interest ever since the Fall.

The *Legend* is the supreme popular compendium of the Bernardine theology and imagery that the Crucifixion inspired. It gives meaning (for example) to a visual pattern laid out by St. Augustine (in the *Liber de Virgine*) that remains constant for centuries: Christ's head bowed—to kiss, his arms spread—to embrace, his feet nailed—to signify that he will abide: 'abide' is the term regularly used in this context in English writing and so adopted by Caxton, and in the fifteenth-century *Speculum Devotorum*. One manuscript anthology gives first the original passage as St. Bernard quoted it (in Sermo 31, 'De Passione Domini'),

then a French version of it, chiefly in rhyme, and a third
'Anglice ad idem':

> Man, folwe seintt Bernardes trace[a]
> And loke in Jhesu Cristes face,
> How hee lut[b] hys heved to the
> Swetlike for to kessen the,
> And sprat[c] hise armes on the tre,
> Senful man, to klippen[d] the.
> In sygne of love ys open his syde:
> Hiis feet ynayled with the t'abyde.
> Al his bodi is don[e] on rode,
> Senful man, for thyne goode.[42]

> [a] path [b] bows [c] spreads [d] embrace [e] placed.

This is indeed *Anglice*: after the second line only one
word is not native English.

If the language as well as the imagery of such poems is
limited, even at times monotonous, it is because they had
both been fixed by St. Bernard: Bernardine devotion is
their fountain-head. They would be developed, but not
radically altered.

As it became mandatory to dwell on the whiteness of the
flesh, the pallor of the face,[43] so, in the poems of reproach,
the constant term is *unkind*: not to be given its modern
sense but the original meaning of 'unnatural':

> Unkynde man, gif kepe til[a] me
> And loke what payne I suffer for the.
> . . .
> Of all the payne that I suffer sare,
> Within my hert it greves me mare
> The unkyndenes that I fynd in the.[44]

> [a] give heed to.

'Sweet' is the counterbalancing epithet. Christ addresses
man as 'sweet brother', or 'sweet lemman', the poets speak
of his sweet passion: 'Sweet the nails and sweet the tree and
sweeter the burden that hangs upon thee' ran the earliest

rendering of Fortunatus' *Crux Fidelis*.[45] The constant recurrence might be cloying did not the simple monosyllables and short lines make for a dominant purity of tone:

> The naylis beit[a] al to longe,
> The smyt his al to sleye,
> Thue bledis al to longe,
> The tre his al to heye.
> The stonis waxin wete—
> Allas! Jhesu mi suete,
> Feu frendis hafdis neye,
> Bot Sin Jon murnind
> And Mari wepind,
> That all thi sorue seye[b].[46]

> [a] are   [b] saw.

Here is no description of suffering or action or circumstance, no word from Christ or any bystander. Only the wet stones show that blood is dripping from the wounds. The single phrase of pity—'Few friends haddest nigh'—is a curt contraction of the last verse of a Messianic psalm: 'Lover and friend hast thou put far from me and mine acquaintance into darkness' (Ps. 88:18).

The bare simplicity of such poems contrasts markedly with the amplitude of their prose counterparts, which have no restriction of form or rhyme. In prose the sweetness does now seem excessive: 'Jesu, swete, Jesu, mi druth [beloved], mi derling, mi drihten [lord], mi healend [saviour], min huniter [drop of honey], min halewei [balm]'; 'mi honibrid, mi sweting, mi honilif'; 'sweter than milc in muthe, mede, methe or pyment [mead or spiced wine]'; though again native, indeed archaic, appellatives (*drihten, healend*) provide an offsetting element. When the famous hymn *Jesu dulcis memoria*, often ascribed to St. Bernard but thought by Dom Wilmart to have been written by an English Cistercian, was translated in the fourteenth century as 'Jhesu swete is the love of the', it was rendered in just such plain native English. And so with the Bernardine extension of the Reproaches quoted earlier from the *Legend*, which

takes lyrical form in simple short-lined yet by no means
artless stanzas:

> Jesus doth him bymene,
> And speketh to synful mon;
> 'Thi garland is of grene,
> Of floures many on;
> Myn of sharpe thornes,
> Myn hewe it maketh won.
> 'Thyn hondes streite gloved,
> White and clene kept;
> Myne with nailes thorled[a]
> On rode, and eke my feet.

> 'Acros thou berest thyn armes,
> Whan thou dauncest narewe;
> To me hastou non awe,
> But to worldes glorie—
> Myne for the on rode
> With the Jewes wode
> With grete ropis todraw.

> 'Opyne thou hast thi syde—
> Spaiers[b] longe and wide—
> For veyn glorie and pride,
> And thi longe knyf astrout[c]—
> Thou ert of the gai route[d]:
> Myn with spere sharpe
> Ystongen[e] to the herte;
> My body with scourges smerte
> Biswongen[f] al aboute.

> 'Al that y tholede[g] on rode for the,
> To me was shame and sorwe;
> Wel litel thou lovest me,
> And lasse thou thenkest on me,
> An evene and eke amorwe[h].

'Swete brother, wel myght thou se
Thes peynes stronge in rode tre
Have y tholed for love of the;
Thei that have wrought it me
May synge welawo.
Be thou kynde pur charite,
Let[i] thi synne and love thou me,
Hevene blisse y shal yevc[j] the,
That lasteth ay and oo[k].'[47]

[a]pierced   [b]slits (in gowns)   [c]sticking out   [d]company   [e]stabbed
[f]beaten   [g]suffered   [h]in the morning   [i]leave   [j]give   [k]for ever and ever.

The English poet has picked up the sense of Bernard's 'side and breast open in sign of vainglory': he sees that it alludes to fine clothes, 'spaiers longe and wide' being (presumably) fashionable slashed jerkins or pleated pourpoints, and he develops the contrast by adding the young spark's 'long knife', juxtaposing it to Longinus' spear. In this he may have been prompted by plays of the Passion presented in streets thronged with gaily dressed youths or even acted by them, just as Chaucer's foppish Absolon 'played Herodes upon a scaffold high'. Certain it is that by the fifteenth century Northern European painters and carvers were peopling Crucifixion scenes with just such elegant young men. There is an unusual but not wholly inappropriate touch of fine language in the last stanza, where Christ adjures his 'sweet brother' to be 'kynde pur charite' (and where the French phrase indicates that 'kind' is approaching its modern meaning).

Of the other prose texts that played a major part in shaping the patterns of devotion to the Cross in England, St. Edmund's *Speculum* had been translated three times by the fifteenth century, and one of these versions (which includes long interpolations) is ascribed in two manuscripts to Richard Rolle. St. Edmund was one of the first to enjoin meditation on 'the Manhood' of Christ—'the meekness of his Incarnation and the Charity of his Passion'. Throughout the passages of the *Speculum* keyed to the liturgical hours these two aspects of the *humanitas* are kept in balance—a balance that later meditative books do not always preserve. At times the English text (like the French) takes on a lyrical rhythm, as in this chapter:

Now, dere frende, before matyns sall thou thynke of the swete byrthe of Jhesu Cryste alther-fyrste[a], and sythyne[b] eftyrwarde of his passione. Of his byrth sall thou thynke besyly[c] the tyme, and the stede[d], and the houre that oure lorde Jhesu Criste was borne of his modir Marie. The tyme was in myd-wyntter, whene it was maste calde, the houre was at mydnyghte, the hardeste houre that es, the stede was in mydwarde the strete, in a house with-owttene walles; in clowtis was he wondene and also a childe was he bundene, and in a crybbe by-fore ane Oxe and ane Asse that lufely lorde layde was, for thare was na nother stede voyde . . . Of the passione, sall thou thynke how that he was at swylke[e] a tyme of the nyghte betrayed of his descyple, and takene als a traytoure, and bowndene als a thefe, and ledde als a felone . . .

   Be-fore pryme[f], thou sall thynke of the passione of Jhesu and of his joyfull ryssynge. Of his passyone sall thou thynke how the Jewes ledde hym in to thaire counsaile, and bare false wytnes agayne hym, and put appone hym that he had saide blasefemé, that es sclandyre in godde, and that he had said that he suld haue distroyede the temple of goddc and make agayne another with-in the thirde day; and thane thay bygane to dryfe hym till hethynge[g] and to fulle[h] hym als a fule, and spite one hyme in dispyte in his faire face; and sythyne thay hide his eghene[i], and gafe hyme bofetes grete and sythene asked hyme whate he was that hym smate; and sythene thay ledde hym dreryly to the dede[j], and yitt never he sayde till thaym anes[k] why thay swa dyde. Many othyre wykkydnes thay dide hym, that lange ware to telle.[48]

[a] first of all   [b] then   [c] earnestly   [d] place   [e] such   [f] 9 a.m.   [g] treat him with scorn   [h] beat   [i] eyes   [j] miserably to death   [k] once.

St. Edmund, in fact, like the translator, rarely enlarges on the biblical record. He is content to assert that 'if alle the sekenes of this werlde and all the sorowe ware in the body of a man anely, and that man myghte consayle alls mekyle noye [hurt] and angwysce and sorowe in his body alls the men of this werlde moghte thynke, yitt it ware full littill or else noghte to regarde of [in comparison with] the sorowe that he sufferde for us ane houre of the daye'.

   The *Meditations on the Passion* ascribed to Rolle, though perhaps influenced in style by the *Speculum*, were not intended for religious but for beginners in the contemplative life. They are fuller and more fervent; more dramatic, in a word, more 'Bonaventuran':

A, Lord, thi sorwe, why were it not my deth? Now thei lede the forthe nakyd as a worm, the turmentoures abowtyn the, and armede knyghtes; the prees of the peple was wonderly strong, thei hurled[a] the and haryed the so schamefully, thei spurned the with here feet, as thou hadde been a dogge. I se in my soule how reufully thou gost: thi body is so blody, so rowed[b] and so bledderyd[c]; thi crowne is so kene, that sytteth on thi hed; thi heere mevyth with the wynde, clemyd[d] with the blood; thi lovely face so wan and so bolnyd[e] with bofetynge and with betynge, with spyttynge, with spowtynge; the blood ran therewith, that grysyth in my syght[f]; so lothly and so wlatsome[g] the Jues han the mad, that a mysel[h] art thou lyckere than a clene man.[49]

[a] harassed [b] made raw [c] blistered [d] clotted [e] swollen [f] makes me shudder to see [g] repulsive [h] leper.

'I see in my soul how ruefully thou goest.' Julian of Norwich was to have just such sights, and to describe them in just such similes and alliterative phrases.

The Bonaventuran chapters on the Passion, whilst making much of the Agony in the Garden, which rarely figures in English verse except in two homely stanzas,[50] dwell on the sorrows of Mary almost as much as on those of her son. And the new occasion for pathos thus introduced proved prolific, partly perhaps because Mary thus became the mouthpiece of human protest and human compassion. These chapters were rendered in sometimes pedestrian verse (unfairly ascribed by their editor to Robert Mannyng of Bourne), in which Mary beseeches the Father to redeem Man in some other way, and Christ cries

> On thys cros she ys with me
> Y shulde be crucyfyed and nat she.

The translator seems almost to relish describing the contumely Christ suffers:

> They punged[a] hym furthe thurgh every slogh
> As an hors ys prykked that goth yn plogh.[51]

> [a] pricked.

The prose translation of the major part of the Bonaventuran *Meditationes* made *c.* 1410 by Nicholas Love, prior of the Carthusian house of Mount Grace in Yorkshire, bears the title 'the Mirrour of the blessed lyf of Jesu Crist'. It renders in full (*inter alia*) Chapters XL to XLVIII of the Latin. Love marks in the margin passages that he has rearranged or interspersed with comments of his own; and the margin also gives certain key phrases that by now had a fixed place in the theology of the Passion; for example, opposite the passage on the Agony in the Garden is the Old Testament text 'Oblatus est quia ipse voluit', which we have met already. Love preserves throughout the work exhortations to the 'simple souls' for whom it was destined. So, having reached the apocryphal episode in which John, Mary, the Magdalene, and others gather in the Magdalene's house, he says, 'Take now intent to them and have compassion of them'. This insistence on inward meditation leading to emotional identification with the actors in the drama characterizes the whole sequence, and is of a piece with the regular use of the dramatic present and with the direct authorial address to some of them ('O Pilat, Pilat! woll thou reprehende and chastice thy lord God?'). Here is the mocked Christ, seeking after his clothes that had been cast in divers places and quaking for great cold, 'for as the gospel witnesseth [John 18:18] it was than harde cold'; the smiting of the forehead 'full of thornes'; the throng of 'the foulest ribalds and winedrinkers who made their songs of him'; the Virgin covering his nakedness with her kerchief; the ascent of the Cross by a short ladder (though Love finds room also for the *jacente cruce* tradition); the 'ghostly' intent of *Sitio* ('he threstede ayeyne the hele [thirsted for the salvation] of soules; neverthelesse also in sothenesse he threstede bycause of the grete passynge out of blood . . .'). *Consummatum est* is not only given a full gloss: the Heavenly Father replies, 'Come now/my swete loved sone: thou hast wel done all thinges . . .'. Then 'Oure Lord Jesu . . . wex al pale; now stekynge [closing] the eiyen and now oponynge; and bowed his hede/now on to that oon side and now onto that other'.[52] Such descriptions affected all classes of readers; and Love's *Mirror* remained popular till the eve of the Reformation.

The *Meditationes* have been described as Bernardine in their theology, Franciscan in their piety: 'Mihi absit gloriari nisi in cruce' (Far be it from me to glory except in the Cross) was a Franciscan motto, and the saint's stigmata were unimpugnable proofs of his identification with the Divine Agony. The prime concern of the original work and all the later variants of it is to stimulate compassion, and so devotion to the Crucified. The rhapsodical prose is deliberately patterned to move the reader's feelings. In this art the Franciscans were skilled, as their verses and their sermons show. Yet until the fifteenth century the vernacular works in this kind, being aimed at the hearts of 'simple creatures', remained plain in syntax and vocabulary, tender in feeling. The contrast with the vast Latin *Vita Christi*, a learned and all-embracing compilation made *c.* 1350 by Ludolf of Saxony (like Love a Carthusian) is very marked.[53]

The influence of the Bonaventuran work was in part due to the dramatic and pictorial possibilities afforded by its multiplication of incident. The Latin manuscripts were often illustrated; Émile Mâle purported to trace their impress on late Gothic art; and the writers of the mystery plays probably drew upon them. Love's translation even provided costume directions: thus the purple robe becomes 'an old red robe, foul and mis-shapen'. It should be noted, however, that in these plays Christ has a largely passive role: in the Wakefield *Coliphizacio* (Buffeting) out of 450 lines he speaks only four. They tend to present his torturers as constantly making game of him. Thus, in the same play, when he sits on a stool it is for a 'new play of Yule' and when he kneels it is for the game of hot cockles, in which the victim, like Christ, is blindfolded. The scene may be compared with the account of the tortures in the fourteenth-century *Siege of Jerusalem*. The Jews, says the alliterative poet, had scourged Christ with whips of *cour-bouilli* till he ran with red blood as rain runs in the streets, blinded him like a bee (a common medieval simile), and 'unbekastyn hym with a crye'—surrounded him as the huntsmen in *Gawain* surround their quarry. It was to avenge this 'villainy' that Titus besieged the holy city.

Powerful and pervasive as the Bonaventuran and Bernardine influences were, they did not inhibit fresh and direct apprehension of the central scene. Working against the vogue for dramatic realism is a liking for cryptic images that have a shock-effect:

> Men rent me on rode
> With wndes woliche wode;
> Al blet[a] mi blode—
> Thenk, man, al it is the to gode!
>
> Thenk who the first wroghte,
> For what werk helle thow sowhte,
> Thenk who the ageyn bowhte[b]—
> Werk warli, fayle me nowhte.
>
> Biheld mi side,
> Mi wndes sprede so wide;
> Restles I ride.
> Lok upon me! Put fro the pride.
>
> Mi palefrey is of tre,
> With nayles naylede thwrh me.
> Ne is more sorowe to se—
> Certes noon more no may be![54]

> [a] bleeds   [b] redeemed.

Much of this is common form, even commonplace: one or more of the Capital Sins are frequently named in Passion poetry. But the sharply ironic image of the Rood as a palfrey has earlier parallel only in fourteenth-century sermons on the Christ-knight who 'pro equo habuit crucem super quam pependit'. It reappears in the later Towneley Play, where a torturer jeers:

> Stand nere, felows and let se
> How we can hors oure kyng so fre!

It might be the mockery aimed at the unkinged Richard II as he was taken through the streets of London.

Rolle thinks of the wind stirring Christ's hair, and in his *Meditations* (on the strength of John 18:18 and *tempestive* in the Latin *Meditationes*) makes much of the cold of Good Friday. Julian of Norwich describes the same wind blowing bitterly over Calvary: 'Each time that our Lord and Blessed Saviour died upon the rood it was a dry, harre [bitter] wind and woundy cold, as to my sight.' In two carols of a later time it sounds through the refrains:

> Blow the winde styl and blow nat so shyl;
> My blode, man, I shed for the al at wyl.
> Blow the winde styl and blow nat so shyll;
> *This paine to suffre is my Father's wil.*

> There blows a cold wynd todaye, todaye,
> The wynd blows cold todaye.
> Cryst sufferyd his passyon for man's salvacyon,
> *To kype the cold wynd awaye.*[55]

The fact that the later verses of the second carol allegorize the cold wind as temptation does not weaken the force of the repeated refrain, which sets the Crucifixion firmly in a harsh northern landscape. Another phrase of Julian's has similar reverberations. 'This long pining', she wrote in the chapter just cited, 'seemed to me as if he had been seven nights dead, dying, at the point of out-passing away, suffering the last pain ... seven nights dead ... seven nights dead. . . .' The repetition parallels that in a fragment of Shetlands verse:

> Nine nichts he hang pa de rutless tree ...
> Nine lang nichts in da nipping rime;

which seems to represent a Christian transmutation of a Norse belief about the god Odin, who in the *Verse Edda* says: 'I hung on the windy tree nine nights long: wounded with a spear and given to Odin: myself, to myself, on that tree of which none knows from what roots it springs.'

A more bizarre image, found in Walter Hilton's *Stimulus Amoris*, a diluted version of a luxuriant Latin work by James of Milan, is that of the Cross as an altar on which Christ's flesh is baked to feed starving men; a variant of the figure in which it is a charger bearing 'the lamb of love, rosted ageyn the sun'.

The medieval reader would not label such lines as

'conceits', and they were easily accommodated to the terse affective mode, which remained dominant till Skelton's time. A poem formerly attributed to him embodies most of the earlier themes and motifs in four elaborately devised stanzas, outgrowths of the devotion to the *imago pietatis* popularized in the late Middle Ages by vernacular primers and by Books of Hours.

> Wofully araide,
> My blode, man,
> For the ran,
> Hit may not be naide[a],
> My body blo[b] and wanne,
> Wofully araide.
>
> Beholde me, I pray the, with all thyne hole reson,
> And be not hard hertid, for this encheson[c]:
> That I for thi saule sake was slayne, in good seson,
> Begilid and betraide by Judas fals treson,
> Unkindly intretid,
> With sharp corde sore fretid,
> The Jues me thretid,
> They mowid[d], they spittid, and disspisid me,
> Condemned to deth as thou maiste se.
>
> Thus nakid am I nailid, O man, for thi sake.
> I love the, thenne love me. Why slepist thou? awake!
> Remember my tender hert-rote for the brake,
> With paynes my vaines constrayned to crake.
> Thus was I defasid,
> Thus was my flesh rasid[e],
> And I to deth chasid,
> Like a lambe led unto sacrefise,
> Slayne I was in most cruell wise.
>
> Of sharpe thorne I have worne a crowne on my hed,
> So rubbid, so bobbid[f], so rufulle, so red,
> Sore payned, sore strayned, and for thi love ded,
> Unfayned, not demed, my blod for the shed,
> My fete and handis sore,
> With sturdé naylis bore;
> What myght I suffer more
> Then I have sufferde, man, for the?
> Com when thou wilt, and welcome to me.

Dere brother, non other thing I desire,
But geve me thi hert fre, to rewarde myne hire.
I am he that made the erth, water, and fire.
Sathanas, that sloven and right lothely sire,
Hym have I overcaste,
In hell presoune bounde faste,
Wher ay his woo shall laste.
I have purvaide a place full clere
For mankynde, whom I have bought dere.[56]

   [a]denied [b]livid [c]cause [d]grimaced [e]torn [f]buffeted.

Some of the phrasal patterns here are reminiscent of Nicholas Love, who had described Christ as 'so falsely accused, so enviously pursued, and so despitously slain'. It is only when, as in the last stanza, such verses enter the realm of the moralistic, the assertive, or the denunciatory that they dwindle in power. Lydgate's flamboyant poems on the Passion provide all too many object-lessons of this kind. By this time too, moreover, concern with the sorrows of the Virgin comes near to outweighing that for the sufferings of her son: witness the Bridgettine Breviary.[57] Complaint poems likewise grow tediously didactic. Yet Lydgate's popular *Testament* (surviving in fourteen manuscripts) has some tender and moving stanzas, concluding with the appeal:

> Cum on, my frend, my brother most entire,
> For thee I offered my blud in sacrifice.

To a modern reader it sometimes seems that in the fifteenth century (when devotion to the Five Wounds also reached its height)[58] piety is becoming fevered, and that Christ's *humanitas* has become synonymous with his passibility. One may ask whether the result was not a sterile religion, practicable only for those with leisure to read and to pray, and inaccessible to the 'poor labourers and busy husbandmen' who made up the bulk of society. *Piers Plowman* (which survives largely in fifteenth-century manuscripts) will provide one answer to this question. Another lies in the classic devotional books themselves. None of their writers regarded meditation on the Passion as anything but an early step in the Christian life. 'Blessed is the man', says Rolle, 'who may in any point follow thee here with the shadow of thy Cross.' If you wish to come to knowledge of the Divinity, says Ludolf, the *humanitas* of the Passion is the royal road: 'Imitatio Christi est summa et perfecta religio'. The lessons of the Cross are to be applied not only in penitential prayer but in daily practice. Rolle makes a personal moral *applicatio* of each scene of the Passion. Walter Hilton is equally insistent on this, and rich withal in saving common sense: 'Don't spend all your time meditating on the Passion to the neglect of your fellow Christian. Wash Christ's feet by attending to your subjects and your tenants. . . . If devotion comes not with mind of the Passion, strive not to press too much thereafter.'[59] This is the gist of his counsel, and even Margery Kempe, for all her extravagances, did not neglect it. It would be presumptuous to question the validity of such devotions as hers simply because we cannot practise them ourselves. Her piety is not essentially different from St. Thomas More's; yet no one knowing his life or reading his *De Tristitia Christi*, or the notes in his Book of Hours, could say that his meditations were self-centred, or irrational, or without profound effects on conduct. Nor do they differ in essence from those that Ignatius Loyola was to enjoin. The central doctrine of the Incarnation, of which the Passion was the summation, remained immutable in the Missal; and the Easter Liturgy, familiar in the Middle Ages to every child, lies behind every poem here considered.

Finally, we should remember that throughout the Middle Ages the Church's emphasis on the Corporal Works of Mercy (which had their own iconographical expression) kept alive the truth that the suffering Christ was to be found in the least of his brethren, the poor, the imprisoned, the halt, and the lame: 'How', one poet imagines Christ asking—with clear reference to the scenes of the Passion—

> 'How mihtou eny merci have
> That never desyredest non to do?
> Thou seye[a] me naked and clothes crave,
> Barehed and barefot gan I go:
> On me thou vochedest[b] no thing save
> But beede me wende thi wones fro[c] . . .'[60]

[a] sawest   [b] didst vouchsafe   [c] badest me leave thy dwellings.

Ludolf of Saxony tells the tale of a hermit who in prayer sees a naked man shivering with cold and carrying a cross. It is Christ, who tells him: 'to carry my cross is to carry my words in your heart'. The recurring emphasis in the opening chapters of the *Meditationes* is on Christ's voluntary poverty. Changes in cultus and theology are powerless to erase the picture of Langland's Christ who 'in poor man's apparel pursueth us ever'. Not the least result of the meditative movement was the revivifying of this scriptural figure of the Son of Man who had not where to lay his head. The ancient *mandatum* of Maundy Thursday, when monks and abbot kissed poor men 'with mouth and eyes' and set drink before them, has never lost its power. If in the Middle Ages the sufferings of men came to be concentrated on those of one Man, his suffering in turn came to give meaning to those of all mankind. 'When he was in pain,' said Julian, 'we were in pain.'

III

CHRISTUS MILES

LIFE is a warfare. The conviction and the metaphor are as old as the Book of Job: 'Militia est vita hominis super terram' (The life of man on earth is hard service).[1] St. Paul was the first to Christianize it, and 'Onward! Christian Soldiers' is still sung, if only by the Salvation Army. In Anglo-Saxon England the archetypal hero was the warrior, and Anglo-Saxon poets presented the Apostles as heroic thegns whose valour did not fail when banners clashed, 'frome folctogan and fyrdhwate'—brave leaders and active in war. It is these conceptions that would give the figure of the heroic Christ in *A Vision of a Rood* its appeal and link it with the world of *Beowulf*. There is nothing specifically Christian about Beowulf himself. But Christian conceptions can be detected in the poem, and its hero is more than a famous fighter, just as the courts he visits are more than mead-halls. They have their own etiquette and decorum, adumbrating the forms and ceremonies of Knighthood. It is high praise in this epic to say of a retainer: 'cuþe he duguþe þeaw'—'he knew what courtly etiquette required'. Here already and well before the Conquest, we have glimpses of a courtly system, an incipient chivalry. That term connotes the *mounted* knight; and already in *Beowulf* prestige attaches to the mounted leader.

But the Normans not only introduced a new language; they represented a new concept of knighthood. The Crusades strengthened the links of chivalry with the Church, and the Arthurian romances of Chrétien de Troyes gave it a glamour that it has never wholly lost. Chrétien directs us away from the world of the epic hero surrounded by loyal thegns or retainers to the lonely, questing knight seeking adventures. Yet it was perhaps the martial rather than the romantic elements of chivalry that first appealed to the descendants of those Danes and Saxons who had listened to minstrels reciting *Beowulf* or *Andreas* or *Elene*. Anglo-Norman poetry was martial before it was chivalric. There is little that is knightly about the Arthur of Wace's *Brut*, written in Normandy *c.* 1155: its sole hint of the new age is a mention of tournaments where already ladies' bright eyes rain influence. But the Crusades that mingled Norman knights with French and Provençal fighters affected the social system as well as the erotic. They bring us to the era of the troubadours' *amour lointain* and the castle where the lord is often absent and his lady becomes both more powerful and more the object of love. It is also the era when the works of Bernard and Bonaventure were making familiar the figure of a suffering God dying in wretchedness, ignominy, and pain.

By the end of the twelfth century the lover-knight had an established role in English aristocratic life and literature: witness that sophisticated verse-dialogue, *The Owl and the Nightingale*. And when about 1230 an anonymous priest compiled a spiritual guide for well-born West Country anchoresses, he could use knightly images and *exempla* with the certainty that they would be acceptable, and understood. In England, such references should remind us, warfare between nominal Christians had been going on intermittently for some two centuries; the Crusades, blessed by St. Bernard, had made knighthood holy, and the Crusaders' galleys floated to Palestine on floods of penitential tears. Hence artists illustrating that perennially appealing text, Prudentius' *Psychomachia*, could now represent the Virtues battling with the Vices as feudal knights, and the Rheims sculptor of Abraham receiving the sacrament from Melchizedek could dress him as a Crusader.[2] So the English priest could quite naturally depict an anchoress as a lady in a castle, and follow up an allusion to a 'gentil wellborn man' with the rhetorical question: 'Is not he a foolish knight who seeks rest in the fight and ease in the place of battle?', and thereupon cite in Latin first, and then, for the sake of weaker sisters, in English, the very verse from Job cited above. A few pages later the author of *Ancrene Wisse* returns to this figure, and develops it, again appealing to the refined sentiments of the anchoresses, first by telling a tale

of a king who loved a poor but high-born lady and then by
launching into a more elaborate *exemplum* of another such
lady besieged in an 'earthen castle': for the purposes of the
parable it has to be a castle built of earth in the primitive
Old English style, not of stone in the Norman manner. A
mighty king who is in love with her first sends her succour,
then does signal deeds of prowess before her very eyes—we
are to envisage her watching him from the battlements as he
unhorses his foes; yet she remains indifferent, though he
offers to crown her as his queen. Knowing he will perish in
the fight, he vows to rid her of his assailants, once for all;
hoping thus to win her love after death, if not before. He
keeps his promise, is slain—but miraculously raised to life.

One hardly needs the gloss that follows this parable, but
the language of the gloss is novel, and arresting. The lady is
of course the soul, that dwells in a tenement of clay, and the
king is Jesus, who showed through *knightship* that he was
love-worthy, 'as were whilom knights wont to do'.
'Knightship' is itself a new though native term for this new
chivalry, first used in a twelfth-century homily to translate
the Vulgate *militia* in that verse of Job, next by Layamon in
his version of Wace: 'cutheth eouwer knihtscipe', says one
of Layamon's heroes—'Show your knightly valour'. The
king, in the *Ancrene Wisse*, 'put him in tournament, and his
shield was pierced on both sides'. This is much the earliest
use of the French term *turneiment* in any English text; it is
not found in romances for a century or more. The pierced
shield is the human body of Christ that concealed his
Godhead. It was stretched on the Cross in the shape of a
Norman shield, broad at the top, and narrowing to a point,
where the feet were nailed with a single nail, as represented
in the paintings of the period—notably in the Crucifixion of
Giunta Pisano, where the face of Christ first shows something of the agony that had become a feature of Byzantine
representations. This, says *Ancrene Wisse*, is the shield
given us against temptations, according to Jeremiah: 'Dabis
eis scutum cordis, laborem tuum' (Lam. 3:65: 'Thou shalt
give them the shield of the heart, thy labour'—a text
variously interpreted): an early example of the moral
application of every facet of the Passion to personal life,

which becomes a major concern of the meditative writers. Further, a shield is made of wood, leather (*courbouilli*), and paint (*liturge*): the wood is the Rood, the leather is God's body, the paint the blood that ran down it. When a knight died his shield was hung high up in church as a memorial (like the hatchments still to be found in parish churches). This knight's shield is the crucifix, set high up (i.e. on the 'great rood' or rood-screen) to remind his *Lemman* that his shield had been pierced and his side opened to show her his heart and inward love.

It is only the *sens*, the delicate application, of this *conte moralisé* that is new in the English text. The *matière* is found in several Latin sermons; of which one by a Franciscan, Albert of Metz, is representative.:

There was a certain maiden who was daily harassed by a tyrant; she had no one to defend her against him and he was intent on robbing her of her inheritance. Daily she prayed the Lord to free her from his power. At length there came a young warrior who offered to fight for her, saying that he wanted nothing of her but that if he should vanquish the tyrant and survive, she would remember him; but that if he died she would keep his tunic and cherish it in memory of him. The day of battle came. The young warrior fought with the tyrant from morning to evening and overcame him, but was gravely wounded, and died of his fifth wound. Then, as he had asked, the maiden took his tunic, stained as it was with his blood and put it in her chamber in such a position that she saw it whenever she entered. Going and coming she would weep for love of him and she went in the more often to gaze upon it and remember her friend.

Albert moralizes the tale much as *Ancrene Wisse* does. But he includes a vernacular sentence which suggests that the story was already old when he applied it: 'Il prist la cuirée blanche, à la croix de geules.' His conclusion: 'Tu ergo, o anima christiana, accipe tunicam, sc. *passionis suae memoriam*, et pone ante oculos tuos. . . .' (Therefore you, Christian soul, take the tunic, that is the remembrance of his Passion, and set it before your eyes.)[3]

In a fuller Latin version which puts the moralization in the mouth of the *domicella*, the *juvenis miles* is a *baccalarius*, an aspirant for knighthood. The term makes it clear why

another French preacher can compare the death of Christ
with the death of the brave Roland, and urge that if
Roland's death can excite a just compassion, so must
Christ's. 'Ad litteram Christus sitivit in cruce, ubi mortuus
est morte Rolandi, sitiendo et clamando. Multi compatiun-
tur Rolando et non Christo.' (Literally Christ thirsted on
the Cross, where he died the death of Roland, thirsting and
crying out. Many feel pity for Roland and not for Christ.)[4]

In English the tale is found in a dozen forms, a few of
which will find a place in a later chapter. It would be
tedious to collate them here, and some of the versions
themselves grow tedious—like that in the Northern Homily
Cycle, which allegorizes every item of the knight's armour,
sometimes gauchely, as in

> A peire gloves he wered of plate,
> Two nayles thorwh his handes sate.
> His basenet was, is nouht to layn[a],
> A crowne of thorne sat to the brayn.

> [a] conceal

It takes a little time to work out the sense of these lines:
instead of gloves of plate he had nails in his hands and
instead of a basinet (a pointed headpiece) a crown of thorns.
Lyric poets, who allude to the tale rather than repeat it, are
far more effective, as shown in a stanza that forms part of a
Complaint of Christ, who bids the 'sweet lemman' for
whom he has laid down his life to

> take myne armes pryvely
> And do tham in thi tresory
> In what stede sa thou dwelles
> And, swete lemman, forget thou noght
> That I thi lufe sa dere have boght
> And I aske the noght elles.[5]

Here *tresory* denotes the safe and secret part of the castle,
where a dead knight's arms would be stored, and *pryvely*
ensures that we read the verse as a trope for the acceptance
of Christ within the heart; whilst 'Forget not' will become
an adjuration of many a lover to his mistress, exemplified in

one of Wyatt's finest lyrics. Religious verse gave to secular
verse as much as it borrowed from it.

An Anglo-Norman variant of this story, told by Peter
Langtoft, gives a different twist, which readers of *Piers
Plowman* will recognize: 'A king who loved a lady who had
been traitorously seduced took the arms of one of his
[knight] bachelors, called Adam, and had a *maiden* arm him
with them. He entered the chamber of this beautiful damsel
so softly that no one knew save the maiden herself. For
"aketoun" [quilted jacket worn under mail] she gave him
white and pure flesh. . . .'[6] If any clue were necessary to
elucidate this, the song 'He cam also stylle/To his moderes
bowr/As dew in Aprille/That fallyt on the flour' would
provide it. But even in Pope's day the central motif would
have been intelligible, for he can allude to it in *The Rape of
the Lock*:

> So Ladies in Romance assist their Knight,
> Present the spear, and arm him for the fight.
>
> (iii. 129–30)

Yet another variant of the tale introduces a scene which is
more reminiscent of ballads such as 'Lord Randal' than of
romance, and which reduces the element of the super-
natural. The lover does not die but, weak from wounds,
reaches his mistress's door. His plea is now slightly
different:

> Beholde myne woundes how sore I am dyght,
> For all the wele that thu hast I wan hit in fyght.
> I am sore woundet, behold on my skyn,
> Leve lyf, for my love, let me comen in.[7]

That last phrase recalls, and may well have been suggested
by, a verse in the Canticles—whose language and sentiments pervade so much of Passion poetry: 'Aperi mihi,
soror mea, amica mea' (5:2: Open to me, my sister, my
love). But to the tender beseeching of that plea the new
context adds a sense of urgency, as well as the suggestion of
a lover pleading for admission. Like the errant hero of
knightly romance this Christ is essentially a solitary figure;
his wounds and his suffering touch the same springs of pity

that Meditations on the Passion were at this very time releasing.

The same motif, with further colouring from the Canticles, shows in two stanzas cited in some thirteenth-century Latin notes for a sermon on the Passion: the first introduces the image of Rev. 3:20 ('Behold, I stand at the door, and knock') but develops it in amorous terms:

> Undo, my lef, my dowve dere,
> Undo, wy stond I stekyn out here?
>   Ik am thi make.
> Lo, my heved and myne lockys
> Ar all bywevyd wyt blody dropys
>   For thyne sake.[8]

The image is from that same verse of the Canticles, which goes on 'my *dove*, my undefiled—for my head is filled with dew ...': a verse that Henry Vaughan was to inform with his own calm, hermetic feeling; but here the drops of midnight dew have become drops of blood.

The situation is, indeed, almost too pregnant with poetic possibilities. One fourteenth-century verse suggests a tale of the *Decameron* rather than the Cross:

> So longge ich have, lavedi, yhoved at the gate
> That my fot is ifrore, fair lavedi, for thi luve faste to the stake.

Here only that last phrase takes us back to the feet nailed to the Cross.

This figure of the lover-knight is so dramatic that it may distract our attention from the object of his love, namely the soul. Yet is has meaning only insofar as it implies a particular concern for the individual *anima*. It is as if with Anselm's questioning of the older theology—in which the soul was almost a pawn in a game between God and the devil—the soul had taken on a wholly new value: the value that a knight of romance attached to the love of his mistress. The topos required that mansoul should be treated throughout as feminine and so brought the theme of salvation into touch with a new world of romantic feeling. The appeal to woman's pity, in particular, was now doubly strong. It is noteworthy that when the *exemplum* makes a last flickering appearance in a Victorian hymn, the soul is replaced by the Church (warrantably enough, for exegesis of the Canticles had long represented the Bride as Ecclesia):

> From heaven He came and sought her
> To be His holy bride;
> With His own blood He bought her,
> And for her life He died.
> (Samuel John Stone, 'The Church's one foundation')

The stanza beginning 'Beholde myne woundes' is found in a Franciscan preaching book, the *Fasciculus Morum*, the English version of which has lately been edited.[9] It reminds us that it was the Franciscans who exploited this vein of piteous appeal. But the context also reminds us of another source of romance-feeling that Christian poets were soon to tap. The first romance, it might be argued, was not the tale of Tristan and Iseult, but the *Roman d'Eneas*, which presents Aeneas in the medieval armour that he was to wear in late medieval tapestries, and Lavinia as a desperate self-questioning inamorata: each sends letters to the other as Troilus and Criseyde were to do. The *Fasciculus Morum* not only introduces an Eneas of this tradition but supports it by citing two lines said to be from Ovid's *Metamorphoses*, though in fact from the *Amores*, III. viii. 19–20, with one slight alteration:

> Cerne cicatrices veteris vestigia pugnae,
> Quaesivi proprio sanguine quicquid habes;

Behold wounds that are relics of ancient strife. I have sought to win you with my very blood.

'Veteris vestigia pugnae'—the very phrase that *A Vision of a Rood* seems to echo when the dreamer makes out 'marks of ancient strife' (*ærgewinn*, l. 19). It is these elegiacs that are expanded into the English stanza, which blends the classical appeal and one consonant with the *exemplum* in the *Ancrene Wisse*. A later Franciscan, the indefatigable Nicole Bozon, who probably belonged to the Nottingham Friary, put into Anglo-Norman verse and romance-form the same story, varying its pattern to the extent that he made Christ a king whose Amie (Mankind) was abducted by the giant Belial. Borrowing from his squire Adam the arms with which a maiden accoutres him for fight, he attacks the giant, who deals him five wounds but surrenders the Amie, whom the king forgives and weds.[10]

It will be clear by now that if Christ was to be presented in the thirteenth century as a lover of mansoul, the courtly associations of love, and the chivalry which required a knight to joust to win his lady's favour, demanded that he should assume a knightly role. Once this equation was accepted, a wide range of figurative possibilities opened up. The weapons, the wounds, the armour, the manner of combat, all can be made to yield poignant images. And as the medium of romance is as often as not the rhymed stanza, and the lover expresses his emotions in song, so the new religious verse will be stanzaic. This makes for a simplicity of diction, as well as a general economy of utterance; both features that extended the appeal of this verse far beyond the confines of the courtly classes. And the expansion of the basic martial metaphor developed along much the same lines as the expansion of the brief Gospel narratives into the minute particularization of every stage of the Passion, every incident of the torture, that we shall find to be the distinctive feature of the Bonaventuran meditations: though the poets who developed the *Christus miles* figure had, so to speak, to set aside or ignore many incidents of the Passion narrative as not appropriate to their framework, just as medieval artists pass over whole areas of Gospel narrative that have no links with the liturgy.

In *Quia Amore Langueo*, that haunting and chameleon-like fourteenth-century poem, which takes its refrain from a text beloved of St. Bernard, these images are put to new purposes.[11] The poet finds a wounded man of kingly countenance sitting on a *mount* beneath a tree (like the mourning Man in Black in Chaucer's *Book of the Duchess*, though here the genre of the poem soon helps us to identify the mount as Calvary), suffering most of all—as in *Ancrene Wisse*—from his fair love's unkind ingratitude. And like the Man in Black he utters his Complaint:

I clothed hyr in grace and hevenly lyght
   This blody surcote she hath on me sett
. . .

Loke unto myn handys, man!
   Thes gloves were geven me whan I hyr sowght.
They be nat white, but rede and wan,
   Embrodred with blode (my spouse them bowght)
   They will not of—I lefe them nowght!
I wowe hyr with them wherever she goo.
   Thes handes full frendly for hyr fowght,
     Quia amore langueo.

Marvell not, man, thof I sitt styll—
   My love hath shod me wondyr strayte
She boklyd my fete, as was her wyll
   With sharp nailes (well thou maist waite!) . . .

We glimpse here such a scene as is depicted in the Luttrell Psalter, where ladies of the knight's household equip him for the tourney. So far the deliberate double-sidedness of the knightly references is obvious enough. But in the second half of the poem we leave a knight's language for a lover's. Thus he says, 'If she be dawngerouse, I will hyr pray', which takes us at once into the world of courtly love, where *dangerous* means stand-offish. Soon we are in the rarer world of the Canticles; and, as often, the rich imagery of that love-song goes to the poet's head. In the Canticles the beloved 'looketh forth at the windows, shewing himself through the lattice'. Here he beseeches the lady (mansoul) to 'look owt at the wyndows of kyndnesse' (a phrase found also in a version of the Psalms). As often the imaginative impulse falters and flags as the poet presses the figure dry. But one line links it with the Complaints from the Cross that bulk so large in devotional poetry of the period: 'Myn armes ben spred to clypp hyr to'. From St. Bernard's time and earlier the arms stretched out on the Cross had been read as a gesture of love, 'spread to love-clipping' as the head was bowed to 'sweet kissing'.[12] By the same token, the Complaint that St. Bernard according to the *Golden Legend*[13] puts into the mouth of Christ had already suggested, if only by way of contrast, how he could be presented in terms of courtly society. He wore a garland

not of flowers but of thorns, not white gloves but dark nails,
not fine array but garments of mockery.

In a Latin sermon on the same text from the Canticles—
'Quia amore langueo': a verse by the fourteenth century
impregnated with the deepest devotional and even mystical
feeling—one sees the particularizing method being sedu-
lously applied to the figure of the Christ-knight; and its
appeal may be gauged from the fact that the sermon is
extant in three manuscripts, each (apparently) introducing
into the Latin a few English technical phrases for which the
writer could think of no Latin equivalent: thus in the
sermon Christ's body is his 'aketoun' or quilted jacket, the
crown of thorns his helm (*galea*), the nails in his hands his
'arothea de plate'—an extraordinary phrasal mix, apparently describing gauntlets, though *arothea* does not appear
in the *Medieval Latin Word List*. The single nail piercing
the feet represents spurs. His horse is the Cross. For a
shield he proffered his side—and so he proceeded against
the enemy with a spear 'non in manu sed stykand in his
side'! This Northern preacher is evidently envisaging the
Crucifixion as depicted in miniatures that show Longinus in
the act of pressing the spear into the side.[14]

Such attention to weaponry is precisely what characterizes the English romances of the period: witness *Sir
Gawain*, and the parody of such romances in Chaucer's *Sir
Thopas*, which provides the best description of these pieces
of armour. It is not by accident that more than one of our
knightly poems uses the same jaunty tail-rhyme stanza as
Sir Thopas. One of these transfers the terminology in
skimble-skamble fashion to the Christian knight, the *miles
Christi*, saying:

> 'At the y mot myn armes borwe,
> My sheld [*sic*] shal be the sword of sorwe
> *Marie* that stong to the herte.
>
> The holi cros my baner biforn
> myn helm thi garland of sharpe thorn
> Mi swerd thi scourges smerte' [etc.].[15]

This achieves merely a vague suggestion of combat,
without regard for sequence or consistency: a desperate bid

for novelty. More effective is the injunction in the same
metre addressed by another poet to the Christian cast down
by the fiend:

> Oup and be god champioun!
> Stond, ne fal namore adoun
> For a luytel blast.
> Thou take the rode to thi staf
> And thenk on him that thereonne yaf[a]
> His lif that was so lef[b].
>
> . . .
>
> Of rightte beleve thou nim[c] that sheld
>
> . . .
>
> And kep thy fo with staves ord[d].[16]
>
>   [a] gave   [b] precious   [c] take   [d] point.

Perhaps the most thorough and deliberate extension of
the figure is the fourteenth-century *Treatise of Ghostly
Battle*, otherwise entitled *Milicia Christi*. It begins with the
familiar verse from Job, now glossed in medieval terms: 'All
man's life on earth is but fighting and *knighthood* against the
flesh, the world, the devil', followed by St. Paul's 'Clothe
you in the true armour of God', with the rather strained
gloss: 'Man's body is a cloth wherewith the soul is clothed'.
In fact the body is at once likened to a *horse*: 'the soul may
not fight against the fiend unless the horse be meek and
mild and bridled [a hint of Plato here?] with Abstinence and
honest occupation'. The two reins should be tied with the
knot of Discretion. 'Sit sadly ['firmly': Chaucer's term for
knightly posture] in thy saddle and keep well thy stirrups.
Take the basinet of health, going and gathering upward to a
little *coppe* [he is describing a pointed helm], and the sword
of the Holy Spirit [we are now back to St. Paul: Heb. 4] and
put on the habergeon of righteousness': where fourteenth-
century linked mail replaces Paul's Roman breastplate. The
shield is triangular, symbolizing the Trinity. So it goes on,
specifying the vanbrace and rerebrace and gloves of plate,
the 'jakke of fence'—the earliest occurrence of that name for
a quilted jacket or 'aketoun', here representing both Charity
'that endureth all things' and the 'seamless coat' of Christ.
The sword is the sword of separation that Christ brought,

the spear the symbol of Passion, the most effectual weapon against one's foes. And with that we come, or rather digress, to a picturing of the Passion in all the traditional and unchangeable detail. The allegory dwindles away into commonplaces about the prison of this life, etc., though still keeping an eye towards knightly concerns—for example: 'It is perilous to fight in marshy ground or stubbly ground or pitty ground; a wise knight will have with him the sun and the wind.'[17]

The very deliberateness of all this makes it tedious. But it is a convenient backcloth for the contemporary verses in which Christ himself is presented as speaking in these very terms: verses that usually have the merit of brevity and simplicity and that by choosing one or two of the chivalric conceits produce more striking effects. Thus in the poem already considered in another context a simple knightly reference arrests attention: 'Restles I ride . . . My palefrey is of tre'; and the stark brevity of the lines sorts with the firm final soldierly injunction:

> Fal noght for fonding[a]
> That shal the most turne to goode
> Mak stiff withstonding—
> Thenk wel who me rent on the rode.

> [a] temptation.

This didactic and exemplary application of the pains of Calvary belongs to the tradition of the prose *Meditations*, though in the *Meditations* the plea 'Make stiff withstanding' is addressed to Christ himself, when Michael the Archangel appears to him in Gethsemane saying, 'Be now of good comfort, my lord, and work right manfully. For it is seemly to him that is in high degree to do great things and worthy.'[18] In just such terms might a young squire or knight address his lord as he entered a tournament or battle. Later in the *Meditations* St. John is described in the same mode when reproaching bystanders at the Crucifixion: 'He took to him a man's heart and rising against them said: "Ye wretched ones, why do ye this cruelty?" '—hardly the utterance one would expect from the almost girlish youth

('Christ's darling' in the *Meditations*) of so many Crucifixion scenes.

In the fifteenth century Lydgate, the Benedictine poet of Bury St. Edmunds, characteristically, and awkwardly, elaborates the basic image in terms of a jousting, in which Christ speaks of 'My platys severed, totorn myn aventail [beaver]/Lik as witnesseth this dolorous pité'.[19] It is just like Lydgate, who could never keep his eye on the object, to add that inapposite reference to a material *pietà*: a picture of Mary beholding the body of her son. Indeed this may be the earliest English reference to the *imago pietatis*; Margery Kempe of Lynn describes one in a Norfolk church as if she had not seen one before. It so moved her that a priest had tried to restrain her tears by saying, 'Damsel, Jesus is dead long sithen.'[20]

It is time to recall the ultimate scriptural origins of all this knightly symbolism, and to go beyond the Pauline passages to the Messianic prefigurings of a kingly saviour, a Lord mighty in battle. A key text here is the lesson from Isaiah 63 which is or rather was read on the Wednesday of Holy Week. It should be read in the Vulgate, for its force is weakened in English renderings, though the Authorized Version is more familiar:

Who is this that cometh from Edom, with dyed garments from Bozrah? this that is glorious in his apparel, travelling in the greatness of his strength?/I that speak in righteousness, mighty to save./Wherefore art thou red in thine apparel, and thy garments like him that treadeth in the winefat?/I have trodden the winepress alone; and of the people there was none with me . . . mine own arm brought salvation unto me.

It is perhaps the most remarkable piece of dramatic dialogue in the whole of the Old Testament, and it must have early played a part in the extension of the dominical utterances beyond those set down in the Gospels. In the seventh century Isidore of Seville had associated the red apparel with the garments that the soldiers had put on Christ in mockery, and the winepress with the Passion (*De Fide Catholica*): the carver of the Bury Cross in the twelfth century had placed the second verse in the centre of the first

medallion. But it is the Vulgate rendering of the first verse
that provided the essential link with the Christ-knight
figure. The English 'mighty to save' hardly conveys the
effect of 'propugnator sum ad salvandum'. What that meant
to a fourteenth-century Franciscan we can see from this
poem:

'What ys he, thys lordling, that cometh vrom the vyht
Wyth blod-rede wede so grysliche ydyht,
So vayre ycoyntised[a], so semlich in syht,
So styflyche yongeth[b], so douhti a knyht?'
'Ich hyt am, ich hyt am, that ne speke bote ryht,
Chaunpyon to helen monkunde in vyht.'

'Why thoenne ys thy shroud red wyth blod al ymeind[c],
As troddares[d] in wrynge[e] wyth most[f] al byspreynd?'

'The wrynge ich habbe ytrodded al mysulf on,
And of al monkunde ne was non other won.
Ich hoem habbe ytrodded in wrethe and in grome[g],
And al my wede ys byspreynd[h] with hoere blod ysome[i],
And al my robe yvuled[j] to hoere grete shome.
The day of thylke wreche[k] leveth in my thouht,
The yer of medes[l] yeldyng ne voryet ich nouht[m].
Ich loked al aboute som helpynge mon,
Ich souhte al the route, bote help nas ther non.
Hyt was myn oune strengthe that thys bote[n] wrouhte,
Myn owe douhtynesse that help ther me brouhte.
Ich habbe ytrodded the volk in wrethe and in grome,
Adreynt[o] wyth shennesse[p], ydrawe doun wyth shome.'

On Godes mylsfolnesse[q] ich wole bythenche me,
And heryen[r] in alle thyng that he yeldeth me.[21]

[a] adorned   [b] strongly advances   [c] mixed   [d] treaders   [e] winepress
[f] must   [g] anger   [h] sprinkled   [i] together   [j] defiled   [k] vengeance   [l] reward
[m] I shall not forget   [n] remedy   [o] drowned   [p] humiliation   [q] mercy
[r] praise.

The preservation here, though in a new context and in
Chaucerian terms, of the Anglo-Saxon figure of a
courageous lord—a 'doughty' knight who goes boldly to the
fray (Chaucer uses *stiffly* and *doughty* of knightly combat)—
is more significant than the introduction of the quite
different notion of Christ as *healer* (l. 6), which may seem

incongruous; and we must not be misled by *shroud* in the next line (rendering *indumentum*): it means simply 'garment', not 'grave-clothes', the latter sense not appearing till two hundred years later.

Still, this is not, strictly speaking, a Passion poem. It is the Resurrected Christ who here speaks. There is a curious echo or reminiscence of the fifth line in Ch. 26 of Dame Julian's *Revelations*, where he says: 'I it am, I it am, I it am that is highest, I it am that thou lovest, I it am that thou likest ... I it am that is all. ...' But Christ is there appearing, says Julian, 'more *glorified*, as to my sight, than I saw him before'. And likewise in the poem: he speaks *after* he has trodden the winepress: the blood is not his own but of those trampled on in Isaiah 63:3. This must control our reading of the opening lines of *Piers Plowman* B XIX where Langland's genius unerringly adapts the Messianic verses to the context and sequences of his poem, in a scene that follows directly on the ringing of the Easter Resurrection bells. The joyful sound wakes the dreamer, and he goes to church to make his Easter Communion, only to fall asleep again, this time to dream

> That Pieres the Plowman was paynted *al blody*
> And come in with a crosse bifor the comune peple,
> And righte lyke in alle lymes to owre lorde Jesu:
> And thanne called I Conscience to kenne me the sothe.
> 'Is this Jesus the Juster', quod I, 'that Juwes did to deth?
> Or is it Pieres the Plowman? Who paynted hym so rede?'
> Quod Conscience, and kneled tho, 'Thise aren Pieres armes
> His coloures and his cote-armure; ac he that cometh so blody
> Is Cryst with his Crosse, conqueroure of Crystene ...'[22]

That it is the Resurrection Christ, carrying his banner of the Cross, is clear from the very use of the title, Christ, pre-eminently his Resurrection name as against the Jesus of his suffering humanity. But our present concern is with Jesus the jouster. The peculiar appropriateness of that description will appear from the fuller account of *Piers Plowman* in later pages. For the present we need only know why Jesus is given arms, and colours. The *arms* must be his coat-of-arms (as in the *Knight's Tale*, 2046). It is a heraldic term, applied presumably to the drops of blood with which his body is bespattered, as (for example) a heraldic shield is marked with tails of ermine. 'Coat-armour' could be used either of an armorial shield or of a vest embroidered with the same arms. We must not press the terms too hard. This is, in fact, practically the first recorded use of 'coat-armour', if we date *Piers* earlier than *Sir Gawain*, which uses the term quite literally. Similarly, this is the first instance of *colours* as applied to the cognisance or insignia of a knight, the next coming in *The Destruction of Troy*, a text notable for its additions of heraldic and knightly detail to Guido delle Colonne's original: the line containing it in that poem runs: 'All their colours to ken were of clean yellow'. In *Piers*, as in the *Edom* poem, the colours are not only red, but *blood-red*: not so common a term as one might imagine—in fact only once instanced in Middle English as used for the colour of a garment. These heraldic allusions illuminate the phrase 'vayre ycoyntised' in l. 3 of the poem, where again we are dealing with a first instance: the participle, meaning 'adorned', probably derives from the noun *queyntise* in the specifically heraldic sense of a 'device, cognisance, or cloth bearing such a device', found only in fourteenth-century romance and in Barbour, whose *Bruce* was in part romance.

Christ carries the Cross as symbol of his triumph. In the earliest representation of his entry into Hell he carries it across his shoulder, in the posture of the Roman Christ who in the Ravenna mosaic tramples under foot the lion and the basilisk. In the *Angelus ad Virginem* (sung by Chaucer's 'hende Nicholas') Christ, issuing from the Virgin's womb, 'iniit conflictum/affigens humero/crucem qua dedit ictum/ hosti mortifero' (entered the conflict bearing on his shoulder the cross with which he struck a blow to the mortal enemy). Already in the St. Alban's Psalter and the South Porch at Malmesbury (both early twelfth-century) it becomes a standard bearing his banner—the red cross, as Piero della Francesca and many others will show it. Whether or no Langland envisaged his Piers–Christ figure with such a banner, there is no doubt that he is thinking of Christ in feudal terms. For in this poem Conscience (who has just

knelt in acknowledgement of Piers's knighthood) forthwith
explains that

> To be called a knighte is faire, for men shal knele to hym;
> To be called a kynge is fairer, for he may knightes make;
> Ac to be conquerour called—*that* cometh of special grace.
>
> (xix. 28–30)

And Langland at once relates these three grades to the
Passion, saying that the Jews whom John baptized became
'gentel men with Jesu': for Jesus was 'yfulled' (baptized)
'and uppon Calvarye on cross ycrouned Kynge of Jewes'.
That last phrase is here to be taken at more than its face
value. The Fathers and medieval exegetes pondered much
over the *titulus* on the Cross. Thus Jerome, in his commentary on Matthew 27, says:

> I cannot wonder enough that, having suborned false witnesses
> and stirred up the people to sedition, the Jews could find no other
> cause to put him to death than that he was King of the Jews.
> Perhaps they put up this superscription in mockery. But when
> they objected Pilate answered: 'What I have written I have
> written'. Whether you like it or not, you Jews, the whole crowd of
> peoples will answer: 'Jesus *is* King of the Jews', that is ruler of
> those who believe and confess him.[23]

'Imperator credentium et confidentium': that is why on the
twelfth-century Bury Cross the inscription runs not *Rex
Judaeorum* but *Rex Confessorum*.[24]

But before expanding and expounding the phrase *Rex
Judaeorum* Langland adverts to the attribute of Christ as
healer that is presented also in the *Edom* poem: there the
champion claims 'to helen monkunde in vyht' (l. 6). In *Piers
Plowman* 'He fended [the Jews] fram foule yveles, feveres
and fluxes' (xix. 46). Langland goes on to present him,
proleptically, as a conqueror:

> And tho conquered he on crosse, as conquerour noble.
>
> (50)

He conquered death. Since that victory was not complete
till he harrowed Hell one may think of the Cross itself as a
weapon. Thus it figures in Anglo-Saxon art and in later
English depictions of the Harrowing as of the Resurrection,

when it appears as a proper attribute of the Christ who
tramples the prostrate bodies of soldiers in knightly armour.
In a French thirteenth-century verse-sermon it is 'le bas-
ton/Dont il parmata il felon' (sc. Satan).[25] It becomes a
lance with a pennant sometimes showing the red cross. A
popular poem of the mid-fourteenth century, which alludes
to the image of the lover-knight ('Thus wald my spouse for
me fyght/And wounded for me he was full sare'), extends
the chivalric allusion:

> To heven he went with mykell blys,
> When he had overcomen his batail.
> His baner full brade dysplaid is,
> When so my fa will me assail.[26]

To 'display one's banner' was the knightly signal for war
(made, for instance, by Duke Theseus in the *Knight's Tale*
(line 966). If Langland conceives of the Harrowing of Hell
in martial terms it is because he is drawing on the apocryphal Gospel of Nicodemus, accessible in his time in a
Middle English version, and long before in Latin. The
account in *Piers Plowman* XVIII and XIX develops from
the question that Hell and Death in that Gospel ask Christ
at the gates of Hell:

'Who art thou that art so great and so small, both humble and
exalted, both soldier and commander, a marvellous warrior in the
shape of a bondsman, a King of glory, dead, yet living . . .? At thy
death all creation quaked, and all the stars were shaken. And thou
hast become free among the dead and dost rout our legions . . .'[27]

Lydgate was to pick up this figure, and set it in an
unexpected context, namely his interminable *Life of Our
Lady*. This introduces a vision of Grosseteste (Bishop of
Lincoln and Chancellor of Oxford) in which Christ the
Lamb vanquishes the wild beasts:

> But or that thay avayle myght in fyght
> The Lambes power made hem for to dye;
> And hem venquyschede through his humble myght,
> That man and angell, when thay this conqueste seye,
> Thay fell downe streght and the lambe obeye,
> That was sent of God, this *meke werryour*
> . . .

And acordyng with this avysion,
This lambe of God, clad in our armoure,
This day was borne of a mayden pure.

(iii. 932–43)

Appropriately enough, Lydgate describes these beasts arrayed against the Lamb as drawn up in a 'shield troop', just
like the *scyldtruma* used by Saxon warriors at Maldon and
Hastings:

Aforcyng hem by *sheltroun* in batayle
By felle malice, the fayre lambe to assayle.

(iii. 930–1)

This is almost the last example in our literature of that old
heroic word.[28] If it surprises us to find such a term coming
from the pen of a learned monastic poet we should remember that he had also translated (and expanded) the
Vexilla Regis, most martial of all Latin hymns. And he had
precedent in a fourteenth-century versifier who in translating another early hymn, *Conditor alme siderum*, renders the
line 'Christe redemptor omnium' as 'Crist that bouhtest
mon wyth fyht'.[29]

Finally, Lydgate's lines bring us face to face with a
paradox that has been pursuing us from the outset. How to
reconcile the imagery of Christ as knightly warrior with the
meek and suffering servant—the Prince of Peace who put
up Peter's sword? Augustine's gloss on Jesus' answer to the
mob, *Ego sum*, presents him as at first repelling the armed
mob by the power of hidden Divinity: 'Deus enim latebat in
carne' (for God was concealed in the flesh); and the
Bonaventuran *Meditationes* repeat this. An alliterative
Northern poet is keeping decorum when he writes:

My fender of my fose, sa fonden in the felde
Sa lufly lyghtand at the evensang tyde,
Thy moder and hir menyhe[a] unlaced thy scheld.
All weped that thar were, thi woundes was sa wide.[30]

[a] companions.

Here the martial image of a princely defender tried in the
field and surrounded by a knightly retinue (*meinie*) blends
with that older figure of the body (*caro*) as the shield: the

'unlacing' is the deposition, by now firmly associated with the liturgical hour of evensong. Christ is pictured as showing love even when 'lovingly lighting' (descending). Again, a fifteenth-century preacher can say that 'Christ set up his banner when he stretched his body on the Cross'.[31] There is no difficulty whilst the terms of weaponry and combat are plainly figurative.

But when a stanza begins:

> I am Jesu, that cum to fiht
> Withouten seld[a] and spere

> [a] shield.

we are moving to another dimension, with the emphasis not on weapons but on their absence.[32] It so happens that this verse was written down at the very time that Langland was penning the eighteenth passus of *Piers Plowman*. There he accepts and exploits all the theological richness and poetic possibilities of this paradox. It is, to be sure, only another facet of the inescapable paradox of the Cross, and of the Incarnation; a paradox necessarily reflected in the doctrine of the Eucharist. Langland will recall us to the true intention of St. Paul when he wrote (2 Cor. 10:4): 'The weapons of our warfare (*arma militiae nostrae*) are not carnal'. The Pauline metaphors were deeply impressed on the medieval mind. When Chaucer's Cecilia addresses converts as 'Cristes owene knyghtes leeve and deere',[33] she bids them, in the words of Romans 13 and Ephesians 6, to

> Cast alle awey the werkes of derknesse
> And armeth yow in armure of brightnesse.
> Ye han forsothe ydoon a greet bataille . . .
> (*CT* G 384–6)

And when his Constance finds herself without a knightly defender, the Man of Law prays:

> But he that starf for our redempcioun
> And boond Sathan (and yet lith ther he lay)
> So be thy stronge champion this day!
> (*CT* B 633–5)

It is this same Constance who shows her devotion to the

Cross in a prayer that Chaucer had inserted into Trivet's narrative and that peculiarly befits her case: the Cross was always invoked in votive masses for travellers by sea, and she is about to be launched in a rudderless boat. Based on antiphons sung at the Feast of the Exaltation of the Cross (14 September), it conjoins the ancient figure of the Rood as a *sigebeam*, a tree of victory, with that of an altar, red with the blood of the Lamb who had routed the hosts of hell (just as they were conjoined by medieval artists: the Bury Cross, carved in the stylized form of a tree, bears a medallion of the Lamb as it had been slain on the side opposite from that where the crucified figure once hung).

> 'O cleere^a, o welful auter, hooly Croys,
> Reed of the Lambes blood ful of pitee
> That wessh the world fro the olde iniquitee,
> Me fro the feend and fro his clawes kepe,
> That day that I shal drenchen^b in the depe.
>
> Victorious tree, proteccioun of trewe^c,
> That oonly worthy were for to bere
> The kyng of hevene with his woundes newe,
> The white Lamb, that hurt was with a spere,
> Flemere^d of feendes out of hym and here,
> On which thy lymes feithfully extenden
> Me kepe, and yif me myght my lyf t'amenden.'
>
> (*CT* B 451–62)

^ashining ^bdrown ^cthe faithful ^ddriver-out.

There breathes through this prayer not only the spirit that had animated the author of *A Vision of a Rood* but also the fervour that characterized the piety of the meditative movement.

The infiltration of martial modes of thought went far beyond the few poems that have here served as samples: when the *Gawain* poet, for example, wishes to illustrate the piety of his knightly hero he represents him as anxious to hear his Christmas mass:

> To se the servyse of that syre that on that self nyght
> Of a burde^a watz borne oure baret to quelle.
> (*Sir Gawain and the Green Knight*, 751–2)

^amaiden.

Editors seek to substitute for *battle*, *strife* (the normal meaning of *baret*) a contextual sense of 'sorrow'. But the poet, having shown Gawain as armed with Christian virtues, would have us think not only of the angels' *Pax hominibus* (peace to men): in conquering Satan, who warred against Mankind, Christ 'made peace through the blood of his cross' (Col. 1:20). In a late carol of Christ's pleading, by James Ryman, he says:

> Have myende, man, how I toke the felde,
> Upon my bak bering my shelde;
> For payne ne dethe I wolde not yelde;
> O synfull man, yeve me thyn hert.

And on the very eve of the Reformation another carol, with a refrain that harks back to the beginning of Christian hymnody, translates *Vexilla Regis prodeunt*:

> The Kinges baner on felde is playd;
> The crosses mistry can not be nayd.[34]

IV

THE PASSION IN PIERS PLOWMAN

THOUGH *Piers Plowman* has been read and circulated for six hundred years, its position as the supreme English testament of Christian faith and practice has still to be recognized. Only in our day has it received the scholarly attention that reveals the sources of its spirituality. Had the fifteenth-century Church taken heed to it, England might still have been a Catholic country: the popular religion, tinged with superstition, and the intellectual slackness that 'played into the hands of Protestant critics' have no place in Langland's poem.

Chaucer himself, as I have elsewhere argued, felt the spell of this *Visio*, and would strongly have disputed the notion that Langland was a minor figure. Strictly speaking, he was Chaucer's predecessor rather than his contemporary. He had probably drafted his first version before Chaucer had penned a line. One reason for its tardy recognition is that its author could never let it alone, nor could his copyists. But his main drift is clear. His central theme is latent in his title: *Petrus Plowman* is a name of multifold meaning—or rather two names, in balance, one scriptural, Latin, and hieratic, the other solidly human, functional, and English. In the course of the poem the name comes to be a synonym for the *humanitas* of Christ, making this the most Christocentric poem ever written. We may conceive of it as a great cone of which the Cross, as supreme expression of that *humanitas*, is both axis and apex. Round this cone we make our slow circular ascent in almost Dantesque fashion, halting at three points of rest that turn out to be points of vantage, altering our whole perspective.

It is not by accident that at each of these points we (through the Dreamer) are given new insights into the meaning of the Passion, the second passage unfolding the first, and the third the second. Never is the Passion presented—as sometimes in devotional writings of the period—as an isolated event, or in abstract theological terms, but always as the sublime and culminating expression of God's love for man; so that it is related directly— even forcibly—to the concerns of every day.

Nowhere does Langland offer a full-scale picture of the Passion. Nor, for that matter, does Dante (whose references to it are nowhere so extensive). In the fourteenth century, no such depictions were necessary—for they were everywhere to hand, in wood, in manuscript, in paint, in glass, in alabaster, and in the mystery plays; not to mention the vogue of the *Meditationes*. The absence of a Bonaventuran strain in Langland is noteworthy. In *Piers Plowman* the Virgin has no role, nor John; and the sufferings are merely alluded to, synecdochically. Yet each presentation is unimpeachably orthodox.

I

The first, in the opening passus (i. 150 ff.), is in the simplest terms, though it follows a dense cluster of pregnant images (including a beautiful adaptation of the Messianic text of Isaiah 53 whereby 'the tender plant' becomes a plant of peace that takes its potency from earth). The passage begins, as Langland always begins such exposition, with Creation:

> alle his werkes he wroughte with loue, as him liste.
> (B i. 148)

It is the Divine Father who

> Loked on us with love and lete his sone deye
> Mekely for owre mysdedes to amende us alle.
> (B i. 165–6)

The first half-line looks before and after: the love was manifest in Creation as much as in Redemption; and *lete* is a carefully chosen word which can mean both 'caused' and 'allowed', or even 'saw fit'. Langland has compressed into a line the whole force of 1 John 4:9: 'In this was manifested the love of God toward us, because that God sent his only

begotten Son into the world, that we might live through
him.' The Son is not otherwise named in this passage, nor
the Father: the repeated third-person-singular pronouns
suggest an identity of purpose. Of the words from the
Cross, only 'Father, forgive them . . .' are referred to, but
paraphrastically, and without any form of address:

And yet wolde he hem no woo that wroughte hym that peyne,
But mekelich with mouthe mercy be bisoughte
To have pité of that poeple that peyned hym to deth.

(B i. 167–9)

Mercy (perhaps personified) and *pity* are the key-words.
The torture is mentioned only in the course of showing that
Christ acted out to the bitter end his own injunction: 'do
good to them that despitefully use you':

Here myghtow see ensamples in hym-selve one,
That he was mightful and make and mercy gan graunte
To hem that hongen him an heigh and his herte thirled[a]

(B i. 170–2)

[a] pierced.

—though we should not overlook the force of that last line,
alluding as it does to the traditional view (repeated by
Ludolf of Saxony) that the Cross was as much as fifteen feet
high, and to Longinus' side-piercing spear: Langland
writes *heart* rather than *side* partly doubtless out of alliterative necessity but partly because of its metaphorical force;
the riven heart figures in illustrations of contemporary
devotional pieces.

We must, in fact, adjust ourselves at once to Langland's
mode of compression. He is writing for a highly literate
'clerisy', and has no need to spell out his descriptions or his
theology. Thus the alliterative 'mightful and meke' (171)
glances back to the conception of the Father being the
potentia ('might') of the Trinity (163–4), whilst the meekness is that of the Son who in unity with the Father
humbled himself. It is a first glimpse of the doctrine of the
Two Natures, the *communicatio idiomatum*, that will bulk
larger later. But, for the present, Holy Church, as teacher,
has a more urgent concern, so urgent that it breaks through

the frame of formal doctrine in which the opening dialogue between Church and Dreamer is set, and jolts us back into the quotidian world of the Field of Folk.

Meditations on the Passion often include a didactic strain; a warning against the Seven Capital Sins, or a plea to show love for one's 'even-Cristen'. In a striking passage in the Old English *Christ*, the Saviour's reproach to Man for ignoring the torment he had undergone for Mankind's redemption concludes:

'I charged you to cherish well my brothers in the world with those goods that I gave you on earth to aid the wretched. Ill have ye done in that regard, but with hard hearts have denied raiment to the naked, food to the hungry . . . in scorn of the King of Heaven. For that ye shall suffer sore torment for ever.'

So here Holy Church's logic, and the social context of her discourse, lead her to voice a very precise and (as Von Hügel would say) 'costing' injunction (173–6):

For-thi I rede yow riche haveth reuthe of the povere;
Though ye be myghtful to mote beth meke in yowre werkes . . .

As God in the Cross has displayed his mercy to all men, rich and poor alike, so must the rich show pity to the poor. It is as if we are being directed to 2 Corinthians 8:9: 'For ye know the grace of our Lord Jesus Christ, that though he was rich, yet for our sakes he became poor, that we through his poverty might become rich.'

But Holy Church goes further, resuming in the next line the legal figure that had opened the paragraph (l. 157).[1] The literal sense of the first clause is 'Though you have the power to summon them to court . . .'; but the repeated *mightful*, which at 171 stood for the *potentia dei patris*, points to the true purpose of the line, which offers a subtle extension of its antecedent. The argument runs, 'As God shows mercy to you, you should show it to others. As he has the power to summon you before his judgement court, yet shows you mercy and even pays your fine, *to the same extent* must you show that mercy.' The Ruskin who so much

admired the Gothic church but so much misconceived the
religion that built it, would have commended this forth-
rightness. And we shall see that it is the abrupt alignment of
the Divine with the everyday, of the mystical with the
mercantile, that gives Langland his distinctive character.
Caritas for him is not a personification of an abstract noun:
it exists only in action. And his Mercy is that for which
Isabella pleaded:

> Why, all the souls that were, were forfeit once,
> And He that might the vantage best have took
> Found out the remedy. How would *you* be,
> If He, which is the top of judgement, should
> But judge you as you are? O, think on that,
> And mercy then will breathe within your lips,
> Like man new made.
>
> (*Measure for Measure*, II. ii. 72–9)

Shakespeare's 'man new made' is St. Paul's 'new man in
Christ Jesus' (in contrast to the 'old man' of Eph. 4:22 and
Timon of Athens, III. vi. 60). And it is this re-creation that
Langland celebrates when he next presents the Passion, in
the great prayer that Repentance offers on behalf of all
penitents, in Passus V.

II

And thanne had Repentance reuthe and redde^a hem alle to knele,
'For I shal biseche for al synful owre saueoure of grace,
To amende us of owre mysdedes and do mercy to us alle.
  Now God,' quod he, 'that of thi goodnesse gonne the worlde
    make,
And of naughte madest aughte and man moste liche to thi-selve,
And sithen suffredest for to synne a sikenesse to us alle,
And al for the best, as I bileve what evere the boke telleth,
  O felix culpa! O necessarium peccatum Ade! etc.
For thourgh that synne thi sone sent was to this erthe,
And bicam man of a mayde mankynde to save,
And madest thi-self with thi sone and us synful yliche,
  Faciamus hominem ad ymaginem at similitudinem nostram;
  Et alibi: qui manet in caritate, in deo manet, et deus in eo;
  And sith with thi self sone in owre sute deydest

On Godefryday for mannes sake at ful tyme of the daye,
There thi-self ne thi sone no sorwe in deth feledest;
But in owre secte^b was the sorwe and thi sone it ladde,
    Captivam duxit captivitatem.
The sonne for sorwe ther-of les syghte for a tyme
Aboute mydday whan most lighte is and mele tyme of seintes;
Feddest with thi fresche blode owre forfadres in derknesse,
    Populus qui ambulabat in tenebris vidit lucem magnam;
And thorw the lighte that lepe oute of the Lucifer was blent^c,
And blewe alle thi blissed in-to the blisse of paradise.
The thrydde daye after thow yedest in owre sute,
A synful Marie the seighe ar Seynte Marie thi dame,
And al to solace synful thow suffredest it so were;
    Non veni vocare justos, set peccatores ad penitenciam.
And al that Marke hath ymade, Mathew, Iohan and Lucas,
Of thyne doughtiest dedes were don in owre armes;
    Verbum caro factum est, et habitavit in nobis.
And bi so moche, me semeth, the sikerere^d we mowe
Bydde and biseche if it be thi wille,
That art owre fader and owre brother, be merciable to us,
And have reuthe on thise ribaudes that repente hem here sore,
That evere thei wratthed the in this worlde in worde, thoughte, or
    dedes.'   (B v. 485–513)

    ^a counselled   ^b company   ^c blinded   ^d more confidently.

This scene, and this prayer, grow naturally out of the prayer of the last of the penitents, who had compared his own plight to that of Dismas the penitent thief, the first soul, according to the *Gospel of Nicodemus* and the *Golden Legend*, to gain entrance to heaven from the blood that flowed from Christ's side.[2] The penitent's prayer had been faltering, but it at once picks up the note of mercy earlier sounded by Holy Church in the first passus:

'Cryst, that on Calvarye uppon the crosse deydest,
Tho Dismas my brother bisoughte yow of grace,
And haddest *mercy* on that man for *memento* sake,
So rewe on this robbere that *reddere* ne have,
Ne nevere wene to wynne with crafte that I owe.
But for thi *mykel mercy* mitigacioun I biseche;
Ne dampne me noughte at Domesday for that I did so ille'.
                                               (B v. 472–8)

With the full meaning of that prayer we are not here

concerned. The immediate point is that it adumbrates the general prayer that follows hard upon it and is prompted by the same hope of grace and mercy.

Repentance's prayer begins with a phrase that serves *inter alia* as a connection with Holy Church's earlier instruction on *deus caritas* (i. 86 ff.) There the pre-Adamic history of the cosmos is sct forth, with Lucifer's disobedience and fall:

> Til God *of his goodnesse* gan stable and stynte,
> And garte the hevene to stekye and stonden in quiete.
>
> (B i. 120–1)

Lucifer, the liar, could not thwart the purpose of the Trinity, which is Truth (i. 131).

It will be evident at a glance that Repentance's sublime and measured utterance owes its power to Langland's apprehension of the Incarnate Word as the ultimate expression of God's goodness as first seen in creation. Here (amongst much else) is the warrant for Dame Julian's 'Sin is behovely' (so Our Lord himself says in her vision). The Latin is integral to the text, and fills out the argument, besides tying it firmly to the ritual of Easter. For *felix culpa* is the canticle sung at the blessing of the Paschal candle; *faciamus hominem* is part of the first *lectio* for Holy Saturday; *qui manet in caritate* alludes both to the 'Ubi caritas et amor Deus ibi est' of Maundy Thursday—to which Blake gave faultless lyrical form—and to the post-communion prayer on Easter Day: 'Spiritum nobis, Domine, tuae caritatis infunde...'. Langland was impregnated, divinely intoxicated with the Offices for Holy Week; and to read them now in their ancient form is to uncover the deepest sources of this passage.

But Langland is a logician before he is a liturgist. For did not Holy Church teach that re-creation and reason go together and that we should pray on Holy Saturday:

Deus, qui mirabiliter creasti hominem, et mirabilius redemisti: da nobis, quaesumus, contra oblectamenta peccati, mentis ratione persistere. [3]

Wondrous our creation, still more wondrous our redemption; may Reason remain sovereign in our minds and be proof against the allure of sin.

So here Langland appeals to reason, hinging the prayer on conjunctions like 'for', 'since', 'by so much the more' (v. 509). And there is a logical nexus implicit in 494 ff.:

God is Love.
Christ is Love, as is shown supremely in the Passion.
Therefore God remains in Christ even in the Passion.

Which brings us to the age-old dilemma: can Omnipotence suffer, as the Monarchians and Patripassians asserted?

Langland clearly accepts the orthodox answer that Christ suffered in his human nature, but not in his divine: a doctrine promulgated by the Greek Fathers and taken over by St. Augustine, who in one place says:

Just as soul is united to the body in the unity of the person so as to constitute man, so is God united to man in unity of Person so as to constitute Christ: in the former there is a mixture of soul and body, in the latter a mixture of God and man.

(Letter 137)

And in another place:

It is because of the Unity of the two natures that the *Lord* [of Glory] is described in 1. Cor. 2:8 as being crucified when only the humanity was crucified.

(*De Trinitate,* 1)

St. Thomas (*ST* III, q. 46, art. 12) had merely restated this in scholastic terms: 'The Lord of Glory is said to be crucified, not as the Lord of Glory, but as a man capable of suffering.' The *Meditationes* repeat it, and the fourteenth-century English verse-rendering of the *Meditationes* has:

This wo he suffred yn hys manhede
Bot God suffred noght yn hys Godhede.[4]

(411–12)

There is some evidence that this doctrine of the hypo-static union, so far from being a difficulty, held a special place in devout minds in Langland's time. Thus Julian of Norwich writes (Ch. 20): 'The one-ing [union] of the Godhead gave strength to the manhood [i.e. Christ's human nature] for love to suffer more than all man might...'. Christ brings to her mind 'the height and the nobility of the glorious Godhead, and therewith the precioushead and the tenderness of the blissful body which be together *oned*, and also the loathness that in our kind [our human nature] is to suffer pain. . . . for as long as he was passible he suffered for us and *sorrowed* for us. And now he is uprisen and no more passible; yet he suffreth with us.' That at least is what the text as printed says, but perhaps the wording should not be pressed.

Writing some thirty years after Langland, Nicholas Love goes out of his way to add to his version of the *Meditationes* the following emphasis (p. 216):

Thou must in thy mind depart in manner[a] for the time the might of the Godhead from the kindly[b] infirmity of His manhood— though it so be in soothness that the Godhead was never departed from the manhead. . . . To have true imagination and inward compassion of the Passion of Our Lord Jesu, very God and man, we shall[c] understand that as His will was to suffer the hardest death for the redemption of mankind, so by the self-same will He suspended in all His Passion the use of the might of the Godhead from the infirmity of the Manhood. . . .'

[a] distinguish, so to speak   [b] natural   [c] are to.

Love is elaborating on the affirmation that Christ suffered sensibly as a man; and as he was 'cleanest of complexioun'—*optimae complexionis*, meaning not that he was of fair skin but that in him the elements were perfectly mixed—so the pains were harder to bear: the cry, 'Eloi, Eloi!' was taken as convincing proof that he was very man.[5]

Of English divines, Lancelot Andrewes was perhaps the last to express adherence to this doctrine in patristic terms, in a Good Friday sermon in 1604, preached before James I:

Leo it is that first said it (and all antiquite allow of it); *Non soluit unionem, sed subtraxit visionem* [from St. Leo, *De Pass. Dom. Sermo* 17: Andrewes took some of his verbal tricks of style from St. Leo]; 'The Union is not dissolved; true, but the beames, the influence, was restrained, and for any comfort from thence His Soule was even as a scorched heathground without so much as any drop of dew of divine comfort. . . .'[6]

Modern critics of the doctrine who seek some new 'model' perhaps forget something that Andrewes knew—namely, that in patristic and later times the prophetic psalms played a decisive part in shaping views of the Passion; their images of suffering were read literally and left no room for doubt about the reality of Christ's pain. And they are deliberately grouped together in the Offices for Holy Week.[7]

It may now be clear why Langland leads up to Good Friday by quoting 'Faciamus hominem . . .' from Genesis 1. That verse was traditionally interpreted as meaning not (of course) that man's body was like God's but that his soul was divine. So Julian speaks of Christ's love of the soul that he has made to his own likeness (Ch. 6); and Gower prays to him

> which withinne dayes sevene
> This large world forth with the hevene
> Of his eternal providence
> Hath mad, and thilke intelligence
> In mannes soule resonable
> Enspired *to himself semblable,*
> Wherof the man of his feture
> Above alle erthly creature
> After the soule is immortal.
> [i.e. man is immortal because his soul is].[8]
> (*Confessio Amantis,* viii. 2975 ff.)

Similarly with the still more pregnant verse 'Verbum caro factum est', cited, at the conclusion of this 'movement' (508), from the last Gospel for Easter Day, and familiar because in Langland's time it was read at every Sunday mass. It is in regard to the hypostatic union that the pseudo-Cyril expounds this text: 'The Flesh is said to have become deified . . . and God the Word is said to have become incarnate and to have been made man.'[9]

Because of the nature of this union it is possible to say that God was seen on earth and conversed with men and that this *man*, Jesus, is uncreated and impassible and uncircumscribed (the term reserved for the Trinity, and applied to it by Dante and so by Chaucer). John of Damascus had put it thus:

The Word (*Verbum, Logos*) appropriates to Himself all that is human, for all that pertains to His holy flesh is His. Hence it is that the Lord of Glory is said to have been crucified [1. Cor. 2:8] and the Son of Man [he has in mind John 3:13] is declared to have been in heaven before the Passion.[10]

The doctrine of impassibility stands or falls with 'the Myth of God Incarnate'. Perhaps, like Christianity itself, that doctrine has not been tested and found wanting but has been found difficult and not fully tested. Langland's whole purpose was to put it to the test, and on the most rigid terms. His Jesus—the Christ from heaven—'in a poor man's apparel' (he later says) 'pursueth us ever';

> And loketh on us in her[a] liknesse and that with lovely chere,
> To knowen us by owre kynde herte and castyng of owre eyen,
> Whether we love the lordes here byfor owre lorde of blisse.
>   (B xi. 180–3)

> [a] their (i.e. poor men's).

In Langland God dies in our human flesh, and in our cause (*sute*, 415, may convey both meanings), when the fullness of time has come (496): full time is *plenitudo temporis* (Gal. 4:4) as well as 'high noon'.

The term 'word-play' is wholly inadequate to describe the fashion in which Langland here as elsewhere makes all the words do double work, squeezing them, overlaying them, revolving them like a kaleidoscope. Because of this, ll. 494–5 are almost untranslatable, representing as they do the upshot of another line of logic:

> God made man in his own image.
> Christ, Son of God, is also man.
> Therefore God is like man.
> And therefore, when Christ died in human form, God died.

But *sute* in its legal sense suggests that he died to meet the demands of justice. Like Anselm and others, Langland conceived of the Redemption in legal terms, as Passus XVIII will show. The affirmation that 'in owre secte was the sorwe and thi sone it ladde' (498) is intelligible only if we break the line sharply in two; the first half speaking primarily of Christ's human nature, his suffering on the

Cross. The verbal iteration of *sorwe* (497, 498, 499) may disconcert us but is surely deliberate: Christ is the Messianic man of sorrows; Calvary was the place of sorrow; and with it all would associate the sorrowing few at the foot of the Cross. It is their sorrow that Nature reflects on a macrocosmic scale, here indicated by the darkening of the sun, hiding its light as the mourners veiled their eyes. It is part of Langland's technique of concentration that he here strips away all the other signs of the shock of the cosmos as its Creator seems to expire—the shock which the Anglo-Saxon poet had likewise expressed in terms of grief: 'Weop eal gesceaft'.[11]

We are still in the context of Creation. God made the sun for a light: in a sermon for Holy Saturday St. Amphilochius had said, 'The elements mourned, as though it wanted little for them to dissolve in chaos and bring disaster to the world, *were it not* that they could see the purpose of their Maker, namely, that of His own will He suffered.'[12] Langland too perhaps interpreted the darkness at noon as a sign of mourning restrained only by such an awareness. Historically the darkness may not have begun at noon, but the whole mode of medieval interpretation would make for midday as the time. As it is Christ, the true sun, *sol justitiae*, the sun of righteousness, who has died, the sympathy of nature would be most fully shown if the sun was quenched in the full blaze of its glory.[13]

It remains to consider that second half-line: 'thi sone it ladde'. As in l. 495, this is a gloss *preceding* the Latin text. But there is an unexpected nexus with the first half-line:

Christ suffered pain and sorrow in his human nature.
But sorrow and pain were the penalty of the Fall.
In suffering them he was destroying the effects of the
   Fall, freeing man from the captivity of Satan and turn-
   ing sorrow into joy (503).

The text itself is from Ephesians 4 (v. 9)—a chapter that must have had a particular appeal to Langland—and St. Paul is there reading Psalm 68 as prophetic of Christ's return from Hell rather than of the Harrowing. Hence Bede applies this text to the parable of the strong man armed (Luke 11:21), saying that the *spolia* are men deceived by the devil 'which the Victor, Christ, distributed, for that is the mark of a conqueror (*insigne triumphantis*)'—a passage that Ælfric had expanded, saying, 'He distributed his spoil (*here-reaf*), which he released with his death when he took Adam and Eve and their offspring . . . and led them from hell up to the heavenly kingdom.'[14] So 490b is proleptic: 'it' being 'oure secte'—now to be read as 'the human race before Christ'.

There is no close link between the two parts of l. 500. We are not to conceive of saints taking a meal at noon. The phrase is expanded and explained by the following line—the blood dripping from the Cross revives the saintly souls in Limbo: in miniatures of the period (e.g. one in the Arundel Psalter) Adam, their representative, catches the blood in a chalice. *Fresh* emphasizes the immediacy of the effect. It is when Julian sets down her revelation of Christ's bleeding body (though bleeding from the scourging, not the wounds) that she says: 'The precious plenty of His dereworthy blood descended down into hell and burst their bands and delivered all that were there which longed to the court of heaven.'

This takes us beyond the Passion. But as we turn from the scene we may recall that the prayer is offered for penitents kneeling, one might say, in a dream-church. At l. 518 they cry *upward* to Christ and his pure Mother. We should perhaps think of them as looking up to a great rood, shrouded in Holy Week but now, on Easter Day, once more revealed, where the Blessed Virgin stands on the left hand, and St. John, holding his Gospel, on the other. Langland's intent is to fix men's minds on the real meaning of the Cross—to substitute for that superstitious trust in such local relics as the Rood of Bromholm, glanced at in an earlier passage (v. 231), a true and saving faith.

Before leaping over twelve passus and several thousand lines to the climactic vision of the whole poem in Passus XVIII, we may pause to consider how far the Christology deducible from this and the earlier scene reflects that current in Langland's day. Few definite conclusions can be drawn. Fourteenth-century theology was far from static. Ever since Anselm and Abelard there had been disputes about the doctrine of the Atonement. In the Schools Scotists and Thomists were still at odds, and Wyclif was raising new issues. On the other hand, many priests and more laymen probably accepted without question the traditional teaching of Peter Lombard and Peter Comestor, or 'the Gilt Legend'. One's impression is that Langland's general doctrine was eclectic without being idiosyncratic—that he was neither Thomist nor Scotist nor Predestinarian. His insistence on *Redde quod debes* (xix. 254, etc.) smacks of St. Anselm's teaching about Satisfaction. He does not emphasize the voluntary action of Christ as much as the Scotists, and St. Bernard, had done; yet it is implicit in the prayer that we have just considered. *Necessarium peccatum Ade* perhaps implies an Anselmian rather than an Abelardian position; for Anselm held that it was sin that made the Incarnation necessary. On the other hand, in presenting the Incarnation as a free exhibition of love Langland is close to Abelard and to Robert Pullen, Abelard's great Oxford contemporary; whilst the suggestion in Passus I that God the Father always looked on men with love is consonant with Peter Lombard's view that he loved before the world was made, and with Duns Scotus' belief that the Incarnation would have occurred if man had never fallen—which the Greek Orthodox Church has ever maintained.

What gives force to Langland's presentations of the Passion, however, is not their theological antecedents but the contexts in which he places them. The beliefs that colour them inspire and inform the whole of his poetry, and the fervour of these convictions fuses diverse literary modes into a new and unique form. It was perhaps the novelty of the form as much as the demands of the doctrine that prevented *Piers Plowman* from having a greater impact. The history of what one might call 'vernacular' theology in the later Middle Ages is of a drift away from the dogma of the Incarnation and towards meditation on the Passion: hence the *Devotio Moderna* that was to hold sway in the Netherlands. Reading some of the so-called mystical writers

of the fourteenth century, one sometimes feels that the
Passion absorbs all their minds. Langland beautifully, if
belatedly, restores the balance.

III

The two passages that we have so far considered, though
they have a logical place in the scheme of the poem, appear
without warning. The preparation for the climactic scenes
of Passus XVIII, on the other hand, is deliberate and
prolonged. They are presented as fulfilments of prophecy
(so the Church had always seen them), and if Christ here
figures as a knight it is because prophets themselves have
earlier in the poem been presented in knightly terms. Thus
Faith, alias Abraham, has figured as a *herald* seeking

> A ful bolde bacheler; I knewe hym by his blasen[15]
>
> (xvi. 179)

—where *bachelor* denotes a young knight who has yet to win
his spurs. Hope has a like role. And the Samaritan, who
embodies Charity, had earlier (xvii. 48–51) entered riding
hard to a *joust* in Jerusalem (though neither the Gospels nor
the Fathers anywhere name his destination). This of itself is
enough to relate him to one 'whose face was as he would go
to Jerusalem' (Luke 9:53). It does not prevent the
Samaritan from stopping to explain to the Dreamer in
almost tedious detail the mysteries of the Trinity: Langland
always put doctrinal relevance before 'realism'. But at last
the Samaritan 'pricks lyard' (his steed)—a good romance
phrase, taken over by Spenser and Milton—and dashes off
like the wind as if to make up for lost time. And when, in
the next dream, the Dreamer hears the anthems and the
organs of Palm Sunday, we are already half-prepared for
the sight of one 'semblable' to the Samaritan ('and *some-del*
to Piers the Plowman', xviii. 10), who comes 'pricking',
bootless, spurless, spearless but sprightly (*spakliche*, 12), as
if eager to be dubbed and to win his spurs. The dubbing or
making of a knight often took place before a battle, or on a
High Feast of the Church, such as Easter; and it was a
religious ceremony.

To joust, a knight needed a horse; and the Samaritan's mule easily merges into the colt of Luke 19:30 that the disciples requisitioned. His steed or *capul* has already (xvii. 107) been given the weighted name *Caro*—all good horses then as now had names, but the point of this one has been made clear by the Samaritan's avowal, 'Of mankind I took it'; so Christ had taken flesh (*caro*) and was to take the colt from its owners.[16]

Barefoot, in a knightly context, means simply that he did not wear the shoes of plate that an armed knight would wear. So the Green Knight, in *Sir Gawain*, rides shoeless into Camelot, and armed only with a holly branch.

Everything in this scene suggests a youthful combatant; not least the cry of the herald—whose duty was to identify each entrant by his blazon, which revealed his name (as *fili David* does here, being the Palm Sunday salutation in Matthew 21:9).

The Dreamer, playing his usual role of slow-witted interrogator, now asks 'What's going on?'—'What al that fare be-mente'—a colloquial, perhaps rustic, phrase, certainly betokening his imperfect understanding. But when Faith tells him that it is Jesus, who has come to fetch what the Fiend claims—'Piers fruite the Plowman' (20)—the mere mention of that name at once alerts him; for it is Piers he has been seeking all the while. 'Is Piers in this place?' he asks; and Faith frowns on him, as if he has missed the main point, before giving an oblique and cryptic answer:

> This Jesus of his gentrice wole juste in Piers armes,
> In his helme and in his haberjoun[a] *humana natura*;
> That *Cryst* be nought biknowe here for *consummatus deus*,
> In Piers paltok the Plowman this priker shal ryde;
> For no dynte shal hym dere[b] as *in deitate patris*.
>
> (xviii. 22–6)
>
> [a] coat of mail   [b] harm

Gentrice is formally a doublet of *gentilesse*, the quality of a truly noble knight, like Chaucer's, or like the Theseus whom Chaucer's knight describes. But it is a word of many facets, and Skeat may be pardoned for glossing it here as 'noble birth' yet in the corresponding line in the C text as 'noble nature': a sacred heraldry asserted that Christ was literally of noble birth. 'Of the offspryng of the *gentilman* Jafeth come Habraham, Moyses, Aron and the profettys; and also the kyng of the right lyne of Mary, of whom that *gentilman* Jhesus was borne, very God and Man: after his manhode Kyng of the londe of Jude and of Jues, *gentilman* by his modre Mary, Prynce of Cote armure.'[17] Langland is calling on every connotation of the term, including the sense of 'gracious condescension': for the line alludes to him who took the form of a servant (such as a plowman was)—Piers in Passus V has described himself as '*serving* Truth ever'.

We have met elsewhere a Jesus who comes to fight without weapons and with no shield but his human body. In *Ancrene Wisse* the shield that covered or concealed the Godhead was the dear body which was stretched on the Cross. Langland extends, deepens, and modernizes the image: *paltok*, 'a short doublet' (25), first appears in accounts and romances about this date; *priker*, 'a light horseman', is first evidenced in Langland and the contemporary alliterative *Morte Arthure*. It is particularly appropriate here, where neither horse nor rider is encumbered by armour. But in attending to these technical terms we may overlook the force of simpler words, like *wole* and *shal*. Neither denotes mere futurity: *wole* expresses Jesus' voluntary action; a contemporary reader would recall Isaiah's 'Oblatus est quia ipse voluit' (actually quoted in a label over the Crucifixion in a fourteenth-century Bible Picture Book).[18] *Shal* (which C substitutes as 21) suggests 'is destined *or* determined to'. Similarly, we must note the repeated use of the name *Jesus*; as always, the title for the Third Person of the Trinity in his humanity—*Christ* betokening his Divine nature, here latent or concealed.

Knights undertaking a great enterprise, or wishing to conceal their identity (as Lancelot does on occasion in Malory), took new coats of arms (as Gawain chose the pentangle before setting out to encounter the Green Knight). So here Christ wears a figurative coat (of arms) that belongs to man. He is to joust, but his only weapons will be his sinless human nature. The suggestion is that the Devil will think that this contestant is merely human:

> That Cryst be nought biknowe here for *consummatus deus*
> (xviii. 24)

—that last phrase perhaps pointing to Hebrews 5:8–9: 'Though he were a son, yet learned he obedience by the things which he suffered; *and being made perfect (et consummatus)* he became the author of eternal salvation (*factus est causa salutis eternae*).'

The whole of Faith's speech is clipped, almost breathless—as if this were not the place for formal question and answer. But 'nought biknowe' points clearly enough to the concealment already hinted at—'One semblable to the Samaritan and some-del to Piers the Plowman' (10). Nicole Bozon, following the ancient *Gospel of Nicodemus*, had presented the Incarnation as a design to lure Belial to combat;[19] and Langland seems here momentarily to adopt this belief.

> 'Who shal juste with Jesus?' quod I, 'Juwes or scribes?'
> 'Nay,' quod he, 'the foule fende and Fals-dome and Deth.
> Deth seith he shal fordo[a] and adown brynge
> Al that lyveth or loketh in londe or in watere.
> Lyf seyth that he likth and leyth his lif to wedde[b],
> That for al that Deth can do with-in thre dayes,
> To walke and fecche fro the fende Piers fruite the Plowman . . .'
> (xviii. 27–33)

> [a] destroy　　[b] as a pledge.

Jesus, he is saying, wears the armour of human nature— and we know that to be subject to pain and death (29, 30), although *deitas* cannot die. The courage of the young knight consists most of all in this; that he faces not one enemy, but three. The Jews who will assail him are not his real foes, but agents of the Devil, False-Doom, and the braggart Death.

The contest, then, is unequal, unfair—three against one. But Christ is depicted as the dauntless challenger. Unexpectedly, he is now given the new title of *Life*—though to be sure it is one he had assumed at the Last Supper: 'Ego sum Via, Veritas et Vita'. Line 31 (heavily alliterative) shows 'Life' in the stance of such a challenger as Arthur admired, one whom (according to *Sir Gawain*, 96–9) he liked to see challenge

> sum siker knyght
> To joyne wyth hym in justing, in jopardé to lay
> Lede, lif for lyf, leve uchon other,
> As fortune wolde fulsun[a] hom the fayrer[b] to have.

> [a] favour [a] advantage.

Line 33, syntactically irregular, switches abruptly to *oratio recta* after an implied verb of boasting. A knightly challenger could properly pronounce his purpose in the terms Life uses; about them clings the colour of such manly *beots*, or vaunts, as Beowulf had made before fighting the enemies of man. Life is not saying that he will walk up to the Fiend, but that he will be alive and moving about; he is also rebutting the assertion of l. 30 that *all* who live and move shall die.

The contest is to be first and foremost with Death; the challenge is to Death as 'Fals-dome', the opponent of 'Veritas'. The Easter Day sequence *Victime paschali laudes* is the genesis of this figure, which later blossoms into the fine fifteenth-century alliterative allegorical poem of *Deth and Lyf*:

> Mors et Vita duello
> Conflixere mirando;
> Dux vitae mortuus: Regnat vivus.

Life and Death in wondrous duel fought; dead was the Leader of Life, yet now he lives and reigns.

St. Catherine of Siena, in her book translated in the fifteenth century as *The Orchard of Syon*, has a similar figure: 'theere played deeth with luf, and luf with deeth'.

Langland, unlike Milton, does not give Death material shape. But he presents the Jews' actions as so many strokes aimed by Death at his rival; and Pilate, sitting as judge of the contest just as Theseus in the *Knight's Tale* sits 'full rich and high' above the lists, thinks of Death as a *doughty* adversary (37): the epithet is of knightly colour. Yet Pilate is to 'deme her botheres righte'—to see that the champions do not break the rules? or to judge justly? Again, the language is terse to the point of being cryptic.

There is a textual warrant, as we have seen, for describing this contest as a 'joust'. But as the passus proceeds the 'romance' figure fades, the juridical colour grows stronger. The fight waged against Lucifer is presented as a duel, and is set forth in legal terms that point forward to the debate between the Four Daughters of God in which the demands of Truth and Justice have to be met. It is, indeed, in Grosseteste's version of this debate that we meet the rendering of Philippians 2:7 (*formam servi accipiens*—'He took on him the form of a servant and was made in the likeness of men and was found in fashion as a man') which prompted the image of Christ fighting in human 'arms'; in Grosseteste's *Chasteau d'Amour* Christ says:

> Del serf prendrai la vesture
> En verité et en dreiture,
> Sustendrai le jugement.

The emphasis on Truth and Justice is crucial. And it is tempting to read the fight between Life and Death as a 'Civil Duel of Law', fought (once or twice in the fourteenth century) by champions, to determine title to property; the loser forfeiting some of his own rights, as well as his principal's. Spiritus Sanctus has already told the Blessed Virgin that Jesus was to joust

> 'by juggement of armes,
> Whether shulde fonge[a] the fruit the fende or hymselve'
> (xvi. 95–6)

> [a] take.

—'the fruit' being 'Piers fruite the Plowman' (xviii. 20, 33). It is in terms of legal *seisin* that Lucifer will later maintan his claim:

> 'And sitthen I *seised* sevene hundreth wyntre,
> I leve that *lawe* nil naughte lete hym the leest.'
> (xviii. 281–2)

To which Christ will answer that he is not 'seising' the souls of men 'by maistrie' (by force),

> 'But bi right and by resoun [I] raunceoun here my lyges'.
>
> (xviii. 347)

Distinct from the Duel of Law, and more familiar, is the Duel of Chivalry, the rules of which were set down by Thomas of Lancaster a few years after Langland had penned this passus.[20] It was fought with knightly weapons, and the vanquished knight might be granted as captive to the victor. If the charge was treason, his land would escheat to the King; and in *Piers Plowman* Satan himself admits that Lucifer's enticement of Eve *was* treachery (286; cf. C xxi. 321). In due course Langland will show that the Lucifer who fails to answer Christ's challenge is a craven.

And so we come to the Passion proper:

The Juwes and the justice ayeine Jesu thei were,
And al her courte on hym cryde *crucifige* sharpe.
Tho put hym forth a piloure[a] bifor Pilat, and seyde,   40
'This Jesus of owre Jewes temple japed and dispised,
To fordone it on o day and in thre dayes after
Edefye it eft newe (here he stant that seyde it)
And yit maken it as moche in al manere poyntes,
Bothe as longe and as large bi loft[b] and by grounde.'   45
'*Crucifige*,' quod a cacchepolle, 'I warante hym a wicche!'
'*Tolle, tolle!*' quod an other and toke of kene thornes,
And bigan of kene thorne a gerelande to make,
And sette it sore on his hed and seyde in envye,
'*Ave, rabby!*' quod that ribaude and threw redes at hym,   50
Nailled hym with thre nailles naked on the rode,
And poysoun on a pole thei put up to his lippes,
And bede hym drynke his deth-yvel, his dayes were ydone.
'And yif that thow sotil be help now thi-selven,
If thow be Cryst, and kynges sone, come downe of the rode;   55
Thanne shul we leve that Lyf the loveth and wil nought lete
    the deye!'
'*Consummatum est*', quod Cryst, and comsed[c] forto swowe
Pitousliche and pale as a prisoun[d] that deyeth;
The lorde of lyf and of lighte tho leyed his eyen togideres.
The daye for drede with-drowe and derke bicam the sonne,   60
The wal wagged and clef and al the worlde quaved[e].

Ded men for that dyne come out of depe graves,
And tolde whi that tempest so longe tyme dured.
'For a bitter bataille' the ded bodye sayde;
'Lyf and Deth in this derknesse her one fordoth her other;   65
Shal no wighte wite witterly[f] who shal have the maystrye,
Er Sondey aboute sonne-rysynge' and sank with that til erthe.
Some seyde that he was Goddes sone that so faire deyde,
            Vere filius dei erat iste, etc.
And somme saide he was a wicche; 'good is that we assaye
Where[g] he be ded or noughte ded doun er he be taken'.   70
     Two theves also tholed[h] deth that tyme,
Uppon a crosse bisydes Cryst, so was the comune lawe.
A cacchepole cam forth and craked bothe her legges,
And her armes after of eyther of tho theves.

                                        (xviii. 38–74)

   [a] robber   [b] above   [c] began   [d] prisoner   [e] trembled   [f] for certain
   [g] whether   [h] suffered.

In contrast to the meditative writers, Langland reduces rather than inflates the Gospel narrative. Thus he not only compresses the series of demands and accusations, but also presents them as made by a *pilour*—a pillager of the dead, one who might act in hope of booty later—and a *cacchepolle*—'a petty serjeant'. Likewise, the garland of thorns—'garland' was by now the accepted term in English Passion narratives for the Vulgate *corona*—is made, and pressed deep into the head (another standard detail), by a single 'ribald'. His 'Ave, rabbi!'—the deceitful salutation of Judas in the Gospels—replaces the Roman soldiers' 'Ave, rex!'

   The remainder of l. 50 marks the beginning of a new torture, and the subject of the verb will not be supplied until l. 52. The throwing of reeds has no New Testament warrant—Matthew and Mark say merely 'they took the reed and smote him on the head'; but several verses in the prophetic psalms may have prompted the use of a kinetic verb, so typical of Langland (for example, Psalm 11:2: 'they . . . shoot at the upright'; cf. Psalm 64:3–4). 'Shot reeds at his eyes' in the C text has no such warrant. But the next line in both texts has the sharpness of a nail. The three nails were by now common form; we meet them so often

that we forget that the third, transfixing both feet, made for
a particularly cruel torture—just as we forget that the
nakedness was the worst shame of all. Of the *crucifixio* itself,
and the Cross, Langland tells us no more; whether it was
jacente cruce or *erecto cruce* does not interest him.

The gall and the vinegar are not elsewhere specifically
described as poisons (the C text, indeed, suggests that they
were intended to lengthen life, not to shorten it). In the
following lines (54–5), Langland conflates two verses of the
Gospels, and sharpens the taunts by adding '. . . if you're so
clever' ('sotil') in the apodosis of l. 54. But of Christ's
sufferings he says nothing, noting only that he swoons
piteously and grows pale. The pallor is traditional—we
found it in the lyrics—but here a new simile brings it home;
or would bring it home to readers of Chaucer's Tale of the
Man of Law, who asks:

> Have yet nat seyn somtyme a pale face,
> Among a prees, of hym that hath be lad
> Toward his deeth, wher as hym gat no grace,
> And swich a colour in his face hath had,
> Men myghte knowe his face that was bistad,
> Amonges alle the faces in that route?
>
> (*CT* B 645–50)

For the rest, the lines come closest to John 19 : 30, but the
substitution of 'leyed his eyen togideres' (59) is not just a
poetic variation. The phrase *may* betoken that the struggle
is ended; or it may be a periphrasis for 'died'. The
Meditationes, in Nicholas Love's version, say: 'And after
that tyme bygan oure lorde Jesu to faille in sight in manere
of deyenge men, and wexe alle pale, now stekynge the eiyen
and now oponynge; and bowede his hede, now in to that
oon side and now in to that other.' English miniatures and
paintings of the period, as opposed to those of pre-twelfth-
century date, show the eyes closed. But the whole of l. 59 is
periphrastic, foreshadowing the next. As the Lord of Life,
dux vitae, dies, so the good things of day withdraw. As the
Lord of Light (*sol justitiae*) dies, so the sun that he created
quenches *its* light. But Langland himself speaks directly of
physical death only in filling out the centurion's words

'Truly, this was the Son of God' with the phrase 'that so
faire deyde'—as if it was the dauntless or patient manner of
his dying that moved the Roman. There is no place here for
'Eloi, Eloi, lama sabachthani'; and *Sitio* will come later,
where there is room and occasion to expand it. The duel is
not yet done. The bodies that rise from their graves (62: cf.
Matthew 27:52–3) testify that it continues in the darkness
of Limbo.

We move back once more to the jouster of heroic temper.
That note is resumed at l. 76 and held for ten lines that are
entirely knightly in feeling.

Ac was no boy[a] so bolde Goddes body to touche,
For he was knyghte and kynges sone, Kynde foryaf that tyme
That non harlot were so hardy to leyne hande uppon hym.
Ac there cam forth a knyghte with a kene spere ygrounde,
Highte Longeus, as the lettre telleth, and longe had lore[b] his
      sighte.
Bifor Pilat and other peple in the place he hoved[c];
Maugre his many tethe[d] he was made that tyme
To take the spere in his honde and justen with Jesus;
For alle thei were unhardy that hoved on horse or stode
To touche hym or to taste[e] hym or take hym doun of rode.
But this blynde bacheler thanne bar hym thorugh the herte;
The blode spronge down by the spere and unspered[f] the knyghtes
      eyen.

                                        (xviii. 75–86)

   [a]fellow   [b]lost   [c]waited   [d]despite himself   [e]feel   [f]opened.

The sense of which is: 'Because he was a knight, indeed of
royal birth (*filius David*), Nature required [i.e. it was wholly
in accord with the fitness of things] that no one of such low
degree as a "cacchepolle" should touch him. Only another
knight was worthy to do that. And even he did it reluc-
tantly. A queer kind of tourney this, in which a blind knight-
bachelor levels his spear at a knight already dead—and in
striking a mortal wound receives his sight.' Here, as in
Passus I, and as in pious literature of the period, Longinus'
spear pierces the heart—though it is always depicted, for
allegorical reasons, as levelled at the *right* side; Christ
himself is to confirm this when, in Passus XIX (166), he
bids incredulous Thomas 'to grope and fele with his fyngres

his flessheliche *herte*'. The centurion's spear has become a knight's jousting lance.

> Thanne fel the knyghte upon knees and cryed hym mercy—
> 'Ayeyne my wille it was, lorde, to wownde yow so sore!'
> He seighed and sayde, 'sore it me athynketh;
> For the dede that I have done I do me in yowre grace;
> Hauc on me reuth, rightful Jesu!' and right with that he wept.
>   (xviii. 87–91)

Langland makes nothing of the symbolic flowing forth of both blood and water. But he insists on Longinus' reluctance, because he represents him as the unwitting and unwilling agent of the Jews, whom Faith now reproaches as wretched *villeins*—a class disdainful or ignorant of the laws of chivalry:

> Thanne gan Faith felly the fals Juwes dispise,
> Called hem caytyves acursed for evere,
> 'For this foule vyleynye venjaunce to yow alle!
> To do the blynde bete hym ybounde it was a boyes[a] conseille.
> Cursed caytyve! knighthood was it nevere
> To mysdo a ded body by day or by nyghte.
> The gree[b] yit hath he geten for al his grete wounde'.
>   (xviii. 92–8)
>
>   [a] churl's   [b] prize.

Once more, readers of the *Knight's Tale* would take the point. For that tale begins with the complaint of the Theban women against Creon, the cruel tyrant who,

> . . . for despit and for his tirannye,
> *To do the dede bodyes vileynye,*

has collected their husbands' bodies and made them food for dogs (*CT* A 941–2).[21]

Faith has taken over Pilate's role as judge. As a herald he knows the laws and terms of feudal chivalry, and proceeds to apply them. In this knightly context the Roman soldier Longinus had to figure as a 'champion chevalier'—he is, indeed, in Langland's time often represented on horseback—who now surrenders as a recreant.[22] 'To yield as recreant' (to confess oneself vanquished) is a phrase of

chivalric romance—compare *Sir Bevis*: 'Ich me yelde recreant to the in this felde', and Malory: 'To yelde me unto thee
as recreant I had rather die to be so ashamed'. *The gree* (98)
is another term of tourney (cf. *CT* A 2733),[23] whilst a line
found only in the C text (94) adds a feudal and juridical
flavour:

> My londe and my lycame[a] at youre lykynge taketh hit.

> [a] body.

The concluding lines of Faith's speech lead beyond our
theme, except insofar as they show Faith, like Holy Church
before him, translating the lesson of the Cross, as Langland
always does, into very practical terms. For the worst penalty
the Jews have to bear is a life of usury (106). Nothing
distinguishes the fourteenth century from the twentieth
more sharply than this condemnation, which Ezra Pound
alone of modern poets dared to repeat.

We have not yet done with Langland's reading of the
Passion narrative. When Christ challenges Satan before the
gates of hell, he contrasts the bitter brew of Death, the
medicine that Satan must now drink himself, with the drink
that nourishes him:

> For I, that am lorde of lyf, love is my drynke.
> And for that drynke to-day I deyde upon erthe.
> I faughte so, me threstes[a] yet for mannes soule sake;
> May no drynke me moiste ne my thruste slake,
> Tyl the vendage[b] falle in the vale of Iosephath,
> That I drynke righte ripe must, *resureccio mortuorum*,
> And thanne shal I come as a kynge crouned with angeles,
> And han out of helle alle mennes soules.
>
> (xviii. 363–70)

> [a] I thirst   [b] vintage.

For reading the *Sitio* of the Seven Last Words as a cry,
not of thirst, but for the 'heal' of man, there was good
patristic warrant.[24] Bede (following Augustine) had written: 'Tu dixisti *sitio, sc.* salutem animarum sanctorum que
in limbo erant, adventurum tuum expectantium' (Thou
saidest 'I thirst', that is for the salvation of the souls of

saints which were in limbo, awaiting thy coming);[25] St.
Bernard says much the same. But in presenting it as a thirst
induced by fighting, Langland is making his last adjustment
of the Gospel narrative to the frame of a tournament.
Knightly combat was thirsty work; and scenes in which the
heavily armed knights retire to refresh themselves with
water or a cooling breeze are the stock-in-trade of romance.

In Langland, then, the figure of Christ the lover-knight has
taken on a new dimension and new depth. Christ's assump-
tion of Piers's arms is an image that brings the Incarnation
within the range of medieval understanding. And in the
last glimpse of Christ fighting on the Cross, parched with
love for the souls of men, we move out of the convention of
spiritualized courtly love to Christian eschatology.

The lines

> 'And thanne shal I come as a kynge crouned with angeles,
> And han out of helle alle mennes soules'
>
> (369–70)

are often quoted as if they made Langland a universalist.
But, though the primary reference is to the release of souls
in Limbo, the larger purpose is to prepare us for the Last
Judgement and the reconciliation of Justice and Mercy in
which the whole passus culminates. The Dreamer takes the
lesson to heart, and with his wife and daughter—now
mentioned for the first and only time—creeps to the Easter
Cross, as the Easter bells ring what Dunbar will call 'the
knell of mercy'. It is always liturgical action that Langland
builds on at his climaxes; and, in the very last lines of the
passus, the three move forward to kiss that jewel of a Cross,
which has indeed 'afered the fende' and vanquished the
power of darkness. The material gems adorning the Anglo-
Saxon poet's rood were symbols of a spiritual value that
Langland invokes, characteristically, in a colloquial phrase:
'Kisseth it for a juwel!'[26]

When Peace appears as the emissary of Love (170 ff.), she
enunciates a doctrine that may be extrapolated from patristic teaching but had surely never before been so boldly
expressed. The Crucifixion as Peace presents it is necessary

not simply to redeem mankind but also in order that God should know the extremities of human suffering and death:

'Ne hadde God suffred of som other than hymselve
He hadde nat wist wyterly whether deth wer soure other sweyte.
For sholde nevere right riche man that lyveth in reste and hele
Ywyte what wo is ne were the deth of kynde[a].
So God that al bygan of hus good wil
Bycam man of a mayde mankynde to save,
And suffrede to be solde to seo the sorwe of deyynge,
The whiche unknytteth alle care and comsyng[b] is of reste.'

(C xxi. 218–25)

[a] know what pain is, unless he had to suffer death like other mortals
[b] beginning.

The phrasing here harks back to Repentance's prayer (B v. 488–98). But Langland never repeats himself: the emphasis and the implications are new; and not readily deducible from such verses as Heb. 2:9–10, though perhaps some commentary known to Langland had expounded that passage in a similar sense.

V

THE SCOTTISH TESTIMONY

OF all the developments in the history of devotion none is
more striking than the force and fervour of the Catholic
poetry written north of the Border in the decades immediately preceding the advent of John Knox and
Presbyterianism. On the very eve of the Reformation
Scotland produces three poems on the Passion as different
in character from any so far considered as their authors are
different from their southern contemporaries and from the
earlier English poets whom they undoubtedly read and
admired. Nor do they have much in common with earlier
northern writers of Rolle's kind. One of them, Robert
Henryson, schoolmaster of Dunfermline towards the close
of the fifteenth century, was evidently a layman. He is, to be
sure, a very hortatory writer. But his *moralitates*, securely
kennelled in the rear of his verses, never mar the brilliance
of his Aesopian fables or blunt the sharpness of his rural
observation or blur our impression of his piety. They
bespeak the dominie rather than the divine.

It is in Henryson's 'Bludy Serk' that we catch practically
the last glimpse of Christ as the lover-knight. Already in
Quia Amore Langueo that knight speaks of his bloodstained
garment as a 'bloody surcoat'; the surcoat being a rich
covering, often heraldically adorned, worn over knightly
armour; but in a late version of this poem the term *scherte* is
substituted.[1] There is good scriptural warrant for the
association of such a garment with Christ. If it was not
suggested by the 'garment dyed red' of the *propugnator* in
Isaiah 63 it would be by the purple robe of the Passion
narrative in the Gospels, or the vesture that replaced it, to
be stained, according to later expansions of that narrative,
with the blood that welled from the wounds inflicted by the
scourges—hence usually represented as purple in
Crucifixion or pre-Crucifixion scenes. But no English

verses do more than mention the surcoat as part of the apparel donned in knightly warfare. Henryson's poem points to his acquaintance not with *Quia Amore Langueo* but with that great thesaurus (or rag-bag) of medieval story, the *Gesta Romanorum*: a collection which appends a moral to every tale in the very manner that Henryson adopts in his *Fables*, and his *Orpheus*. John Gower and the influential fourteenth-century philosopher Robert Holcot had drawn on the *Gesta* for much the same purpose.

The Henryson canon shows him to be a master of a variety of verse-forms; and 'The Bludy Serk' follows a pattern of narrative verse that if not peculiar to Scotland was extensively practised there. It belongs to a group of poems, some running up to sixteen stanzas, usually of from six to eight lines, that tell a brisk tale, usually in dialogue and in simple dialect. Henryson's own pawky pastoral, 'Robin and Makyn', is one example, Dunbar's 'In Secreit Place this hyndir nicht' (which relies as much on alliteration as Henryson does) and 'Bewty and the Prisoneir' are others; the anonymous *King Hart* is a longer allegorical variant. Henryson's opening line firmly sets 'The Bludy Serk' in the secular world of this genre:

> This hindir yeir I hard betald
> Thair was a worthy king . . .

—a conventional romance opening that he at once develops in romance terms, with a fair daughter dwelling in a bower and loved by princes *par amour*. (The complete text is printed at the end of this chapter; see also n. 3 to Ch. III.)

The tale as Henryson tells it is attached in the *Gesta* not to a king but to an emperor. In one of the fifteenth-century English versions of the *Gesta* the emperor dies leaving a beautiful daughter, in the other she is already fatherless when the story opens. In the one it is an earl who beguiles her and then casts her off, in the other an envious king.[2] Whatever version Henryson knew, it is evident he is moulding the tale to his own purposes, whilst adding romance embellishments such as the giant who refuses ransom (like Theseus in the *Knight's Tale*), lives in a dungeon, and has crooked nails five quarters long. From the outset Henryson tips in phrases that at second view reveal a deeper purpose. The father of the lady is described as a lord 'anceane and ald': we think of the Ancient of Days. The giant's claw is perhaps literally 'ane hellis cruk', while his dungeon recalls the dim abode of the devil in Passus XVIII of *Piers Plowman* and in the mystery plays.

One of the English versions of the tale in the *Gesta Romanorum* presents a dialogue between the hapless maiden and the handsome young knight astride a handsome steed. 'I shall fight for thy heritage, and I promise thee victory,' says the knight. 'Ah, lord, alas,' quoth she, 'I have nothing to give thee but myself.' Then spake he:

'If it hap me to die for thee in battle and not to have victory [I will] that thou set out my bloody serk on a perch[3] afore . . . that the sight of my serk may move thee to weep . . . and that when any man cometh to thee for to have thee to wife thou run to the serk and behold the serk and say to thyself: "God forbid that ever I should take any to my husband after the death of this lord which died for my love and recovered my heritage."'

How the knight can have done this if he has failed to win the victory is not clear; but minor inconsistencies abound in such *exempla*.

Henryson's version is far more impressive: partly because of the terseness and speed of his verse—which can yet allow six lines to the confounding of the giant (51–6). Only when the knight lies at the point of death (in the same piteous plight as the enamoured Arcite in the *Knight's Tale*) is the serk mentioned, and only then does the lady avow her love, professing that she would willingly have followed him to beggary. It is the test that the Nutbrown Maid has to pass in the ballad of that name, and again we sense that Henryson is putting secular song to his own high purposes. · It is the essence of ballad that it seizes only on essentials, and so here. That the knight dies of his wounds and that the lady duly hangs up his serk is nowhere stated. Nor, to be sure, is his death mentioned in the second of the English prose versions. But that version does tell us that 'the maiden rose out of the bed of wretchedness and poverty and had her kingdom; and took the coat-armour of her husband that was

all besprinkled with blood, and hung it in her privy
chamber, that it might be alway ready to her sight'. A
rendering of the tale in the fifteenth-century *Dives et Pauper*
puts it somewhat differently: the knight there sends home
his bloodied shirt *with a letter* that runs:

> 'Behold my wounds and have them in thy thought
> For all the goods that be there
> With my blood I have them bought.'

The application, the *sens*, of this *matière*, is evident
enough, even if one has never read of Christ as the lover-
knight before: the 'privy chamber' is the maiden's heart,
her 'goods' are her salvation and spiritual treasure. We
hardly need the flat explicatory lines of Henryson's twelfth
stanza; and the appended *Moralitas*, which spells it out still
more plainly, only recovers the original thrust of the tale as
it draws to its close:

> Borrowit with Chrystis angell cleir,
> Hend men, will ye nocht herk?
> For His lufe that bocht us deir,
> Think on the bludy serk.

The title-phrase, repeated in that closing line, has worked
powerfully throughout the poem, bringing to it that same
enigmatic element that operates in *A Vision of a Rood*; and
the appeal to 'hend men' (gentlefolk) is a last touch of
romance colouring, preceded by a more cryptic phrase that
eludes exact translation (? 'preserved, protected by St.
Michael against the Devil'). In fact, Henryson has merci-
fully reduced the *moralitas*, which in the Latin text of the
Gesta includes the gloss: 'Miles qui iuxta eam equitabat erat
filius dei, qui in equo humanitatis mundum istum intravit et
humano generi compaciebatur' (the knight who rode beside
her was the Son of God, who on the horse of human nature
entered the world and suffered with mankind): a passage
that links the figure to Langland's knightly Samaritan who
rode on the mule of humanity.

It seems unlikely that Henryson had an immediate verse
model. But he may have known an English text similar to
the second English version of the *Gesta*, the closing lines of

which, though printed as prose, fall into rhymed couplets (and are intended for general application):

> Whilst I have in mind
> The blood of him that was so kind,
> How should I him forsake
> That the death for me would take?
> Nay, forsooth, I shall not so,
> For he bought me from mickle woe.

Such a verse-passage may well have prompted the Scottish poet to pour the whole tale into a verse-mould. It seems to reflect the words written in the margin of a Harleian manuscript of the *Gesta*: 'In camisia sua, secundum quosdam, erant haec verba scripta [on his shirt, according to some, these words were written]: "Thynke on hym and have good mynde/that tho [then] [to] the was so kynde".'

One other detail suggests that Henryson may have owed his knowledge of the *exemplum* to an English version of the *Gesta* rather than to the diffused tradition of Christ the lover-knight as disseminated in sermons: the term *serk/sark* is last recorded in English use in the *Oxford English Dictionary* from one of the aforesaid English renderings of the *Gesta*, whilst the first quotation from a Scots source is from Dunbar; it may well have caught Henryson's eye in an English text as the *mot juste*. His poem, in any event, bears witness to the appeal of the tale to a poet whose natural bent was to the tragic and the austere.

To catch the full flavour of the poem, to sense its contemporary appeal, we should read it alongside a knightly romance by a knightly English writer of Henryson's own time. In Malory's tale of Alexander the Orphan, a widowed mother approaches her son on the day he is to be knighted, and at the offering of the mass 'pulls out a bloody doublet and a bloody shirt that was bebled with old blood'. Starting back and growing pale, he asks, 'What may this be to mean?' They are the garments his father had worn when King Mark slew him 'for his good deeds', before her very eyes. She charges him, on the high order of Knighthood, to take revenge. The motif evidently derives from the story of La Cote Mal Taillée, nickname of a knight who wore the rent coat that his father had worn when an enemy slew him as he slept. In the French version of Malory's tale the father's squire, having buried his body at a hermitage, takes his shirt and armour and brings them to his widow. For Henryson's readers the associations of 'a bloody shirt' would not necessarily be with Christ the lover-knight: they may well have been, primarily, with themes such as Malory's; possibly, also, with the 'Corpus Christi' carol, in which a maiden weeps beside the bed of a bleeding knight. [4]

Early in the seventeenth century an anonymous English versifier (rightly conscious of his 'want of skill') found in the ancient theme a subject for a piece befitting the Christmas season, when men 'strange adventures tell'. His pace and proportions are very different from Henryson's. Three stanzas go to the lady's beauty and virtue, three to her ravishment:

> her pearls and tyre
> are trod in myre

and she is set by the roadside, bound hand and foot, so that all men might her 'plumèd [*sic*] corpse deride'. The knight-errant to whom she plights troth vanquishes her foes in open field, but is mortally wounded, leaving her 'Cy testament', his armour bright and clothes besprent with blood. She is to set them by her bed:

> In thy closet
> let them be set
> and chambred in thy soule
> my memory let never dye
> but it in heart enrole.

The last three stanzas produce the expected *moralitas*, but go no further than identifying the 'cumly creature' with Mankind, the knight with Christ. They might seem to mark the dead end of the tradition. [5]

Yet four hundred years after Henryson wrote, a poet of a very different milieu and sensibility gave the romance elements in the basic story a new, high-toned setting. Dante Gabriel Rossetti's 'Staff and Scrip' derives from a variant found in another chapter (25) of the Latin text of the *Gesta*, one that may indeed have been known to the poet of *Quia Amore Langueo*. In this version the damsel, far from cherishing the memory of her deliverer, gets rid of his relics, which (as in the unpublished *Sermones Dominicales* of Friar Felton, in MS Harley 4) consist not of a surcoat but of a staff and scrip. Rossetti's brilliant blend of the two versions adopts these symbols. His carefully structured stanzas are distinctly Pre-Raphaelite in flavour, yet retain a certain power: witness those on the dead knight:

> 'Oh what do ye bring out of the fight,
>> Thus hid beneath these boughs?'
> 'Even him, thy conquering guest tonight,
>> Who yet shall not carouse,
>>> Queen, in thy house.'
>
> . . .
>
> His sword was broken in his hand
>> Where he had kissed the blade.
> 'O soft steel that could not withstand!
>> O my hard heart unstayed,
>>> That prayed and prayed!'

And so the verse rises with mounting force to the last cryptic lines:

> The lists are set in Heaven today,
>> The bright pavilions shine;
> Fair hangs thy shield, and none gainsay;
>> The trumpets sound in sign
>>> That she is thine.
>
> Not tithed with days' and years' decease
>> He pays thy wage He owed,
> But with imperishable peace,
>> Here in His own abode,
>>> Thy jealous God.

Modern poetry yields few more impressive witnesses to the persistent power of an ancient theme than this strange re-creation. Yet if the theme persists it is perhaps more for its appeal to the deepest human feelings than for its literary antecedents. A garment that bears signs of a beloved's wounds in battle acquires its own aura, as a modern soldier implies when describing his dismay that friends should think of washing the bloodstained shirt that he wished to take back to his wife as it was.[6]

'The Bludy Serk' was written, probably, about the turn of the fifteenth century. It prepares us to consider the most substantial collection of vernacular verse (and prose) devoted to the Passion now extant, compiled two or three decades later. To those who think of Scotland as the natural home of the Reformation and of John Knox as the mouthpiece and epitome of Scottish religious feeling it may come as a surprise to learn that the anthology in question, made on the very eve of the break with Rome, is a wholly Scottish compilation, even though we owe its preservation to Lord William Howard of Naworth Castle, Cumberland, where it found a home when the old religion was stamped out north of the Border. It is this Arundel manuscript that provides the best guide to early sixteenth-century piety and devotional practices, though it has been hitherto overlooked by historians of Catholic devotion in Tudor times.[7] From this miscellany it is not practicable to select for study more than a few poems, but these will suffice to show its representative character for they come from the pens of two of the best-known poets of the time. On paper bitter rivals, William Dunbar and Walter Kennedy stand here next to each other, united in a common poetic and a common faith.

Dunbar is often dubbed a Scottish Chaucerian. 'Scottish Lydgatian' would be nearer the mark, for Lydgate's influence was more pervasive than Chaucer's in northern parts. In the Arundel collection, some verses of Lydgate's on the Passion follow those by Dunbar on the same theme, and Dunbar's other devotional poems have something in common with those of the Monk of Bury. Two of them—on the Nativity, and the Resurrection—have found their place in anthologies and literary histories. His verses on the Passion, ignored even by C. S. Lewis, lie midway in every-sense between these two. (The verses are printed at the end of this chapter. A full commentary is now available in J. Kinsley (ed.), *The Poems of William Dunbar* (1979), pp. 230–4.) Like the two better-known poems, the verses have no close equivalent in English—unless we count a Tudor 'carol', to be considered shortly. Superficially they may seem to be yet another synopsis of the pseudo-Bonaventuran *Meditationes* that formed the basis of chapters in Ludolf of Saxony's *Vita Christi* and Nicholas Love's *Meditations*; the latter had been partly incorporated in the fifteenth-century *Speculum Devotorum*, the former put into English in Dunbar's time; at least one copy of the Latin *Vita* had reached Scotland by then, though the title is not found in sixteenth-century library lists. His poem does in fact present in little the same deliberate movement through the major scenes of the Passion that characterizes the Latin works. Almost every phrase of the first twelve stanzas can be paralleled in earlier meditative prose or verse, whilst the opening lines:

> Amang thir freiris within ane cloister
> I enterit in ane oritorie,

testify to the role of the friars in propagating the cultus of the Passion in the North, as in the South: the vision that then befalls the poet as he sleeps prostrate before the Rood is just such a vision as Margery Kempe had in a friar's oratory at Lynn. Critical as Dunbar is of the friars in his satirical verse, this poem in all its parts shows that he had learnt from them the art of emotional compression, which appears in every line.

Not till the very last line are we told specifically that the image before which he kneels hangs on a rood, and that it is Holy Week, though we might have guessed it from the likeness to the Anglo-Saxon *Vision of a Rood*. Not that this 'crose of sweit Jesu' was necessarily a wooden image, or on a rood-screen: it might have been a reredos carved with Passion scenes, or a mural fresco of the Crucifixion, or an alabaster panel. Lydgate, at the end of Part IV of his *Testament*, describes how

> Myd of a cloyster, *depicte* upon a walle,
> I saugh a crucifyx, whos woundes were not smalle,
> With this word *Vide* wrete there besyde[8]

—where *Vide* would stand for 'Homo, vide quid pro te patior'. In Holy Week such images would presumably be veiled, but that would not diminish recollection of the figures daily vivid to the eyes of worshippers. Dunbar's phrase 'michtie king of glorie' (l. 4) perhaps implies that the *Christus crucifixus* was crowned, with an INRI label above. Whether it were a rood or a *pietà*, the Virgin Mother to whom the poet next pays reverence (l. 6) would be represented beside her son; and the invocation *gaude flore virginali* with which he at once addresses her—the *incipit* of a familiar Latin hymn—attests the deep devotion to the Virgin that flowers in his richest and most aureate poem, 'Hale, sterne superne'. The economy of the present piece, however, allows no further space for her—though the 'sweit Jesu' of the last two stanzas may echo the *Jesus dulcissimus* of this same hymn.

It is, then, Easter Eve, the time of vigil after a week of fasting, and the sleep that brings the vision is the sleep of exhaustion. The account of the vision is to be read not so much as strict autobiographical record as conforming to the established genre of dream-poetry, which required the immediate occasion of the dream to be stated, as here. Dunbar was devoted to this genre, and seized on its possibilities as a frame for religious feeling to a degree unparalleled since Anglo-Saxon times. It allows him to present the essential scenes in the Passion sequence without repeating all the details and directions that figured in the books of Meditations. As a dream-poem about Calvary only one lyric of similar date approaches Dunbar's: the so-called carol with the refrain

> My fearfull dreme nevyr forgete can I:
> Methought a maydyns childe causless can dye.

But that is remarkable chiefly for its elaborate stanza form and its concentration on the griefs of the Virgin as the sword of sorrow pierces her heart.[9]

It is no part of Dunbar's purpose to paint vivid word-pictures or vie with the Gothic realists in their manner of actualizing gruesome detail. Rather, he eliminates all local colour, all personal emphasis. Judas at once merges with the other Jews who led the Heavenly Prince before the judge. Herod is nowhere named, nor Pilate, nor Longinus. But the

ignominies inflicted are intensified, now by similes recalling
the Psalms:

> . . . as lyounis with awfull ruge[a]
> In yre thai hurlit him heir and thair;
>
> [a] roar.

now by underlining malicious motive:

> Thay terandis[a], to revenge thair tein[b],
> For scorne thai cled him in to quhyt[c].
>
> [a] tyrants　　[b] anger　　[c] white.

The blindfolding hides the face of him whom angels desired
to behold (28)—a motif that recurs a few lines later (54) and
that depends ultimately on the *panis angelorum* of Psalm
78:25.[10]

Dunbar achieves his most telling effects by deft use of
common phrases, often alliterative phrases that smack of
Edinburgh wynds: 'tell us tyt', 'large and lang', 'back and
side', 'brim as wild bores' (fierce as mad boars), 'fall down
with a swak'. The emphasis is repeatedly on the shedding of
innocent blood, which flows copiously at every stroke. The
crown of thorns is thrust down till the blood blinds the eyes
and mingles with the sweat. Stones pierce the feet. Dame
Julian and others had made much of the skin torn roughly
off with the cloth that 'thai raif away with ruggis [tugs]
rude' (60) so that blood flows afresh. The mystery plays had
made more of the stretching of the limbs to meet the cross-
ends or nail-holes. The yearly repetition of that scene on the
pageant-wagons would make it so familiar to his readers
that Dunbar need merely allude to the action—indeed he
conflates it so far as to apply the verb *tie* (properly used of
the ropes that bound the limbs before the nailing: a piece of
business made much of in the plays, and reflected in
alabasters) to the nails themselves: 'Syne tyit hym on with
greit irne takkis' (69). The laden cross is deliberately let fall
'with a swak': we almost hear the crack of wood, and bones.
Here for once Dunbar's language does resemble that in 'My
fearfull dreme', which has, to the same effect,

> Full boistously in the morter he was doune cast,
> His vaynys all and synouis to-raff and brast.

It is the 'game' of putting Christ on the Cross and raising it that had called forth all the dramatic powers of the writers of the mystery plays, compelled, as devotional poets were not, to provide dialogue that would occupy the considerable space of time the action required. Thus in the York Play such dialogue occupies more than 250 lines. Dunbar certainly witnessed such plays, and this poem suggests that he could well have written them.[11]

Yet much that other poets made poignant or that dramatists made circumstantially grim, Dunbar omits altogether. The actual moment of death passes almost unnoticed:

> Thus Jesus with his woundis wyde
> As martir sufferit for to de
>
> (93–4)

—where 'martir' has an almost reductive force until we recall that the meditative writers present the Crucifixion as both model and comfort for all martyrs.

Cumulatively the effects up to this point are impressive enough. The narrative is terse, the compression of incident intensifies rather than diminishes the horror of the scene. But now comes a sudden change of mode and direction, signalled by a second 'methought' (97) and by a change of refrain.

The first refrain ('O mankynd, for the luif of the') had not been integral to the verse, indeed fits awkwardly into dream-narrative. Not so the second ('Thy blissit salvatour Jesu'), which in each case provides a clinching and climactic line, with the distinctive Scots form *salvatour* repeated like a chime. And now the refrain pertains not to mankind but to the dreamer. The violent action of the earlier verses is now wholly internalized. It is now the dreamer, not Christ, who is struck, pulled, tugged, accused, oppressed. The cross, nails, scourge, lance become instruments of *his* torture; but the *tortores* are Compassion and Contrition, Ruth (Pity) and Remembrance, going alliteratively hand in hand, displaying yet again that medieval genius for vivid abstraction that was to survive in Herbert's religious verse and that at this very time was reflected in didactic art. Here they represent the essence of the Meditative Exercises.

Despite the bright celebratory and nobly formal verse by which Dunbar is best known, he is essentially an introspective poet, indeed anticipatory in this respect of many later Tudor poets: witness his verses on a migraine ('My heid did ache yistirnicht'), his *Timor Mortis Conturbat Me*, and the briefer yet equally moving 'In to their derk and drublie dayis'—in which he presents himself as 'vexit with havie thocht', whilst Despair says 'Provide', Prudence whispers, 'Why keep what will vanish?', Age bids him, 'take me by the hand', and Death casts his gates wide open. To read that poem, or the more sprightly 'Bewty and the Prisoneir', a concise but masterly re-enactment of the *Roman de la Rose*, with Scorn as Jester and Good Fame drowned in a sack, is to see why at this point in the Passion poem Dunbar moves into what critics pedantically classify as Personification Allegory.

He is in fact dramatizing all those patterned and detailed *documenta* of Ludolf of Saxony and his kind, that require the reader not only to apply to his own soul the lessons of each 'station' of the Passion but at each stage, in Nicholas Love's words, 'to have ymaginacioun and inward compassioun'; in modern phrase, he is inducing devotional empathy. It is for this reason that after the Crucifixion (the Deposition is not even mentioned) the dreamer is assigned the role of a Joseph of Arimathaea who is to prepare a place of repose for his Lord:

> 'Ordane for him ane resting place
>   That is so werie wrocht for the,
>   That schort within thir dayis thre
> Sall law under thy lyntell bow,
>   And in thy hous sall herbrit be
> Thy blissit salvatour Chryst Jesu.'

Here the 'resting place' suggests not only the tomb but the Easter altar of repose to which the crucifix is carried on Maundy Thursday, whilst 'weary' likewise recalls the figure of Christ the warrior who fought on the rood from which, in the Anglo-Saxon *Vision* (63–6), he is lifted down 'limb-weary as he was', to rest, exhausted after the fight, whilst the tomb is prepared. Yet Dunbar's image conveys something more than this. Preserving decorum by putting the words into the mouth of Grace, he interiorizes the scene by adapting the ancient figure of the house of the soul, whilst allowing the domestic image of Christ at rest on a bed to provide its own multifold suggestions.[12] And as in the early homily *Sawles Warde* Wit, the master of the house, is troubled when his froward wife, Will, fails to keep it tidy and in order, so here Conscience and Repentance take pains to cast out cankered sins and make all ready for the King of heaven, whose advent was to be imaged by an anonymous seventeenth-century poet in just such terms:

> Yet if his Majesty, our sovereign lord,
> Should of his own accord
> Friendly himself invite
> And say 'I'll be your guest tomorrow night'
> How should we stir ourselves . . .[13]

He will come, in one epiphany, humbly as he did at Emmaus, when the doors were shut and he was made known in the breaking of bread; which means that he will also come in the communion of Easter morning, 'within thir dayis thre' (117). 'Low-latched in leaf-light housel' (Hopkins has put a line from Milton's abortive Passion poem, 'His starry front low-rooft beneath the skies', to a Eucharistic use that he would hardly have approved), he comes as he came to the centurion who said, 'Domine non sum dignus ut intres sub tectum meum' (Lord, I am not worthy that thou shouldst enter under my roof)—the very words of the mass, said (or formerly said) before Communion.[14]

To one versed in the techniques of meditation this sort of imaginative extension is easily within reach. Space and time cease to matter, the events of Calvary assume cosmic significance and perpetually recur. So now the dreamer feels himself shaken by the very earthquake that rent the rocks when Jesus yielded up the ghost:

> For grit terrour of Chrystis deid[a]
> The erde did trymmill quhair I lay . . .

> [a] death.

The effect corresponds with that achieved in a very different context at the close of Dunbar's 'Golden Targe', where the ship's guns fire off so violently that

> For rede[a] it semyt that the raynbow brak;
> Wyth spirit affrayde apon my fete I sprent[b]
> Amang the clewis[c], so carefull[d] was the crak.
> And . . . I did awake of my sueving[e].

> > [a] fear   [b] sprang   [c] cliffs   [d] dismal   [e] dream.

It was almost obligatory in dream poetry that a noise or violent shock should wake the dreamer. But this dreamer wakes 'halflingis in effray'. He shares the earth's horror that men should murder the Creator Lord. The streak of darkness, of nightmare and foreboding, that runs through much of Dunbar's poetry here shows in a unique setting. Countless poets and preachers had pointed to Nature's grief and amazement at the Crucifixion: only with the Scottish poet does it induce personal terror. The contrast with the last scene in the English 'carol' 'My fearfull dreme' is notable, even if the phrasing is similar. In those verses, as Christ cries 'Hely, Hely' his mother, ruefully weeping,

> > > > wrang her handes fast.
> Upon her he cast his dedly loke.
> Wherwith sodenly anon I awoke
> And of my dreme was sore agast.

The English poet's afflatus has failed and the gratuitous 'dedly loke' barely redeems these final lines from banality. In Dunbar dream and reality have become one. Once more a rood seen with the natural eye has become the Rood perceived with the spiritual eye. The soul shakes before the *mysterium crucis*.

The Arundel manuscript that includes Dunbar's 'Passion' and other verses by him on cognate themes includes also poems on the Passion by other hands. In fact almost every item, whether in verse or prose, testifies to the strength of Northern devotion to the Rood, and its persistence long after Rolle's influence had waned. One of the prose pieces, a 'Remembrance of the Passion', is a series of exercises somewhat in the manner of the *Bridgettine Hours*, and still more in the manner that Loyola was to adopt, being divided into numbered articles; it is a translation of a Latin text known to me only in a manuscript written in 1518 by or for Jasper Fylott, a London Dominican associated with the Bridgettine house at Mount Syon.[15]

The very first item in the Arundel anthology is Dunbar's 'Table of Confession'—a confession made not to a fellow-priest but

> To *the*, O marcifull salviour myn, Jesus,
> My king, my lord, and my redemer sueit.

More precisely, it is made before a crucifix, and shows the poet in the same posture as that described in the first stanza of his 'Passion':

> Befor thy bludy figour dolorus
> I schrife me cleyne, with humile spreit and meik
> . . .
> Falling on face full law befor thy feit.

'Thy bludy figour dolorus' preserves for us a picture of the typical crucifix or *pietà* of a thousand Scottish parishes before Knox and his brethren swept away such papish ornaments.

The 'Table of Confession' is followed at once by the *Passioun of Crist* of Walter Kennedy, the longest and the latest poem in the Bonaventuran tradition. It is headed by a woodcut of the scourging at the Pillar, from a Netherlands devotional work printed at Antwerp *c.* 1505, and similar cuts are mounted at intervals throughout the manuscript: testimony to the date of the compilation as well as to unexpected links between Scots and Continental piety.

Kennedy was a king's clerk (and so doubtless in orders) and himself of the blood royal. Dunbar's abuse of him in his famous *Flyting* is simply high-spirited burlesque, good dirty fun of the Goliardic and Skeltonic kind. His is the last name in Dunbar's still more famous 'Lament for the Makaris', which voices both Dunbar's respect for Kennedy and his grief at his imminent death. The two Passion poems show each rivalling the other as they had done in the

Flyting, but now on a different plane. They are contrasting exercises in the art poetical, though the craft displayed does not diminish the devoutness they express. The most obvious conrast is in length. What Kennedy takes twelve hundred lines to tell, Dunbar compresses into a hundred. Yet Kennedy is far from prolix and like his rival can be both dour and tender. And he is just as unmistakably Scottish. The Jerusalem of his Holy Week is an earlier Edinburgh in which Pilate's hall is a 'tollbooth' and Christ, 'a bonny bairn', is in Scots legal phrase 'put to the horn', and tells his disciples in Gethsemane, with typical laconic Scots meiosis, 'heir to duell it is na ganand tyme' (322): sc. 'it is hardly sensible for us to stay here'. The prose devotions in the Arundel manuscript have the same Northern flavour as the petition 'For thy gret powerte, contempcioun and *hething*: Have marcy' (ed. cit., p. 207); *hething*, 'contumely', is a word found elsewhere chiefly in Northern accounts of the Passion.

The scribe of the manuscript describes the poem (which makes 1715 lines in all) as '*compilit* be maister Walter Kennedy', and a compilation it certainly is, inasmuch as he inserts into a frame deriving ultimately from the Bonaventuran *Meditationes* such separate pieces as Mary's Complaint to the Cross (1095) and the *Responsio Crucis* (1121). At one point (196) he cites as authorities 'Lendulphus and others': a form that suggests confusion between Ludolf of Saxony, whose *Vita Christi* had been printed in 1474 and often thereafter, and 'Lentulus', who in the thirteenth century was credited with a supposedly eye-witness description of Christ's life and physiognomy.[16] Certainly Kennedy does not follow Ludolf *ad litteram*, or in full; if he seems slow-paced it is because the seven-lined stanza pattern itself makes for deliberateness. But like Ludolf he follows the pattern of the so-called Hours of the Passion. At what date an episode of the Passion was allotted to each of the monastic hours is not certain. Such an assignment is found already in England in the Anglo-Saxon Benedictine Office, and in St. Edmund of Abingdon's *Speculum Ecclesie*, later translated into Middle English. Ludolf took the structure from the Bonaventuran

Meditationes. English lyrics and, later, English primers reproduced it with variations.[17]

The programme in Kennedy's poem begins with the Vespers for Maundy Thursday ('Skyriss Thurisday', 'Sheer Thursday', elsewhere in the Arundel manuscript: ed. cit., p. 183) and runs on till Compline for Good Friday:[18] the purpose being to induce the reader at each of the liturgical hours to apply the Passion to his own soul, as thus, at Matins on Good Friday:

> Walk[a] of thi sleip, O man, at matyn hour;
> With bitter teris remember, gif thou may,
> The cruell panis quhilk Crist thi salvitour,
> The to redeme, sustenis nycht and day.
> With hert forthink[b], syne with gret piete say:
> 'I am gret caus of all the cruell pane;
> I staw[c] the frute, thocht thou restorit agane.'
>
> (393–9)
>   [a] wake [b] repent [c] stole.

That last image, which Herbert will reapply, comes in unexpectedly, as if Kennedy needed to round off his stanza: the later *Responsio Crucis* (1129 ff.) will explicate it.

Similarly at Evensong (Vespers):

> With reuthfull hert remember at evin sang
> The cruell dede quhilk deit[a] hes thi king.
> Behald quhat pane, quhat tyme, quhat place he hang,
> He hes tholit to bring the to his ring[b];
> And quhat pane and pyne dreit[c] hes this ding[d],
> Is for thi saik; be nocht thairfor unkind . . .
>
> (1191–6)
>   [a] died [b] kingdom [c] endured [d] worthy one.

Even in a stanza that the scribe has mangled, 'unkind' still stands out as the key word as it had been in lyrics of the Passion two centuries before.

More remarkable than the liturgical pattern that Kennedy has thus imposed on the narrative is his resort, with only the very slightest inducement from the late meditative literature, to the imagery that clusters round the persistent figure of *Christus miles*. That Christ after the Last Supper should exhort the disciples 'stifly to fecht aganis adversité' (318) is not in itself surprising. But Kennedy picks up the martial metaphor when describing Gethsemane:

> Me think this king had bot ane sempill gard,
> That yeid[a] to sleip quhen he to battall wes.
>
> (339–40)
>
> [a] went.

Later he presents Christ not only as 'that fair young prince ... in manly natour the prent of perfitnes' but also as 'veriour [warrior] for man' (589–92). Later still he is the wounded knight:

> Thus in the graif lyis this woundit knycht
> Under the cure[a] of dedis dirk umbrakill[b].
>
> (1394–5)
>
> [a] cover [b] shadow.

We are accustomed by now to the participants at Calvary being described in knightly terms. Kennedy addresses the reader himself as a knight:

> O knycht, behald now thi king furth is led.
>
> (617)

He stiffens and enlarges his narrative with yet another ingredient. In England, by the turn of the fifteenth century, allegory was dying from overwork and mechanical exploitation. But Gavin Douglas's *Palice of Honor* and the anonymous *King Hart*, not to mention Dunbar's courtly poems, suggest that in Scotland at this time it took on a new, vigorous, and independent life. Some of Kennedy's most individual stanzas are replete with so-called Personification Allegory. This is the means he uses to give fresh point to the cruelty of Christ's tormentors, whose 'game' had been a stock constituent of the mystery plays: .

> Ire is thair gid, Feid[a] flemes[b] him fra ressoun,
> Will is thair law, Inwy thai mak schirray[c],
> Prid is the prince quhilk seikis him to slay,
> Cupid is king quhilk him sa mait dois stand[d],
> Falset is faith quhilk herd hankis[e] his hand;
>
> (458–62)
>
> [a] enmity [b] drives away [c] Envy acts as their sheriff [d] causes him to stand so baffled [e] ties.

though here as often Kennedy has had to resort to a desperate device to close up his stanza: Cupid can properly be called a king in Henryson's *Testament of Cresseid*, in view of the role there assigned to him; here he seems to be standing in for Cupidity.

We have met Death in the role of antagonist to Christ in *Piers Plowman*. Kennedy gives him an active, speaking part. He recognizes Christ's royal rank and is even put to fear by his innocence, saying:

> 'O king, thocht ye have done no mys,
> For your pepill ye mone^a bow till our wand,
> For your fader hes gart us understand
> That be your ded man is restorit to grace;
> Bot yow saikles^b I dred to slay, allace.'
>
> (984–8)

^a must　^b innocent.

The second person plural (*ye, yow*) betokens a respect appropriate to a king that the poet himself will not show to Death when he breaks in a few verses later to 'flite' (dispute) with him as 'foull of reif' (robbery, 1019) and unlawful (1022): Death having wrested Christ from Pain as being *his* special prisoner (775).

One other kind of personification, and one that derives from the very earliest strand in our Passion poetry, Kennedy introduces when depicting the Virgin's grief and bewilderment. In the *Vita Christi* she addresses her questions to Christ himself. Here (1095–1120) she complains to the Cross that has unjustly slain her son: 'The fruit you bear is not your own. You should be ashamed of taking such a noble prince. . . .' The lines (1095–1120) are a compendious rendering of the first 36 lines of a Latin poem beginning 'Crux de te volo conqueri', a *debate* in ten nine-lined rhyming stanzas, by Philip de Grève, or 'the Chancellor', written early in the thirteenth century. His stanzas achieved a well-merited popularity, and there are versions in Anglo-Norman, Dutch, and Italian, as well as in Middle English.[19] Kennedy's rendering is only occasionally literal, and he takes several liberties. The Virgin's complaint is followed, as in the Latin, by the *Responsio Crucis*; in which the Cross not only justifies its role as pre-ordained but provides effective comfort for Mary in a viticultural image that comes somewhat strangely into northern verse; indeed Kennedy has to expand the terse Latin of

> Ulmus uvam non peperit
> Quid tamen viti deperit
> Quod ulmus uvam sustinet
> Fructum tuum non genui
> Sed oblatum non respui

The elm does not bear the grape, yet it would perish did not the elm support it. I bore not your fruit, but have not disdained (to bear) the sacrifice.

into

> Thocht fra the stok grew nocht the bob of wyne,
> The bob it helpis, for it the branche up beris.
> Richt so I say to yow, O sueit virgin,
> This nobill frute, quhilk your hert sair deris,
> That God ordanit to ceis Adames weris,
> Grew nocht on me, for I am bot ane stok,
> For saik of man to beir up this wyne blok.
>
> (1149–55)

The complaint of the Virgin is essentially a variant of many an earlier *planctus*, a genre which was already well established in the vernacular by the time of the Montecassino Latin Passion Play and which demands, and has received, separate treatment. But Kennedy's version of this stanza in the *Responsio* stands as one of the few allusions in our vernacular poetry to the Cross as a vine- or fruit-bearing tree, St. Bernard's *Vitis Mystica*. It is so represented in a small sculpture by Eric Gill, now in Oxford.

This Cross acts, like the Rood in the Anglo-Saxon poem, in obedience to 'the nobill prince of price', and carries the message of light into Limbo (1147), as it does in the docetist Gospel of St. Peter.[20] Its *responsio* was perhaps suggested by the example of prosopopoeia given by Philip de Grève's contemporary, Geoffrey de Vinsauf, in his *Poetria Nova*;

where the Cross complains of its seizure by (Saracen) dogs and asks (ll. 472–3):

> Dic, homo, nonne tibi crevi? tibi fructificari?
> Nonne tuli dulcem tibi fructum, nonne salutem?

Say, man, did I not grow for thee? Did I not bear fruit for thee, the sweet fruit of salvation?

Kennedy is not concerned to reproduce every detail of the Passion and of cognate events. He makes his own selection, and his own emphasis. The entry into Jerusalem finds no place. Christ goes to the Upper Room 'followand on fute as a pure sempill man' (277). At his arrest,

> Thai strenyeit thai^a fair handis with a string
> Quhill^b his fingeris, quhilk quhit wes, wox bla^c.
> . . .
> Than but^d delay apoun him all thai schot,
> Preiffand thair pith, quha fastest couth him sair^e.
> That nobill prince thai defoulit^f under fute,
> Birsand his breist, rivand his tender haire.
>
> (379–80, 442–5)

^athose ^buntil ^clivid ^dwithout ^etrying their best to show who could harm him soonest ^ftrampled.

Again we see the impress of scenes in the mystery plays devoted to the *tortores*; whereas Kennedy's gloss on the *Ego sum* with which Christ meets his pursuers follows the traditional patristic view that the words proclaim his latent divinity:

> For the vertu of his godheid, unseyne
> Vnder the claith of his humanité,
> Mycht not susteyne mannis fragilité.
>
> (369–71)

The reed put in his hand in mockery as a sceptre is used (as Giotto and others had depicted it) to strike his head. He is bound on the Cross with sharp cords and

> all the lethis^a on his tendir bak
> Thai sa depart quhill that his ene wox dyme.
>
> (766–7)

^ajoints.

Most of the extra-scriptural tortures (and interpretations thereof) find a place in Kennedy's poem. Flesh and blood and purple cloth cleave together as the skin is torn off from head to foot.[21] The crown of thorn is pressed down hard into the brain, as in contemporary carvings and miniatures. And as in the same paintings, Mary embraces her son, her eyes blinded with bloody tears as she laments,

> 'Thy lufsum lippis with ded ar maid full bla,
> Thy teth is haw[a], changit cheik and chyne . . .'[22]
>
> (1269–70)
>
> [a] dark, leaden.

When the lamp of night expires, Phoebus withdraws his beams,

> As he wald say: 'I sall revengit be
> Apoun the man quhilk garris his maker de.'
>
> (937–8)

The brief agonized cry *Sitio* is expanded at some length:

> 'I spend
> For mannis saule my saule and my body.
> Moir causis mc my lufe na[a] pane to cry.
> Thame to redeme I have sa gret desire
> That lufe and pane my hert birnis in a fire.'
>
> (955–9)
>
> [a] than.

We may take leave of Kennedy with the verse in which he glosses the superscription INRI:

> Thoucht Pilot understude nocht quhat he wrait,
> He commendit Cristis nobillité;
> Calland him king, he extollit his stait,
> For till his crowne all kingis moist sudiet be[a];
> And every man in his realme crownis he,
> Predestinat quhilk is to hevinnis blis,
> For be his ded our realme restorit is.
>
> (827–33)
>
> [a] must be subject.

Predestinate: this Pauline term Kennedy will use again. It was to become the sign-manual of the Scots preachers who in later decades turned the stream of northern piety into channels very different from those fed by the *Passioun*. Apart from one Wycliffite example, it is the first instance of the term, though not recorded in the *Oxford English Dictionary*, where it should precede the quotation from the Scots New Testament.

Kennedy is not a great poet, and his *Passioun* is not a masterpiece. But it is not in masterpieces that we find the clearest mirrors of the characteristic preoccupations and concerns of a period. Like the collection of which it forms a part, it displays the tenor of Scots devotion as it continued almost up to the day that Knox mounted the pulpit of St. Giles; and it is not surprising that Lord Arundel, the recusant into whose hands the manuscript came, should have written verses in the same strain. But the suspicion of Mariolatry, not to mention the implicit acceptance of traditional doctrines of the Eucharist and of Indulgences, would lead to the destruction or disappearance of most such handbooks and aids to devotion. The Orison on the Seven Words spoken on the Cross, of which a notable Scots version in rhythmic and sometimes alliterative prose is found in the Arundel volume, is doctrinally unexceptionable; but it includes the petition 'Make me by thy love and charity that I be joined to thy mother', and so it falls out of use at the Reformation.

In England as early as 1585 the traditional treatment of the emotional elements in the Passion story—reflected in the collection of prayers known as the 'XV Oes', which likewise appear in this volume, and of which Caxton and Wynkyn de Worde printed prose versions—had come under sharp attack:

For the most parte whan they entreate this mater [preachers] lepe out of the frutefull and holsome storie, into these their comenplaces. How Jesus toke his leave of his disciples, and with what dolorous sighes his Mother Mary pitied hym, and suche other thyngs. On these they bable at length and discante their pleasures, rather to the weryenge than edifyenge of the audience.[23]

Ten years later the prayers devoted to the Passion in vernacular primers show a new doctrinal emphasis on satisfaction and redemption, though the *Godly Meditations* of a Marian Martyr, John Bradford (published posthumously in 1562), still keep attention fixed on the figure of the suffering Christ: 'heaven shined not on thee, the sun gave thee no light, the earth was afraid to bear thee, Satan did sore tempt and assault thee, and thine own senses forced thee to cry out: "My God, my God, why hast thou forsaken me?"' It is the restraint that would commend these sentences to Protestant readers. When *Ecclesia Anglicana* began to produce devotional poetry it was suffused with feelings hardly different from Bradford's, who applies his meditations on the Cross in these terms:

O wonderful passions which thou sufferest! In them thou teachest me, in them thou comfortest me; for by them God is my father, my sins are forgiven: by them I should learn to fear God, to love God, to hope in God, to hate sin, to be patient, to call upon God, and never to leave him for any temptations' sake, but with thee still to cry yea, even when very death should approach, 'Father into thy hands I commend my spirit.'[24]

The substance of scores of pages in Ludolf of Saxony or Nicholas Love has been condensed into a few lines.

The Bludy Serk

This hindir yeir I hard [betald]
Thair was a worthy king;
Dukis, erlis and barronis bald
He had at his bidding.
The lord was anccane and ald,   5
And sexty yeiris cowth ring;
He had a dochter fair to fald,
A lusty lady ying.

Off all fairheid scho bur the flour,
And eik hir faderis air,   10
Off lusty laitis and he honour,
Meik bot and debonair;
Scho wynnit in a bigly bour,
On fold wes none so fair;
Princis luvit hir paramour   15
In cuntreis our allquhair.

Thair dwelt a lyt besyde the king
A fowll gyane of ane;
Stollin he hes the lady ying,
Away with hir is gane,   20
And kest hir in his dungering,
Quhair licht scho micht se nane;
Hungir and cauld and grit thristing
Scho fand into hir wame.

He wes the laithliest on to luk   25
That on the ground mycht gang;
His nailis wes lyk ane hellis cruk,
Thairwith fyve quarteris lang;
Thair wes nane that he ourtuk,
In rycht or yit in wrang,   30
Bot all in-schondir he thame schuke—
Thy gyane wes so strang.

He held the lady day and nycht
Within his deip dungeoun;
He wald nocht gif of hir a sicht,   35
For gold nor yit ransoun,
Bot gife the king mycht get a knycht
To fecht with his persoun—
To fecht with him both day and nycht
Quhill ane wer dungin doun.   40

The king gart seik baith fer and neir,
Beth be se and land,
Off ony knycht gife he micht heir
Wald fecht with that gyand;
A worthy prince that had no peir   45
Hes tane the deid on hand,
For the luve of the lady cleir,
And held full trew cunnand.

That prince come prowdly to the toun
Of that gyane to heir,   50
And fawcht with him his awin persoun,
And tuke him presoneir;
And kest him in his awin dungeoun,
Allane withouttin feir,
With hungir, cauld and confusioun,   55
As full weill worthy weir.

Syne brak the bour, had hame the bricht
Unto hir fadir deir;
Sa evill wondit was the knycht
That he behuvit to de;   60
Unlusum was his likame dicht,
His sark was all bludy;
In all the warld was thair a wicht
So peteous for to sy?

The lady murnyt and maid grit mone   65
With all hir mekle micht:
'I luvit nevir lufe bot one
That dulfully now is dicht:
God sen my lyfe were fra me tone
Or I had sene yone sicht,   70
Or ellis in begging evir to gone
Furth with yone curtas knycht!'

He said: 'Fair lady, now mone I
De, trestly ye me trow;
Tak ye my sark that is bludy   75
And hing it forrow yow;
First think on it and syne on me
Quhen men cumis yow to wow.'
The lady said: 'Be Mary fre,
Thairto I make a vow!'   80

Quhen that scho lukit to the serk
Scho thocht on the persoun,
And prayit for him with all hir harte,
That lowsd hir of bandoun,
Quhair scho was wont to sit full merk   85
In that deip dungeoun;
And evir quhill scho wes in quert,
That was hir a lessoun.

Sa weill the lady luvit the knycht
That no man wald scho tak.   90
Sa suld we do our God of micht
That did all for us mak;
Quhilk fullely to deid was dicht
For sinfull manis saik;
Sa suld we do both day and nycht   95
With prayaris to Him mak.

Moralitas

This king is lyk the Trinitie,
Baith in hevin and heir;
The manis saule to the lady,
The gyane to Lucefeir,   100
The knycht to Chryst that deit on tre
And coft our synnis deir,
The pit to hell with panis fell,
The syn to the woweir.

The lady was wowd, bot scho said nay   105
With men that wald hir wed;
Sa suld we wryth all syn away
That in our breistis bred.
I pray to Jesu Chryst verrey,
For us His blud that bled,   110
To be our help on Domysday,
Quhair lawis are straitly led.

The saule is Godis dochtir deir,
And eik His handewerk,
That was betrasit with Lucifeir   115
Quha sittis in hell full merk.
Borrowit with Chrystis angell cleir,
Hend men, will ye nocht herk?
For His lufe that bocht us deir,
Think on the bludy serk.   120

The Passion of Christ

Amang thir freiris within ane cloister
    I enterit in ane oritorie,
And knelit doun with ane pater noster
    Befoir the michtie king of glorie,
    Haveing his passioun in memorie;   5
Syn to his mother I did inclyne,
    Hir halsing with ane *gaude flore*;
And sudandlie I sleipit syne.

Methocht Judas with mony ane Jow
   Tuik blissit Jesu our salvatour,   10
And schot him furth with mony ane schow,
    With schamefull wourdis of dishonour;
    And lyk ane theif or ane tratour
Thay leid that hevinlie prince most hie
   With manassing attour messour,   15
O mankynd, for the luif of the.

Falslie condamnit befoir ane juge,
   Thai spittit in his visage fayr,
And as lyounis with awfull ruge
    In yre thai hurlit him heir and thair,   20
    And gaif him mony buffat sair
That it wes sorrow for to se;
   Of all his claythis thay tirvit him bair,
O mankynd, for the luif of the.

Thay terandis, to revenge thair tein,   25
   For scorne thai cled him in to quhyt,
And hid his blythfull glorious ene,
    To se quham angellis had delyt;
    Dispituouslie syn did him smyt,
Saying, 'Gif sone of God thow be,   30
   Quha straik the now, thow tell us tyt';
O mankynd, for the luf of the.

In tene thai tirvit him agane,
   And till ane pillar thai him band;
Quhill blude birst out at everie vane   35
    Thai scurgit him bayth fut and hand;
    At everie straik ran furth ane strand
Quhilk mycht have ransonit warldis thre;
   He baid in stour quhill he mycht stand,
O mankynd, for the luif of the.   40

Nixt all in purpyr thay him cled,
   And syne with thornis scharp and kene
His saikles blude agane thai sched,
    Persing his heid with pykis grene;
    Unneis with lyf he micht sustene   45
That croune, on thrungin with crueltie,
   Quhill flude of blude blindit his ene,
O mankynd, for the luif of the.

Ane croce that wes bayth large and lang
  To beir thay gaif this blissit lord,   50
Syn fullelie, as theif to hang,
  Thay harlit him furth with raip and corde;
  With blude and sweit was all deflorde
His face, the fude of angellis fre;
  His feit with stanis was revin and scorde,   55
O mankynd, for the luif of the.

Agane thay tirvit him bak and syd
  Als brim as ony baris woid,
The clayth that claif to his cleir hyd
  Thai raif away with ruggis rude,   60
  Quhill fersly followit flesche and blude
That it was pietie for to se:
  Na kynd of torment he ganestude,
O mankynd, for the luif of the.

Onto the crose of breid and lenth,   65
  To gar his lymmis langar wax,
Thai straitit him with all thair strenth,
  Quhill to the rude thai gart him rax;
  Syne tyit him on with greit irne takkis,
And him all nakit on the tre   70
  Thai raissit on loft be houris sax,
O mankynd, for the luif of the.

Quhen he was bendit so on breid
  Quhill all his vanis brist and brak,
To gar his cruell pane exceid   75
  Thai leit him fall doun with ane swak,
Quhill cors and corps and all did crak.
Agane thai rasit him on hie,
  Reddie mair turmentis for to mak,
O mankynd, for the luif of the.   80

Betuix tuo theiffis the spreit he gaif
  On to the fader most of micht;
The erde did trimmill, the stanis claif,
  The sone obscurit of his licht,
  The day wox dirk as ony nicht,   85
Deid bodiis rais in the cite:
  Goddis deir sone all thus was dicht,
O mankynd, for the luif of the.

In weir that he was yit on lyf
   Thai ran ane rude speir in his syde,   90
And did his precious body ryff
    Quhill blude and water did furth glyde:
    Thus Jesus with his woundis wyde
As martir sufferit for to de
    And tholit to be crucifyid,   95
O mankynd, for the luif of the.

Methocht Compassioun, vode of feiris,
   Than straik at me with mony ane stound,
And for Contritioun, baithit in teiris,
    My visage all in watter drownd;   100
    And Reuth into my eir ay rounde,
'For schame, allace, behald man how
    Beft is with mony ane bludy wound
Thy blissit salvatour Jesu.'

Than rudelie come Remembrance,   105
   Ay rugging me withouttin rest,
Quhilk crose and nalis scharp, scurge and lance
    And bludy crowne befoir me kest;
    Than Pane with passioun me opprest,
And evir did Petie on me pow,   110
    Saying, 'Behald how Jowis hes drest
Thy blissit salvatour Chryst Jesu.'

With greiting glaid be than come Grace
   With wourdis sweit saying to me,
'Ordane for him ane resting place   115
    That is so werie wrocht for the,
    That schort within thir dayis thre
Sall law undir thy lyntell bow,
    And in thy hous sall herbrit be
Thy blissit salvatour Chryst Jesu.'   120

Than swyth Contritioun wes on steir
   And did eftir Confessioun ryn,
And Conscience me accusit heir
    And kest out mony cankerit syn;
    To rys Repentence did begin   125
And out at the yettis did schow.
    Pennance did walk the house within.
Byding our salvatour Chryst Jesu.

Grace become gyd and governour,
   To keip the house in sicker stait   130
Ay reddy till our salvatour,
   Quhill that he come, air or lait;
   Repentence ay with cheikis wait
No pane nor pennence did eschew
   The house within ever to debait,   135
Onlie for luif of sweit Jesu.

For grit terrour of Chrystis deid
   The erde did trymmill quhair I lay,
Quhairthrow I waiknit in that steid
   With spreit halflingis in effray;   140
   Than wrayt I all without delay,
Richt heir as I have schawin to yow,
   Quhat me befell on Gud Fryday
Befoir the crose of sweit Jesu.

VI

DONNE, HERBERT, HERRICK

ÉMILE MÂLE, the great historian of French medieval art, once went so far as to assert that after the Reformation there was no such thing as Christian art, only Christian artists; though his later study of Baroque led him to modify this dictum. It would be equally temerarious to declare that after the accession of Elizabeth there was no such thing in England as Christian poetry, only Christian poets. Certainly some of the central dogmas and beliefs that had hitherto shaped that poetry were now denied, and the books and manuscripts that had disseminated it banned or burnt. Yet however sharp the official severance with Rome and with Catholic cultus,[1] long-established habits of private devotion did not at once wither away. If the age-old influence of St. Bernard and his followers waned for a time, he was read in the seventeenth century by such diverse divines as Andrewes, Donne, and Richard Baxter. The *Imitatio Christi*, though truncated, never lost its place in the affections of the devout. The 'XV Oes', a devotion that had been specially popular in England, reappeared in Elizabeth's *Book of Christian Prayers* (1578);[2] and Louis Martz and Dame Helen Gardner have had no difficulty in demonstrating the impress of the Ignatian patterns of meditation and visualization of the Passion upon Herbert, Donne, and (amongst others) Crashaw, whose forms of devotion, we now know, were fixed long before he left Peterhouse and the Anglican fold.

It would be churlish to reproach these scholars for not perceiving that this Ignatian pattern had been set several centuries before and that Loyola merely systematized and rationalized established practices. If Martz barely mentions Ludolf of Saxony, he gives due place to the Bonaventuran *Meditationes*. But when he cites the English Jesuit Gibbons on 'composition of place, and seeing with the eyes of the

Imagination the corporeal place where the thing I wish to contemplate is found', and on reading what 'good authors' write of these places,[3] it is well to remember that such earlier *dévotes* as Margery Kempe, whether or not they read some version of the *Meditationes*, followed exactly this practice, considering themselves to be present at Calvary and, imagining Christ on the Cross, 'made a colloquy with Him', just as Loyola was to suggest. Again, the concept of a 'Spirituall Combat', which Martz associates with an Italian work of that name published in 1589 and with the recusant Robert Southwell's *Short Rule*, was already established in English devotion with the fourteenth-century *Treatise of Ghostly Battle*. Likewise, the value attached in the days of the Counter-Reformation to the gift of tears was no greater than that it had held for the fourteenth-century mystics and their followers; if it was now associated (as in Crashaw) especially with the Magdalene, so had it been in late medieval art; whilst the antitheses that Martz quotes from Fra Luis de Granada are medieval commonplaces: the association of the bleeding face with angels who desired to behold it we have met also in Dunbar; and the grim humour playing about mortality and corruption that Martz sees as characterizing Fra Luis is present abundantly in such popular medieval works as *The Prick of Conscience*.

For further evidence of the same sort we need look no further than Henry Vaughan's *Mount of Olives or Solitary Devotions* (1652), which includes 'an excellent discourse of the blessed state of Man in Glory written by the most reverend and holy Father Anselm Archbishop of Canterbury'. This is not, of course, a work on the Passion, and may not be St. Anselm's; but like others of Vaughan's translations it shows him openly drawing on the Catholic inheritance. Similarly, the title of Crashaw's *Steps to the Temple* echoes the heading 'Per gradus ascendebatur in Templum' in the *Rosetum* of Jean Monbaer (1494), a work that Joseph Hall had used as the basis of his *Art of Meditation* as early as 1606—though without venturing to name its Catholic author. Indeed Bishop Hall (whose verses Gray rated higher than Donne's) in his own prose *Contemplations* (1634) bestrides the Catholic and the

Protestant worlds. The antithesis and parallelisms of his devotions—'I had scorched, if Thou hadst not sweat'—sometimes recall Donne, sometimes St. Bernard. His Christ is still a knightly champion, showing in Gethsemane the divine magnanimity 'wherewith he entered into those sad *lists*'. He evokes the sufferings much as Dame Julian had done, if not in such relentless detail: 'One kicks thee with the foot, another strikes thee with his staff, another drags thee harshly by the cord.' On the Cross the arms 'tendered out beyond their natural reach' embrace all mankind. Are these pierced hands, he asks, those that stretched out the heavens as a curtain? The agony, and the faith, of the Virgin are described in traditional terms. Almost the only new emphases are on the appeasement of the Father's wrath, and on *Eloi, Eloi*: 'How is it with thee, O Saviour, that thou thus astonishest men and Angels with so woful a quiritation?' (the bishop has drawn on Livy for the nonce-word).

Whether we should say, with Dame Helen Gardner, that the English poets in reading recent Catholic works 'took the corn and left the chaff' is another matter. Or rather, it hardly matters at all. For the immediate influence of the poets in question was not destined to be wide or powerful. The Puritans—whom it would be better to call by the contemporary term, Precisians—were generally hostile to any devotions that seemed to emanate from the City of the Seven Hills. Their theology, concentrating on the doctrine of Faith, left little room for the sacred humanity of Christ, and none for a conception of the Eucharist that linked it with the blood flowing from the Cross; *The Pilgrim's Progress*, for example, has no place for such doctrines. This is not to say that the Bunyan who wrote

> Blest Cross, blest sepulchre! Blest rather be
> The Man that there was put to shame for me

was deliberately reducing the role of the Cross in Christian worship; it was when Christian saw One hang bleeding upon the Tree ('as I thought in my mind'—the phrase might come from Julian herself) that he lost his burden. But in Bunyan the focus is certainly on the Man rather than on the Tree, though his allegory retains, if unconsciously, some of the forms and figures of earlier ages. Thus some traces of the lover-knight can be found in the Lord of the Hill, who had been 'a *great warriour*, and had fought with and slain him that had the power of death, but not without great danger to himself, which made me love him the more. For . . . he did it with the loss of much blood.' He is 'such a lover of poor Pilgrims, that his like is not to be found from the East to the West', and had 'stript himself of his glory that he might do this for the Poor'. This is the very language of medieval Meditations; just as Milton's language, in his unfinished 'Passion', combined elements of an ancient strain with allusions to the latent deity who had hidden himself, in the patristic phrase, at the Incarnation and the Passion—'O what a Mask was there, what a disguise!' But this heroic Christ is presented in Spenserian language:

> Most perfect Heroe, try'd in heaviest plight
> Of labours huge and hard, too hard for human wight.

The poem is, in fact, a pastiche. Milton admitted that the subject was 'above the years he had when he wrote it', and one must share his dissatisfaction with the unfinished piece. He was never to return to the theme. In *Paradise Lost* the Cross is given just three lines, couched in Pauline terms. Easter had still less a place in the Puritan year than Christmas. And a glance at the more fervent verses of Samuel Crossman, a contemporary of Milton's who, like him, came into disfavour at the Restoration, suggests that the tenderness and tension that characterized medieval Passion poetry are now weakened and attenuated. In Crossman's 'My Song is Love Unknown' the emphasis is entirely personal, the language self-regarding and a little strained ('sweet injuries'; 'no friendly tomb'; the Prince of Life '*cheerful* to suffering goes/that he his foes/from thence might free'). What power the verses have they owe to Herbert, from whom comes the phrase 'love unknown', and from whose 'Agony' Crossman has adapted two of his last lines:

> Never was love, dear King,
> Never was grief like thine.

True, in the time of the Commonwealth, Richard Baxter, the most perceptive and most open-minded of Puritan writers, recommended Catholic works of devotion and even followed their patterns; appealing to his readers in such terms as St. Bernard himself might have used: 'Hast thou forgotten since He wounded Himself to cure thy wounds and let out His own blood to stop thy bleeding?'[4] Towards the close of the seventeenth century Bishop Ken and Anthony Horneck also speak St. Bernard's language and breathe his spirit.[5] But the temper of the Restoration and, what is more important and more lasting, the tone and structure of the Book of Common Prayer, favoured this type of piety as little as they favoured the revival of Catholicism; whilst later Deism, Rationalism, Comtism, Evolutionism, and Humanism have persistently worked against it. The most striking evidence of this is the practical disappearance for three centuries and more of the Passion as a subject for vernacular art. Blake's notable presentation of the Crucifixion in *Jerusalem* (cf. his *Soldiers casting lots for Christ's vestments*) is the exception that proves the rule: it is to be read as a picture of Satanic selfhood.[6]

What almost perished at the same time and for the same reason was the faculty for religious wit that in retrospect turns out to be a common feature of earlier poems as diverse as *Piers Plowman* and *A Vision of a Rood*. By wit in this context I mean not verbal cleverness but deep delight in the riddling and ambiguous elements of language, and in paradoxes of situation; not mere word-play or paronomasia but that relish for multiple facets of meaning that Langland shows when he speaks of Christ bearing man's arms and dying in his *sute* or *secte* or Lancelot Andrewes when he describes the Incarnation: 'the word within a word, unable to speak a word'. Which last phrase points indeed to the paradox on which all this wit ultimately depends: 'Verbum caro factum est'. Hence it is that Crashaw can write of the Virgin:

> Oh, wit of love that thus can place
> Fountain and garden in one place!

and that Herbert can say, addressing God, 'And if I please

thee I write fine and witty'. It is part of the achievement of both these poets, as it is of Donne, that they win back for English religion this dimension of poetry when it had almost been abandoned to the secular.

In the light of what has been said above, it will be the less surprising that by the second decade of the seventeenth century we can find poems and sermons that seem rather to be extensions or continuations of their medieval counterparts than departures from earlier modes of discourse and devotion. Of the sermons, those by Lancelot Andrewes on the Passion and Resurrection are the most accessible and the most striking. To read them is to see, for one thing, how close a learned Stuart prelate could keep to traditional patterns of exegesis. His very choice of text, for example Sermon II, 'Of the Passion', from Lamentations 1:12, Sermon XVII, 'Of the Resurrection', from Isaiah 63:1–3, each quoted from the Vulgate, displays this connection: both belong to the ancient Liturgy of Holy Week. St. Leo, St. Augustine, St. Bernard are the only *auctores* cited in these sermons, every paragraph of which rests on patristic glosses. This notable translator, who was one of those in charge of the Authorized Version, here rephrases Vulgate texts in such vigorous terms as 'Seized upon the *Chirographum contra nos*, the Roll that made so strong against us; tooke it, rent it, and so rent, nailed it to His Crosse';[7] or, 'They in the Judgment Hall worshipped Him with *Ave Rex*, and then gave him a *bobb blindfold*'; which is John 19:3 rendered in the very phrase of the mystery plays. Jeremiah 22:18: '. . . Vae domine, et vae inclyte', becomes 'Alas, alas for that noble *prince*'. His *Preces Privatae* include a long passage enumerating the sufferings in terms derived from a late-medieval text, *The Golden Litany*. Andrewes' sermons, to be sure, are far more searching, far more comprehensive, and far more learned (witness their Greek and Hebrew) than any in medieval English; but his conceits, his paradoxes, his emphases are thoroughly medieval. It is against the backcloth they provide that we should set contemporary Passion poetry as Donne and Herbert wrote it.

The central place of the Crucifixion in Donne's

Christology hardly needs demonstration; nor, at this date, does the impress made on him by the Ignatian meditations which present the life and Passion of Christ as 'the spring and fountaine of all our Good', and insist on the preparatory 'composition of place'—the seeing with the eye of the imagination a particular place where Christ was found (a prescription partly anticipated in the *Imitatio Christi*, II. ii). The conclusion of Ignatius' First Exercise is particularly pertinent to any reading of Donne's 'Good Friday, Riding Westward' or of his Holy Sonnets, the former of which, we should note, is described in the manuscripts as a Meditation, whilst the latter bear the general title 'Divine Meditations': 'Imagining Christ our Lord *present before me on the Cross*, to make a colloquy with Him, asking Him how it is that being the Creator, He has come to make Himself man . . .'.[8]

In 'Good Friday' Donne moves from the general to the personal. For reasons that he expresses in familiar paradoxes but with new bravura he dares to say that he could almost be glad *not* to have seen the Crucifixion:

> Who sees God's face, that is selfe life, must dye;
> What a death were it then to see God dye?
> It made his owne Lieutenant Nature shrinke,
> It made his footstoole crack, and the Sunne winke.
> Could I behold those hands which span the Poles,
> And tune all spheares at once, peirc'd with those holes?

The poem hinges on the thought that in riding westward he is turning away from the East, where Christ the true Sun was on this day crucified; but if he turns his back on him, it is to receive correction—having in mind the Christ who gave his back to the smiters and who is depicted as doing so in such medieval books of devotion as *Die Negen Couden*, from which came the woodcut that stands at the head of Kennedy's *Passioun* in the Arundel manuscript.[9] The apostrophe 'and thou look'st towards mee, O Saviour, as thou hang'st upon the tree' suggests a crucifix or imagined re-creation of the Passion, and that personal appeal of Christ from the Cross that motivates to many medieval poems. Conceivably 'look'st towards mee' carries also the colloquial sense of 'look with favour' that it still bears in one context.

Staunch Anglican though he is, Donne yet gives a place in his *compositio loci* to the Virgin:

> If on these things I durst not looke, durst I
> Upon his miserable mother cast mine eye,
> Who was God's partner here, and furnish'd thus
> Halfe of that Sacrifice, which ransom'd us?

We shall not hear such language in English verse again—except in Crashaw, Vaughan, and, muted, in Herbert—for almost three centuries.[10]

Donne's poem on 'The Cross' itself is of a different order, and may seem to display some of that very concupiscence of wit that he warns against in the course of it.[11] The rush of images with which it opens—

> Who can deny mee power, and liberty
> To stretch mine armes, and mine owne Crosse to be?
> Swimme, and at every stroake, thou art thy Crosse,
> The Mast and yard make one, where seas do tosse.
> Looke downe, thou spiest out Crosses in small things;
> Looke up, thou seest birds rais'd on crossed wings;
> All the Globe's frame, and spheare's, is nothing else
> But the Meridians crossing Parallels

—these might appear far-fetched conceits if we did not know that they had all been neatly packed together, and illustrated, in the *De Cruce* of the learned Lipsius, who duly traces them back to the Fathers.[12]

Of the Holy Sonnets, 'What if this present were the world's last night?' stands out as a direct fruit of meditation on the Crucified. Addressed to his soul, not to the Deity, it presents the picture of the Crucifixion as imprinted on his heart. The figure, though, is not of a tortured frame but of a body divinely beautiful: *optime complexionis*, in the medieval phrase. For the medieval Meditations had emphasized this bodily beauty, even whilst enumerating the tortures inflicted. So Nicholas Love calls Christ 'the flower of all mankind', and Ludolf of Saxony expands this into 'the most lovely younge man, elegant and shamfast, beautious above all other men'.[13] It is not the marring of this beauty but the pitying gaze that holds the poet. The 'amazing light' from the eyes is quenched—we infer—in the tears of compassion. This is the figure of the Son of Man in Rev. 1 : 13 ff., whose eyes were as a flame of fire and whose countenance as the shining sun. This Christ does not frown, because the blood shed for man fills the creases on his brow. [14] He speaks not in despair but in prayer for his enemies: 'Father, forgive them . . .'.

This is not the greatest of the Sonnets; the opening line, as arresting as Donne's openings usually are, is not clearly related to what follows. But the whole gains from being read in the light of medieval antecedents. As the medieval poet presented Christ as a knight in love with Mansoul, so here Donne presents him as loving his soul, addressed here as the poet would formerly ('in my idolatrie') have addressed a profane mistress. In the Divine poems, as in the love-songs, it is the concision that counts. So in the 'Hymn to God my God, in my sickness' the line 'By these his thornes give me his other Crowne' compresses into a few words the force of a long fifteenth-century meditation that concludes

> And for the thornes thei did the take
> Crounynge thin hed into the brayne
> Yeve us that croune that thou did make
> In heven for us, with all thi payne. [15]

Donne has typically made this into a personal plea.

George Herbert's Passion poetry likewise has a medieval ancestry. In his 'Sacrifice' 'compacted lie' all the figural features that from the time of Prudentius till the printings of the so-called *Biblia Pauperum* in the fifteenth century had come to cluster round the theme of the Passion. It is the summation of all the poetry that the Easter *Improperia* had generated, and its position at the forefront of *The Temple*, as well as its length, testifies to the prominence in Herbert's mind of Christ as the Man of Sorrows. We find no trace of *Christus miles* here. But we do find a more liberal extension of the text 'Popule meus, quid tibi feci?' (Micah 6 : 3) than any medieval vernacular poem affords. The closest analogue is a fourteenth-century refrain poem on the same text, which happens to be by another Herbert, the friar William who wrote the *Quis est iste qui venit de Edom?* that was cited earlier, and a dozen other religious poems or translations. He is at least as good a poet as Richard Rolle: witness his version of *Popule meus*, which begins:

> My volk, what habbe y do the?
> Other in what thing tened the?
>   Gyn nouthe^a and onswere thou me:
> Vor vrom Egypte ich ladde the,
> Thou me ledest to rode tre.
>   My volk, what habbe y do the?
> Thorou wyldernesse ich ladde the,
> And vourty yer bihedde the,
> And aungeles bred ich yaf to the,
> And in-to reste ich broughte the.
>   My volk, what habbe y do the?[16]

> ^a begin now.

Neither the friar's poem nor George Herbert's corresponds completely with the Reproaches as now sung on Good Friday, though some Latin text of the services for Holy Week was undoubtedly the basis of 'The Sacrifice'.[17]

   The Good Friday service is one of the few texts in the Roman Liturgy that is deliberately given dramatic form: the celebrant reciting 'Popule meus, quid tibi feci?', the deacon and subdeacon repeating it in response to each verse. The Reproaches had easily been incorporated into the Towneley Crucifixion play: no sooner has the Cross and its burden been lifted into the *mortice* (the same term is used in Dunbar's 'Passion'), so that it stands up 'like a mast', than Jesus breaks out into alliterative rhyming stanzas suggested by the biblical 'Is it nothing to you, all ye that pass by?' (Lam. 1:12). They take little else from Scripture save the concluding five lines, which expand 'Father, forgive them', and an unexpected application of the text 'The foxes have holes':

> All creatoures that Kynde may kest
> Beestys, byrdys, all have thay rest
>   When thay ar wo begon
> But Godys son, that shuld be best,
> Hase not where apon his hede to rest
>   Bot on his shulder bon

—a posture doubtless suggested by contemporary miniatures of the Crucifixion.

In the play the appeal is first addressed to 'my folk', but
soon to 'sinful man', in the singular, as in earlier appeals
that render 'respice in faciem Christi' as 'Loke, man, to Jesu
Crist', 'man and wyman, loket to me'. The verse of the play
is not memorable in itself, yet the visual impact of the scene
must have been great. The actual hoisting of the Cross with
its living burden, a 'business' taking several minutes, would
attract all eyes, and produce a sudden silence after the
frenzied shouting and cursing. And Christ's appeal to the
executioners as his brethren would be the more poignant
because it was scorned:

> '*Yis*: what we do full well we knaw.
> Yee, that shall he find within a thraw[a].'

> [a] short time.

The monologue of Herbert's 'Sacrifice', by contrast, lacks
dramatic or even liturgical context. But behind it, as the late
Rosemond Tuve forcefully demonstrated, lie centuries of
typological exegesis, which had taken final shape in the
illustrations to the so-called *Biblia Pauperum*, one of the
most influential of early printed books.[18] And we can still
profit from a glance at earlier versions of the Reproaches.

From the oldest extant Middle English rendering I have
quoted above. It begins with 'Ego te de Egypto eduxi':

> Vor vrom Egypte ich ladde the,
> Thou me ledest to rode tre,

and goes on to the striking of the rock and the Kings of
Canaan. Herbert radically rearranges and extends these
typological allusions, intercalating in ordered sequences
incidents of the Passion—as in the verse:

> Then they accuse me of great blasphemie,
> That I did thrust into the Deitie,
> Who never thought it any robberie

—a phrase deriving from Phil. 2:6: 'Who thought it not
robbery to be equal with God', part of the Epistle for Palm
Sunday. But more notable is a new and pervasive ironical

bitterness of tone, as in: 'I, who am Truth, turn into truth their deeds', or:

> Why, Caesar is their onely King, not I:
> He clave the stonie rock, when they were drie;
> But surely not their hearts, as I well trie.

The Jews had cried, 'We have no King but Caesar' (John 19:15)—as if it had been Caesar who had saved their fathers by giving them water from the rock in the wilderness. In the Latin text the juxtaposition is: 'Ego te potavi aqua salutis de petra; et tu me potasti felle et aceto'. St. Paul himself had said 'that rock was Christ' (1 Cor. 10:4); and accordingly it is depicted as a type of Christ's wounded side in the *Biblia Pauperum* and Books of Hours. But for Herbert *rock* also signified stony-hearted hearers of the word (Luke 8:6), impervious to pity; a figure that in 'The Sinner' he applies to himself:

> And though my hard heart scarce to thee can grone,
> Remember that thou once didst write in stone.

The 'fel et acetum' come later in 'The Sacrifice' and their bitterness is now more than physical:

> They give me vineger mingled with gall,
> But more with malice: yet, when they did call,
> With Manna, Angels food, I fed them all.

The 'aungeles mete' figures in the medieval texts,[19] but not in contrast to the gall, though one medieval poem gives, more poignantly, love-potion as counterpart to gall:

> A luf drink I ask of the
> Ayzell and gall thai gaf to me.

Herbert's tone does not change even when Christ prophesies that evil will turn to good:

> Nay, after death their spite shall further go;
> For they will pierce my side, I full well know;
> That as sinne came, so Sacraments might flow.

Sin came first through Eve, taken from man's side; so Eve figures opposite the pierced side in Books of Hours, the *Bible Moralisée*, the *Biblia Pauperum*. The Sacraments in question are Baptism and the Eucharist, the water and the blood which flowed from the riven side: that liquor, as Herbert describes it elsewhere, 'sweet and most divine,/ Which my God feels as bloud; but I, as wine'.[20] The pattern of the last line of the verse follows St. Paul: 'Where sin abounded, grace doth much more abound' (Rom. 5:20). Yet there is strangely little of grace in this poem. The sense of grief, by being extended too far, has, for once, overmastered it.

Christ as a man acquainted with grief is presented more than once in medieval verse:

> Of all the payne that I suffer sare
> Within my herte it greves me mare
> The unkyndenes that I fynd in the:

so run the central lines of *Homo, vide*.[21] But nowhere before Herbert does this grief approach vindictiveness. There is no room in 'The Sacrifice' for the traditional colloquy between Justice and Mercy. Here Christ seems to anticipate the Final Judgement. So, to be sure, he does when he descends into hell in *Piers Plowman*. But there, as in Dunbar's 'Resurrection', the note of mercy is struck repeatedly: 'to be merciable to man then, my kynd it asketh . . . and my mercy shall be shewed to many of my brethren' (*P.Pl.* B xviii. 371, 390). Whereas here Christ spends his last breath in a self-regarding reproach, 'As he that for some robberie suffereth':

> Alas! what have I stollen from you? *Death*.

So even the redemptive work of the Cross takes on a sombre colour that permeates every verse, and not least the last, when Christ answers his own question:

> Onely let others say, when I am dead,
> Never was grief like mine.

The ironies and double meanings that abound in 'The Sacrifice' made it inevitable that the poem should attract the attention of the author of *Seven Types of Ambiguity*. But they are mostly traditional ironies, as old as St. Bernard. That the tree of life is the Cross (l. 203) we know from the

Vision of a Rood; and the Cross was early represented as a tree stripped of its branches, being shown thus in the Winchester Psalter and on the Bury Cross. That the Crucifixion was conceived of as an ascent of the Cross (l. 202), *salire in ligno*, we know from the *Passio* of St. Andrew and the medieval Meditations. And that Christ himself was both the new fruit of the tree ('tam nova poma', as Fortunatus has it in the hymn *Crux benedicta nitet*) and the climber who in the terms of the Canticles 'ascendam in palmam et apprehendam fructus eius'—this we know from passages collected in, or rather scattered throughout, Miss Tuve's study; to which we may add the *Responsio Crucis* in Kennedy's *Passioun*, where the Cross says:

> I lay full low, but now I stand on fute,
> Fresche flurisand in the fruite of sic a kyn,
> Quhilk to ded men is werray medicyne

—this in reply to the Virgin's claim that its fruit was of her body, free from the sin of Adam, who 'staw the frute'. Herbert has it thus:

> Man stole the fruit, but I must climbe the tree;
> The tree of life to all, but onely me:
> Was ever grief like mine?

But he goes no further to suggest that Christ is the 'new fruit' than the opening words of the next stanza: 'Lo, here I *hang* . . .'. The dominant implication is that to steal fruit is easy but to climb this bitter tree is a fatal undertaking; and Empson's insistence that the image is of a child trying to put back apples seems perverse. Yet he was surely right in seeing more in this poem than the survival and continuation of a traditional mode. Its tone is harsher and more ironic than that of any medieval antecedent, or of any contemporary presentation: contrast Francis Quarles's summary use of the figure:

> He did but climb the cross, and then came down
> To the gates of hell; triumph'd, and fetch'd a crown.

The visual aspect too has altered. The appeal is no longer 'Behold my pain, behold my wounds', but 'Look, how *they* runne . . . *See, they* lay hold on me'. The dimension is now triangular; the speaker, the spectators, the actors in the drama.

Actors in the drama: the phrase reminds us of the strictly theatrical terms in which another Caroline poet, Robert Herrick, presents the Crucifixion. His 'Good Friday: *Rex Tragicus*, or Christ going to His Cross', compels us to question the general view of Herrick as a pagan parson, a cheerful bucolic. For one thing it is tinged with contempt for

> the base, the dull, the rude,
> Th'inconstant, and unpurged multitude

who make up the bored audience who wait for the chief actor to appear and

> *Yawn* for thy coming: some ere this time cry
> 'How he defers, how loath he is to die.'
> Amongst this *scum*, the soldier with his spear
> And that sour fellow, with his vinegar,
> His spunge and stick, do ask why Thou dost stay?

Surely this scene is the more vivid because the poet has lived through the execution of the saintly Laud and the martyred Charles, whose emblematic frontispiece to *Eikon Basilike* bore the distich:

> With joie I take this Crown of Thorn,
> Though sharp, yet easie to be borne.

The next lines likewise recall the King and his bearing on the memorable scene:

> Not as a thief, shalt thou ascend the Mount,
> But like a person of some high account;
> The Cross shall be thy stage; and thou shalt there
> The spacious field have for thy theatre.
> Thou art that Roscius and that marked-out man
> That must this day act the tragedian
> To wonder and affrightment: Thou art he
> Whom all the flux of nations comes to see:
> Not those poor thieves that act their parts with thee:
> Those act without regard, when once a King
> And God, as Thou art, comes to suffering.

No, no, the scene from Thee takes life and sense
And soul and spirit, plot, and excellence.
Why then begin, great King! ascend thy throne,
And thence proceed, to act thy Passion
To such a height, to such a period raised,
As Hell, and Earth, and Heaven may stand amazed. . . .

There is more than rhetoric here; there is a strength and
dignity and a full articulation of theme that neither Donne
nor Herbert surpassed. The true place of the poem is
alongside Marvell's Horatian Ode, in which the 'Royal
Actor' is taken from Carisbrooke so that he

The Tragick Scaffold might adorn
While round the armèd bands
Did *clap* their bloody hands.

Marvell's 'scene' is the classical *scena*, the stage or platform
of the Greek or Roman theatre; and Herrick's 'Roscius'
shows that he too is thinking of the classical theatre rather
than of mystery plays. But he can reckon also on all the
associations that the Renaissance had brought to the image
of the world as a Divine theatre: 'The great theatre of the
world', in Calderón's phrase. There is something of a
specifically theatrical, scenic quality in Rembrandt's great
etchings of the Passion. Yet even this conception can be
found adumbrated in Christian writing of far earlier date.
Honorius 'of Autun', in his *Gemma Animae* (*c.* 1100),
writes:

It is known that those who recited tragedies in theatres presented
the actions of opponents by gestures before the people. In the
same way *tragicus noster* [viz. the priest celebrating mass] represents by his gestures in the theatre of the Church (*in theatro
ecclesiae*), the struggle of Christ and teaches them the victory of
His redemption.[22]

Though several of Herbert's poems are dramatic in tone,
none picture the Passion in Herrick's terms. For a counter-
poise to 'The Sacrifice' we must turn to his sonnet
'Redemption', one of a cluster of poems full of allusions to
the Crucifixion, though unique in its parabolic quality. The
title is as near as it brings us to overtly scriptural language

or theme; and even the title is ambiguous. A hint of the
legal sense of 'redemption' (strong in St. Anselm's soteri-
ology) is present in the first quatrain, with its leasehold
image (found also in 'A Friend Unknown'):

> Having been tenant long to a rich Lord,
> Not thriving, I resolved to be bold,
> And make a suit unto him, to afford
> A new small-rented lease, and cancell th'old.

The stance here is not unlike that taken at the opening of
Herbert's more famous 'The Collar' (which must be read as
'yoke', Christ's 'easy' yoke of Matt. 11:30). The suppliant
seeks this lord at his manor, only to be told that he has gone
to take possession of some *dear-bought* land:

> I straight return'd, and knowing his great birth,
> Sought him accordingly in great resorts;
> In cities, theatres, gardens, parks, and courts:
> At length I hard a ragged noise and mirth
> Of theeves and murderers: there I him espied,
> Who straight, *Your suit is granted*, said, and died.

This is Herbert at his finest: dense in suggestion, and
mounting quickly in the sestet to a pregnant climax. Only
the last couplet hints at the parable of the vineyard in the
Synoptic Gospels from which the whole develops. In the
parable, after the householder's husbandmen had beaten,
stoned, and killed his servant, he sends his son, saying:
'They will reverence my son'. Instead they take him and
slay him. Told, in Luke 20, on the eve of the Passion, the
story must early have found a place in Holy Week devotions, and it still has a place in the *Improperia*, where
'Quid ultra debui facere tibi?' is followed immediately by
'Ego quidem plantavi te vineam meam', an allusion amplified in the tract for Holy Saturday from Isaiah 5:1, 2:
'Vinea facta est delecto in cornu' etc. The identity of
reference is confirmed by the illustrated *Speculum Humanae
Salvationis*, where the same opening shows Christ carrying
the Cross, the sacrifice of Isaac, the murder of the son in
this parable of the vineyard, and the grapes brought from

Canaan.[23] No other parable acquires the status of a historical antitype, which this collocation implies.

By the same token, the central passage of 'The Agonie', a
poem that comes shortly before 'Redemption' in *The
Temple*, owes much of its force to traditional typology.
Much—but not all: as so often, Herbert here achieves his
effect by beginning with an almost banal line ('Philosophers
have measur'd mountains') and concluding with a seemingly simple and colloquial phrase ('If ever he did taste the
like'). But in between comes the stanza:

> Who would know Sinne, let him repair
> Unto Mount Olivet; there shall he see
> A man so *wrung* with pains, that all his hair,
> His skinne, his garments bloudie be.
> Sinne is that presse and vice, which forceth pain
> To hunt his cruell food through ev'ry vein.

Knowing the medieval poem in which a champion is asked

> Why thoenne ys thy shroud red wyth blod al ymeind,
> As troddares in wrynge wyth most al byspreynd?

we know that this man pressed by sin is he who cometh
from Edom. The *Golden Legend* cites from Pseudo-
Dionysius' *Celestial Hierarchy* a passage in which the
Angels at the Ascension ask Christ, 'Why is thy clothing red
and thy vestments as trodden or fulled in a press?' To
which the answer is, in the words of Isaiah 63: *Torcular
calcavi*, 'the press I have turned and fouled [*sic*] all alone':
the press being the Cross, with which the body was pressed
'in such wise that the blood sprang out. And after that He
opened the tavern of heaven and poured out the wine of the
Holy Ghost' (iii. 100: Caxton's translation). So in the last
couplet of 'The Agonie',

> Love is that liquour sweet and most divine,
> Which my God feels as bloud; but I, as wine,

liquor is used in a specific sense found (for example) in
Numbers 6:3: 'Neither shall he drink any liquor of grapes'.

Christ had indeed felt it as life-blood welling from him; the Christian, tasting the Eucharistic wine, receives it as life-giving blood. Thus in 'The Invitation' Herbert says:

> Weep what ye have drunk amisse,
>   And drink this,
> Which before ye drink is bloud.

The actual figure of a winepress appears in late medieval miniatures: for example, in the *Hours* of Catherine of Cleves (*c.*1440) now in the Pierpont Morgan Library, New York: beneath a bloodstained figure of Christ standing victorious, and alone, on a reclining cross is a smaller representation of the same figure, holding whip and scourge, crouched beneath a press.[24] Hopkins, in a verse thronged with scriptural images of the Passion, will apply the figure to the wine of the Eucharist:

> For us the Vine was fenced with thorn,
> Five ways the precious branches torn;
> Terrible fruit was on the tree
> In the acre of Gethsemane;
> For us by Calvary's distress
> The wine was rackèd from the press;
> Now in our altar-vessels stored
> Is the sweet Vintage of our Lord.
>   ('Barnfloor and Winepress')

The title of Herbert's poem, some modern readers may need to be reminded, alludes to the Agony in the Garden of Gethsemane: hence it comes first in his Passion sequence, which jumps almost at once to the still more allusive 'Good Friday', of which this verse is typical:

> Since bloud is fittest, Lord to write
> Thy sorrows in, and bloudie fight;
> My heart hath store, write there, where in
> One box doth lie both ink and sinne.

The figure here seems to be transferred from that of

Christ's charter or chirograph, as Friar William Herbert (amongst many others) had applied it:

> Sith he my robe tok[a]
> Also[b] ich find in bok
>   He ys to me ybounde
> And helpe he wol, ich wot,
> Vor love the chartre wrot,
>   The enke orn[c] of hys wounde.[25]

[a] i.e. assumed human flesh   [b] as   [c] ink ran.

Another fourteenth-century poem approaches still closer to Herbert, for it includes the metaphor that we have already met in 'The Sacrifice':

> For thogh my hert be hard as stone,
> Yit maist thou gostly write theron
> With naill and with spere kene
> And so shullen the lettres be sene
>   . . .
> Write upon my hert boke
> Thy faire and swete lovely loke. . . .[26]

A final instance of Herbert's medieval affinities comes, fittingly, from his 'Easter':

> Awake, my lute, and struggle for thy part
>   With all thy art.
> The crosse taught all wood to resound his name,
>   Who bore the same.
> His stretchèd sinews taught all strings, what key
> Is best to celebrate this most high day.

No less a critic than C. S. Lewis has cited this seemingly bizarre conceit as an instance of deliberate Metaphysical shock, *discors concordia*, coupling the sacred Cross with profane 'fiddle-strings'. In fact Herbert was simply rewording a patristic commonplace, derived from a Messianic exegesis of Psalm 57, the Easter psalm, of which verses 8–9 run: 'Paratum cor meum, Deus; exsurge gloria mea, exsurge psalterium et cithara' (My heart is fixed, O God; awake, my glory, awake psaltery and harp'), with which was always coupled Psalm 81:2: 'Sumite psalmum et date tympanum, psalterium jucundum, cum cithara' (Take pipe and tabor, pleasant psaltery and harp). The harp, according to Augustine, signifies Christ as man in His suffering: 'caro humanus patiens' (*Enarrationes in Psalmos, PL* 36. 671–2). Cassiodorus had extended this: 'the harp means the glorious passion which with stretched sinews and counted bones (*tensis nervis . . . dinumeratisque ossibus*—cf. Ps. 22:17) sounded forth his bitter suffering as in a spiritual song (*carmen intellectuale*)': *PL* 70. 404. Sedulius had put this into verse in his *Carmen Paschale*. The conceit reappears in Bede and in the *Vitis Mystica* (see n. 6 to Ch. VII) and, as F. P. Pickering has pointed out, it is the reason why David's ten-stringed harp is presented as a type of Christ in a twelfth-century miniature from south-east Germany.[27] A nameless German poet developed it, affirming that as soon as Christ was stretched on the Cross the sweet sound of the harp resounded through all the world and down into hell (as if Christ were a divine Orpheus?). A German *Passional* says that God the Father spanned the strings on the harp of the Cross and played till the strings broke. The insistence in the Bonaventuran *Meditationes* and the mystery plays (as in Dunbar's 'Passion') on the stretching of the arms on the Cross because the nail-holes had been bored too far apart, and on ropes to pull down the feet, kept this image of the tautened body vividly present. It is found in a fifteenth-century vernacular sermon from Worcester:

But who harpid ther? Truliche Crist himsilf and non other. What was [his] harpe? Nothyng ell but his owne precius bodi. This harpe was wrafte[a] so hie whan it was nailed o the rode tre that al the strengis o the harpe, ye, al the synwes and al the veynes [in] Cristes bodi al to-rayssched and to-brak at tones. . . . whan musyk was first vownde ther wer but fowr strengis e the harpe. . . . Had Crist thes fowr strengis in his harpe? Ye vorsotha a had—the virst streng in his rith arm, the secunde in his left arm, the thrid streng in his rith leg, and te vowrthe in his left leg. Wyth this strengis Crist, for a wulde be vyr[b] herd, wente up on to an hy hil, on to the hil o Calverye, and ter[c] tempred his harpe and song so hie therto that a was herd bothe to hevene and to helle and te al the world over.[28]

[a] tuned, wound [b] far [c] there.

A little earlier Robert Mannyng of Bourne had claimed that the great Grosseteste justified his delight in minstrelsy by saying that 'to the croys by gode skille [with good reason]/Ys the harpe lykened wele' (*Handlyng Synne*, 4755–6). Lydgate compares the Cross to David's harp ('A Seying of the Nightingale', 307) and later in the fifteenth century, in the *Epistle of Othea*, Christ is strained as a harp to make the music of love.

Herbert, then, can properly match the wooden frame of his lute with the Cross and its strings with the stretched sinews of Christ's body: the lute here symbolizing his art, his verse, which must be stretched to the limit in praise and adoration on 'this most high day'.[29]

It remains to take note—for neither Rosemond Tuve nor Louis Martz did so—of Herbert's most formal and deliberate treatment of the Passion, in the twenty-one sets of Latin verses, the *Passio Discerpta*, which merit more than the perfunctory attention that Grosart and Canon Hutchinson gave to them.[30] These epigrams are of a distinctly late Renaissance, almost baroque cast; yet their themes are precisely those of late-medieval devotion: the bloody sweat, the crown of thorns, the purple robe, the *alapes* or striking on the face, the flagellation, the penitent thief, the casting of lots ('against custom, your garments are given to your enemies; but you give us yourself'), the nails, the bowed head, the sun darkened, the opened graves, the earthquake, the rent veils, the sympathy of Nature with its Lord—this last an adaptation of an ancient theme:

> Agnoscitque tuam Machina tota Crucem.
> Hunc ponas animam mundi, Plato: vel tua mundum
> Ne nimium vexet quaestio, pone meam:

a cryptic allusion, which we may render: 'So you may lay aside your world soul, Plato; or, lest that question vex the world too much, lay aside mine.' Donne makes the same Platonic reference at the end of his 'Resurrection': '. . . this body'a soule,/If not of any man, yet of the whole [world]'. More important than an exact rendering is the final phrase: *pone meam*. We should not be dazzled by the wit and metrical facility of the Public Orator of Cambridge into thinking that these accomplished verses are mere exercises. This is not to say that all are equally successful. But it is to remind ourselves that like earlier aureate poems by Dunbar and others they were designed as a form of worship; and the choice of subject itself testifies to Herbert's Christocentric theology. His Country Parson, we remember, 'knows nothing but the Crosse of Christ, his mind being defixed on it with those nailes wherewith his Master was'.

VII

RECUSANTS AND HYMNODISTS

IN the centuries after the Reformation the streams of
Catholic as of Anglican poetry devoted to the Passion came
near, if for different reasons and at different periods, to
running dry. Not only had Protestant theology produced
new doctrinal emphases—for Luther the suffering of the
Cross was a veil in which God hid himself—the views of a
Pico della Mirandola on the dignity of Man were not
reconcilable at once with the *skandalon* of the Crucifixion.
Hitherto it has been no easy matter to choose representative
texts from the hundreds that survive in manuscript or print.
Now selection becomes easier, though it involves exploring
tracts of verse that do not always appeal to modern taste,
even though they may be labelled 'metaphysical'. Much of
the verse in question is fugitive in a double sense, being
composed by recusants who fled their country for religion's
sake and published, when they did publish, abroad. Some of
it has only recently been edited for the first time. It offers its
own distinctive witness to the persistence of medieval
tradition.

William Alabaster (1568–1640), one-time Fellow of
Trinity College, Cambridge, counts as a recusant, though
he returned from Douai to the Anglican fold.[1] His symbols
are as traditional as Herbert's, and the title of a sequence of
sonnets, 'Divine Meditations', at once suggests his affinities, which are made clear when one of them is headed
'On St. Augustine's Meditations'. The *Liber Meditacionum*
was not in fact by St. Augustine, but the Middle Ages had
thought it was, and the ascription contributed to its popularity. The first series sets forth the Portrait of Christ's
Death, beginning with the starless night of the Passion,
'when Christ did sound the onset martial'—an image that
sets the tone for the series. This is the Christ of the Psalms
and early hymns, who rejoices as a giant to run his race. As

sin began in the garden of Eden, so its defeat began in the Garden of Gethsemane. Ten sonnets (the first and perhaps the finest of which is cited below, p. 226) are devoted to 'the "Ensigns" of the Crucifixion', 'sweet and bitter monuments of pain'. The thorns of the coronet are the fruit of the curse on man's sin (Gen. 3:18); they will become the noble wood of the cedar. The Cross sustains a vine: 'Ego sum vitis' (John 15:1 and 5), and a bunch of grapes (alluding, as Herbert will allude, to the grapes of Eshcol, Num. 13, that figure as a type in the *Biblia Pauperum*). 'Intertwined with love entire', the vine provides 'A cool repose from lawless flame'. Another sonnet sets forth the difference between Compunction and Cold (that is, tearless) Devotion in beholding the Passion. Penitential tears are the essence of Alabaster's religion, and in this respect at least he stands as a signpost to later Catholic verse in the seventeenth century.

Of that verse another Cambridge Fellow, Richard Crashaw, is a better-known practitioner. Indeed, he has come to be more highly regarded in the present century than he was in his own, when it was his Anglican father who gave more acceptable expression to Christian devotion. In the elder Crashaw's *Manuall for True Catholics* (1611) the emphatic *true* is meant to affirm the conviction of this Johnian Bachelor of Divinity, 'Preacher of God's word', that 'the Pope's seat and power were the power of the great Anti-Christ'. Yet it is genuinely catholic in its selections, which include renderings of 'holy meditations and prayers gathered out of certain ancient MSS, written 300 years ago or more'. They show him to be well-read in the medieval meditative writers. The conversion of Richard Crashaw thirty years later would certainly have scandalized him. Yet the son was but following the father when he translated—or rather, expanded and adorned in his own baroque style— some of the classic medieval prayers and hymns. It was in temperament rather than theology that the two differed. St. Teresa was Richard Crashaw's favourite saint, and, like Roy Campbell, he might be said to be *anima naturaliter hispanica*: believing, in Santayana's terms, that 'in the service of love and imagination nothing can be too lavish, too sublime, or too festive'.

The Preface to his *Steps to the Temple* says that in St. Marie's Church near St. Peter's College he lodged under Tertullian's roof of angels. Perhaps we should take this literally. When the egregious Dowsing visited Peterhouse during the Civil War he pulled down 'two mighty great angels with wings and divers other angels and about a hundred cherubims'; whilst at Little St. Mary's next door he 'brake down sixty superstitious pictures, some popes and crucifixes, and God the Father sitting in a chair'. With just such pictures and emblems were Crashaw's sacred poems adorned when they came to be printed in Paris. Or rather, the poems were prompted by such images, which themselves exemplified that 'Application of the Senses' to all themes of religion which the Ignatian Exercises had encouraged. Thus at the head of 'The Weeper' is a cut of the weeping Magdalene. 'Epiphany' begins

> Bright babe, whose awful beauties make
> The man incur a sweet mistake

because it stands below the Three Kings adoring the nimbed Holy Child. And the translation of the Office for the Holy Cross is preceded by a striking crucifix filling a whole page: the head bowed and crowned with thorn, but the face compassionate and the body unscarred and unbloody. This Office is found in later medieval Books of Hours, and in the Sarum Primer, which had been translated in Queen Mary's reign. Crashaw's adaptation is of the freest kind. In the English prose prayers and meditations one senses a deliberate approximation to the language of the Book of Common Prayer: as if Crashaw looked to the day when the English Church would become 'truly catholic' in *his* sense. The Hymns of the Office are another matter. Here he seizes with relish on the age-old paradoxes, following the precedent of Donne and of his friend Herbert, and stretches them to the limit. As at Matins:

> The wakeful Matins haste to sing
> The unknown sorrows of our King:
> The Father's word and wisdom, made
> Man, for Man, by man's betrayed,

The world's price set to sale, and by the bold
Merchants of Death and Sin is bought and sold.
Of his best friends, yea, of himself, forsaken;
By his worst foes (because he would) besieged and taken.

'Because he would' has no warrant in the Latin: it represents the ancient text from Isaiah, in the Vulgate form 'Oblatus est quia ipse voluit', that is central in orthodox belief. Again, at Prime:

The early prime blushes to say
She could not rise as soon as they
Call'd Pilate up—to try if he
Could lend them any cruelty.
Their hands with lashes arm'd, their tongues with lies
And loathsome spittle, blot those beauteous eyes,
The blissful springs of joy; from whose all-cheering ray
The fair stars fill their wakeful fires,
The sun himself drinks day.

The eyes to which Donne had given two words—'amazing light'—here take up four lines. But 'blushes' in the opening line is enough to sign the verse as Crashaw's: the conceit is one that he applies differently in the epigram on the Marriage at Cana, where 'the waters saw their God, and blushed' improves on the ancient 'hydriae aquae rubescunt'.

Essentially a poet of wit in the serious seventeenth-century sense, Crashaw gives his own inflexion to the Hymn for Terce:

But there is wit in wrath, and they will try
A 'Hail' more cruel than their 'Crucify':

more cruel because it alludes to the mockery of 'Ave, *rex*', 'in sport he wears a spiteful crown'. At Sext ('the noon of sorrow's night'),

Lo the faint lamb, with weary limb
Bears that huge tree which must bear him.
That fatal plant, so great of fame
For fruit of sorrow and of shame
Shall swell with both for him; and mix
All woes into one crucifix.

According to the ancient legend of the Holy Rood, the wood of the Cross grew from a seed of the fruit of the Tree of Knowledge of Good and Evil—'that fatal plant'.[2] At Evensong Crashaw, like Fortunatus and other early Christian poets, invokes a Cross that bears a royal burden:

> Thy lofty crown
> The King himself is; thou his humble throne
> Where yielding, and yet conquering, he
> Prov'd a new path of patient victory.
> When wondering death by Death was slain,
> Our own captivity his captive ta'en.

He is incorporating the Pauline text that Langland had put into the mouth of Repentance: 'Captivam cepit captivitatem'. 'Patient victory' must likewise be read in a Latinate sense: it is *Christus patiens* (Crashaw had paraphrased, and expanded, Grotius' work of that name) who by suffering achieves victory. These are not new metaphysical paradoxes; rather, the poetic climate of Crashaw's time favoured their rediscovery in such ancient hymns as the Easter *Vexilla Regis*, the fourth verse of which he will amplify thus:

> Tall tree of life! thy truth makes good
> What was till now ne'er understood.
> > Though the prophetic King
> > Struck loud his faithful string,
> It was thy wood he meant should make the throne
> For a more than Solomon.

So too 'Statera facta est corporis' (the tree is made a balance) becomes:

> Even balance of both worlds! our world of sin
> And that of grace heav'n weigh'd in him,
> > Us with our price thou weighed'st;
> > Our price for us thou payed'st.

In the Messianic psalm, as the traditional text ran, David had foretold: 'Regnavit a ligno Deus': God is to reign by a tree. A king must needs have a throne, as Solomon did, and it will be spread, as in Crashaw's next verse, with royal

purple: a greater than Solomon is here. This combination of
ancient typology and liturgical texts characterizes
Crashaw's devotional verse.

Nowhere is the wit more compressed than in the lines on
The Weeper:

> Sententious tears, O let them fall!
> Their *cadence* is *rhetorical.*

More unreservedly than Donne or Herbert can Crashaw
identify himself with the weeping Virgin at the foot of the
Cross, in the manner of Jacopone da Todi. In a stanza of
'Sancta Maria Dolorosa' he applies to that cross a phrase
that Donne had used rather differently:[3]

> Yea, let my life and me
> Fix here with thee
> And at the humble foot
> Of this fair tree take our eternal root
> That so we may
> At least be in love's way
> And in these chaste wars, whilst the wing'd wounds flee
> So fast twixt him and thee
> My breast may catch the kiss of some kind dart
> Though as at second hand, from either heart.

The spiritual wounds of the Virgin Mother (foretold in the
text 'a sword shall pierce through thy own soul also': Luke
2:35) are presented as matching the physical wounds of her
son; just as in medieval painting they are shown as made by
so many darts or arrows in her heart. All of Crashaw's
ardour pulses through that verse, though like Herbert he
does not eschew the everyday phrase ('at second hand');
elsewhere he writes of 'the wardrobe of Christ's side'. If we
still suspect his intensity of feeling as strained it is partly
because we have never wholly recovered from the
Protestant censorship of the sensuous that Crashaw
deplored.

His hymn on 'the bleeding Crucifix', for which, as for
several others, he wrote a parallel Latin version, seems to
have no single source. He cannot have read the medieval

Complaint 'Restles I ride' cited above (p. 56), but he uses a similar conceit:

> Thy restless feet cannot go
> For us and our eternal good,
> As they were ever wont. What though?
> They swim—alas in their own blood.

Another poem on the theme likewise has a Latin version, though one more loosely related to the English, which harks back to *Christus miles*:

> Come, brave soldiers, come and see
> Mighty Love's artillery—

while introducing a further martial image:

> For bow his unbent hand did serve,
> Well-strung with many a broken nerve.

Herbert had proclaimed Love as 'a Man of war/Who can shoot, and can hit from far'—a desecularized Cupid; but for Herbert the stretched sinews had been harp-strings.[4] A late fourteenth-century orison, the scribe of which wrote feelingly that 'a more devout prayere fond [found] I neuer of the passioun', had thus rendered a passage from the *Liber Meditacionum*:

> Lat now love his bow bende,
> And love arowes to my hert sende,
> That hit mow percen to the roote,
> For suche woundes shold be my bote.[5]

The figure of Christ's own arms outstretched as a bow is found only in a few Continental texts, the earliest being the *Liber de Benedictione Jacob* of Gotfrid of Admont in Styria (d. 1169):

A bow consists of a piece of wood or horn, and a string, which is a worthy representation of our Lord and Redeemer. The string may be taken to mean his most holy body, which in his various dire tribulations was wondrously spanned and stretched. By the wood or horn is meant his invincible divinity, which in a manner of speaking remained rigid and unbending to bear the sum of human miseries, until the noble bowstring, his holy body, began to be twisted with insults, drawn in mockery and stretched to the notches [or nails: *affixionibus*] of the Cross for our salvation. This is the bow that the Father promised us when he said: 'I do set my bow in the cloud' (Gen. 9:13).[6]

We may stagger at this last assertion. But support for it can be found, as well as later applications of the figure of the bow. Thus Heinrich of Neustadt (*c*. 1320) says:

> Man legt in uf das cruce nider.
> Da wooden sine reinen glider
> Und sin geeder uf gezogen
> Als die severoe uf den bogen.

He was laid down on the Cross. Then his pure limbs, his sinews and his veins, were drawn up like the string on a bow.

And the *Mystère de la Passion* of Angers (1486) incorporates a verse from Ps. 22:17, which other writers had taken up when applying that verse to the figure of Christ's body as a harp:[7]

> Onques arbaleste bendee
> ne tendit ne telle façon . . .
> onques corde d'arc ne tria
> meis que ses ners foibles et fors
> car nombreroit pur son cors
> ung a ung les os qui y sont.

The Counter-Reformation conversion of Cupid and his bow, illustrated in the *Amoris Divini Emblemata* of Vaenius (1615), would have made this image in every sense accessible to Crashaw.[8] Compare also 'Dinumeraverunt omnia ossa mea' (above, p. 165).

Epigram—witness Belloc, Chesterton, Ronald Knox—has been the forte (and sometimes the foible) of English Catholics: perhaps because the dogmas of their religion made them alert to paradox. Crashaw's Latin *Epigrammata Sacra* should not, any more than Herbert's, be dismissed as merely ingenious.[9] As he relished 'the wit of love' that in the face of the Magdalene could 'trace fountain and garden in one place' so he was quick to seize on the traditional figure of the Cross as support or fulcrum of the True Vine:

> Tu viti succurre tuae, mi vinitor ingens:
> Da fulcrum; fulcrum da mihi: quale? crucem.

> Support thy vine, O tender of my vine.
> Give it a prop, and me. What prop? The Cross.[10]

But I have not elsewhere found the seed that fell among thorns in the parable of Luke 8:5 ff. ('Semen est verbum dei') identified with the *Logos/Verbum* who was crowned with thorns:

> . . . nam sic spinas ah scilicet inter
> Ipse Deus Verbum tu quoque (Christe) cadis.[11]

Nor in any earlier verse is the darkening of the sun at Calvary presented as penance for having accepted idolatrous worship:

> And the Great Penitent press his own pale lips
> With an elaborate love-eclipse.

Compared with Crashaw's divine poetry, in Latin or English, Cowley's translation of a Greek Ode on the Crucifixion remains a frigid exercise; but it may owe something to his friendship with the recusant poet. Alongside it may be placed two 'Pindarique' Odes of John Norris, Fellow of All Souls, who dedicated his *Miscellanies* (1687) to its Warden. In one he bids the 'Bold Licentious Muse' sing 'the unfathom'd Depths of Love'; but she can do no better than rehearse old conceits:

> The *common* Sluces of the Eyes
> To vent his *mighty* Passion won't suffice.
> His tortured Body weeps *all-o're*,
>   And out of every Pore
> Buds forth a precious Gem of Purple Gore.

A loquacious Michael brings comfort in Gethsemane. But

when the 'wearyd Muse' reaches Calvary it has to report that:

> No longer able to *contain*
> Under the great *Hyperbole* of pain,
> He mourns, and with a strong Pathetick cry,
> Laments the sad Desertion of the Deity

—a reference to the *Eloi, Eloi . . .* of Mark and Matthew, which earlier poets had been conspicuously reluctant to take beyond the *Improperia*. Norris's notes to this Ode, bland as they are, reveal that he was not unversed in patristic learning, but do little to redeem it. Nor does he do better in his Pindaric paraphrase of Isaiah 63:

> Why wear'st thou then this scarlet dye?
> Say, mighty *Hero*, why?

or in the quatrains on 'The Passion of the Virgin Mother, Beholding the Crucifixion of her Divine Son'; the wonder is that he should have attempted this last theme at all.

Later poets of Crashaw's persuasion—like him they had to spend part of their life in exile—frequently followed him both in theme and in style. Edward Thimelby—whose verses are found only in a quarto volume called *Tixall Poetry*, published in Edinburgh in 1813 from a manuscript now missing—came of an old Catholic Lincolnshire family, one of whom had become a Jesuit, rector of St. Omer, and a defender of St. Ignatius against the charges of Dr. Stillingfleet. Edward was the friend of John Caryll, who was a friend of Pope and likewise of Catholic nurture. His poem on 'The Expostulation of St. Mary Magdalen'[12] goes a good deal further in rhetorical bravura than Crashaw went in 'The Weeper', as one verse will suffice to show:

> Oh, take Thy blood and pardon back:
> Restore the tears and sins I lose:
> To me hell's dearer for Thy sake
> Than heaven at so dear a cost:
> Though my sight ran astray, is't meet
> My wandering eyes shall draw Thy weeping feet?

There is more here than deft balance, word-play, and covert allusion. A later verse, which introduces the figure of the stricken deer now familiar from its application by a better-known poet, reflects the traditional interpretation of the Crucified's cry of *Sitio*:

> Methinks, in midst of all Thy smart,
> I hear Thee cry Thou thirst'st for me.
> Then, wounded hart, speak to this heart
> That's sick to death as well as thee.

Contemporary with Thimelby was Patrick Cary, whose biography has been traced and whose poems have been edited only recently.[13] A younger brother of the enlightened Lucius Cary, Lord Falkland of Great Tew, Patrick, once a Cavalier, became for a time a Benedictine novice at Douai, where he would have access to a library rich in devotional literature old and new. His *Crucifixus pro nobis*, four stanzas in fourteen patterned lines rounded off with a fifteenth refrain line, suggests that he had learnt some of his rhetoric as well as his mode of piety from Crashaw.

> Why did he shake for cold?
> Why did he glow for heat?
> Dissolve that frost he could,
> He could call back that sweat.
> Those bruises, stripes, bonds, taunts,
> Those thorns, which thou didst see,
> Those nails, that cross,
> His own life's loss,
> Why, oh, why suffered he?
> 'Twas for thy sake,
> Thou, thou didst make
> Him all thy torments bear:
> If then his love
> Do thy soul move
> Sigh out a groan, weep down a melting tear.[14]

Before dismissing 'the rhetoric of a weeping eye' as a conventional 'property' of baroque Counter-Reformation art we should recall Marvell's 'Eyes and Tears', where he adduces the Magdalene's tears for the terms of a comparison:

> So Magdalen in tears more wise
> Dissolved those captivating eyes
> Whose liquid charms could flowing meet
> To fetter his Redeemer's feet.

It is the same poet who in 'The Coronet' preserves the medieval mode of applying the moral lessons of the Cross to the personal snares of 'Fame and Interest' (i.e. Pride). And in the eighteenth century penitential tears would become a sign of grace for the Wesleys, as for Christopher Smart.

To find an Anglican counterpart to Cary amongst his contemporaries we have to look to Traherne. And as his *Meditations* bear but slight resemblance to earlier works with the same title, like that of Nicholas Love, so he conceives of the Passion in a way that Love, or Bonaventure, would hardly have understood:

I admire to see thy Cross in every understanding, thy Passion in every Memory, thy Crown of Thorns in every eye, and thy bleeding, naked, wounded body in every soul. Thy Death liveth in every memory, thy crucified Person is embalmed in every Affection, thy pierced feet are bathed in every one's fears, thy Blood all droppeth on every Soul. . . .

O Thou Sun of Righteousness, Eclipsed on the Cross, overcast with Sorrow, and covered with the Shadow of death, remove the veil of thy flesh that I may see thy Glory. . . .

Who art thou who bleeding here causest the ground to tremble and the rocks to rend and the Graves to open? Hath thy death influence so high as the Highest heavens? That the Sun also mourneth and is clothed in sables? Is thy spirit present in the Temple, that the Veil rendeth in twain at thy Passion? O let me leave King's Court to come unto Thee . . . tear the veil of my flesh that I may see into the Holy of Holies! O darken the Sin of Pride and Vain Glory. . . .[15]

To be sure, Traherne here applies scriptural language in a wholly traditional way. He was well-read in the Fathers— St. Anselm is one of the few authors cited in the *Centuries*— and St. Bonaventure had affirmed long before Traherne that the Universe bears 'the footprints of the Deity'. But there are new elements in Traherne's ecstasy, elements that owe something to Trismegistus and the Renaissance Platonism of Pico della Mirandola, which had only be-latedly made any impress on English minds. It is unlikely he would have relished Julian's *Revelations*, first published in England in his lifetime by Serenus Cressy (1670).[16]

We are moving towards the century of Whiggery and Deism, of Hume and Gibbon—but also of Pope, and Dr Johnson. Pope's Catholicism was not of the kind that centred in devotion to the Passion; essentially a social poet, he contrives to give even to the emblem of the Cross a fashionable setting.[17] The nature of Dr Johnson's religion shows in his wish that when his mother lay dying there should be read to her 'the Passion of Our Saviour'.[18] By that he meant the Gospel narrative: devout as he was, he had strong reservations about religious verse of any kind, and he shows no sympathy with Herbert's or with Donne's. Nor would he have been stirred by the news that Dr Burney had discovered in the Vatican Palestrina's great setting of the *Improperia*, which thus came to be published first in England (1771).[19] Johnson, though he properly distrusted William Law's adherence to the mysticism of Jacob Boehme, thought *A Serious Call to a Devout and Holy Life* (1729) was 'the finest piece of hortatory theology in any language'. Yet Law's theology had no room for vicarious suffering. He preached self-denial, not self-sacrifice. And it has been justly said that his ethical view 'strikes heroism out of religion, casts aside the noblest of motives to which the dullest of men will respond, and turns the spiritual life into a round of unceasing penance'.[20]

When a new spring of devotion bursts forth in England it draws on ancient sources but flows in unexpected direc-tions. Though Evangelicalism found the outward forms and dogmas of the Catholic Church repellent, it yet resorted without a qualm to the traditional modes and figures of Catholic hymnody (in the nineteenth century, by the same token, the Plymouth Brethren, though staunchly Protestant, developed an allegorical exegesis of the Old Testament that hardly differs from St. Gregory's, or St. Bernard's). Cowper sees the Cross as a fountain filled with blood drawn from Immanuel's veins, much as Bonaventure had done in the *Stimulus Amoris*. It had been depicted thus in late medieval miniatures and (for example) in a starkly emblematic Continental engraving to which the community at Little Gidding applied English texts.[21] What books Cowper found on the shelves of his friends the Unwins we do not know; but editions of Herbert had continued to appear until 1723, and he may have read Herbert's 'Love Unknown', in which the heart is washed in

> A stream of bloud, which issu'd from the side
> Of a great rock.

Augustus Toplady, in a famous hymn, addressed that Rock in the very terms of a medieval Latin verse:

> Dignare me, O Jesu, rogo te
> In cordis vulnere abscondere
> Permitte me hic vivere
> In tuo latere quiescere.

This is very close to:

> Rock of Ages, cleft for me,
> Let me hide myself in Thee.
> Let the water and the blood
> From Thy riven side which flowed
> Be of sin the double cure,
> Cleanse me from its guilt and power.

The figure is that of the rock which served Moses both as shelter and as source of living water: a regular type of the Cross, popularized in the fifteenth-century *Biblia Pauperum*.[22] And when this penitent sinner says

> Nothing in my hands I bring,
> Simply to thy cross I cling,

he is adopting the posture of the Virgin or the Magdalene in many a late miniature. The penitent, however, is now a solitary figure beneath the Cross. There is no place now for the Maries or St. John, and none for the soldiery. The concern is entirely personal, and indeed these hymns come near to being egocentric rather than Christocentric. Toplady was well-read in traditional theology, from the

Fathers to the Caroline divines, and their typology and
symbolism would be familiar to him. But he was also a rabid
Calvinist apprehending the Cross entirely in terms of
personal salvation. The Crucifixion has now become an
event of a different order from any antecedent events; and
the dominant image now is the Blood of the Lamb: a phrase
that carries with it Apocalyptic overtones and that will
prove a resource if not an inspiration for scores of revival-
ists. It is only when their verses (like Watts's paraphrase of
Psalm 21) follow the pattern of ancient devotions that they
cease to be sectarian. No one can dispute the power of
'When I survey the wondrous cross', so moving in its
simplicity of stance and diction. If, as David Jones affirmed,
the second line of that hymn originally ran, in defiance of
metre,

> On which the young prince of Glory died,

then the nexus with the Anglo-Saxon poet who had pictured the figure on the Rood as just such a prince is
undeniable.

The Evangelicals were nothing if not hymn-singers. John
Newton, the converted slave-trader who exercised such a
dubious influence on Cowper, wielded a far wider spell by
his verses, easily accommodated as they were to the simple
tunes to which they owed much of their almost hypnotic
appeal. A believer in instantaneous conversion, he presents
himself as halted in his wild career because

> I saw one hanging on a tree
> In agonies and blood
> Who fixed his languid eyes on me
> As near His cross I stood.
>
> Sure never till my latest breath
> Can I forget that look:
> It seem'd to charge me with His death
> Though not a word He spoke.
>
> . . .
>
> A second look He gave, which said,
> 'I freely all forgive;
> This blood is for thy ransom paid;
> I die, that thou may'st live'.

The reproaches of the *Improperia* are here concentrated in one look; and singers preoccupied with personal redemption will not pause to consider how eyes credited with such speaking glances can be called 'languid'.

Cowper's hymns followed Newton's pattern. It is only in *The Task* that we find him revivifying a potent medieval image, to apply it in a characteristically personal and Evangelical way when he turns from his major theme to depict himself as a stricken deer seeking the shade:

> There was I found by one who had himself
> Been hurt by th'archers. In his sides he bore,
> And in his hands and feet, the cruel scars.
> With gentle force solliciting the darts.
> He drew them forth, and heal'd, and bade me live.

His warrant for the image of a Christ shot at by archers lies in the *sagittae*, the arrows of more than one Messianic psalm. The small archer at the top of the south side of the Ruthwell Cross is thought by some to embody this motif. It appears hardly more than once in medieval verse. But the antecedents hardly matter. The gentle Olney poet has given to the figures his own reading and imbued them with a meaning appropriate to the age of anguished consciousness that his poetry ushers in. Here is a Saviour who was indeed afflicted with all our afflictions, yet not as a scapegoat, nor even as a sacrifice, but so that he might learn to heal those wounded as he was wounded: a truly compassionate Christ who is *conpatiens*—suffering *with* as well as *for* us. Ancient dogma here takes on a new dimension and equips itself to meet some of the questionings of the following century; though not those of Matthew Arnold, who in *God and the Bible* was to dismiss the ancient *fabula* of Jesus meeting the claims of Justice as impossible of acceptance even by the religious middle class 'with its bounded horizons'. 'Leave the Cross,' says the Master in Arnold's stanzas on Progress. 'But guard the man within.'

One might have expected that when at last the Anglican revival came, its historical bent would have prompted a rediscovery and reappraisal of pre-Reformation devotions: for its leaders were learned men, and enamoured of ancient

forms. Yet in their approach to the past they were highly
selective; and their learning could prove an encumbrance.
Whatever the faults of Wesleyan hymns, their fervent
language is comparable in its simplicity to that of the best of
medieval religious verse; it is native, and largely monosyl-
labic. But Keble's effusion on the Passion from the very
opening line bears all the marks of a conscious literary
exercise:

> Fill high the bowl, and spice it well and pour
> The dews oblivious. For the cross is sharp,
> The cross is sharp, and He
> Is tenderer than a lamb.
> Fill high the bowl, benumb his aching sense
> With medicin'd sleep . . .

The semi-Miltonic 'dews oblivious', the half-heard echo of
Macbeth, are forerunners of such stilted passages as

> Measuring in calm presage
> The infinite descent.

Much unimpeachable sentiment and doctrine find a place
('emptied of thy glory awhile . . . Thou wilt feel all that
Thou mayst pity all'), but also some gratuitous pathos:

> The very torturers paused
> To help Him on His way.

And finally the soft-centred verse grows both flaccid in
form and dubious in theology:

> Though the strife be sore
> Yet with His parting breath
> Love masters Agony: the soul that seemed
> Forsaken, feels her present God again
> And in her Father's arms
> Contented dies away.

It is bracing to glance back from these mannered lines to
one of the earliest Anglican poems, Giles Fletcher's
'Christ's Triumph over Death' (1610), which I have de-
layed considering, precisely to point the contrast. Fletcher,
like Keble a university man and in orders, was just as much
the conscious literary craftsman—he acknowledged a debt

to Du Bartas—but his touch is altogether surer, his verse more disciplined and confident. He enlarges and juxtaposes familiar themes in his own way, framing them in his favourite near-Spenserian stanza, as in these verses on the Crucifixion:

It was but now their sounding clamours sung,
Blessed is he, that comes from the most high,
And all the mountains with Hosanna rung,
And now, away with him, away they cry,
And nothing can be heard but crucify:
   It was but now, the crown itself they save,
   And golden name of king unto him gave,
And now, no king, but only Caesar, they will have:

It was but now they gathered blooming May,
And of his arms disrob'd the branching tree,
To strew with boughs, and blossoms all thy way,
And now, the branchless trunk a cross for thee,
And May, dismayed, thy coronet must be:
   It was but now they were so kind, to throw
   Their own best garments, where thy feet should go,
And now, thyself they strip, and bleeding wounds they show.

See where the author of all life is dying:
O fearful day! he dead, what hope of living?
See where the hopes of all our lives are buying:
O cheerful day! they bought, what fear of grieving?
Love love for hate, and death for life is giving:
   Lo how his arms are stretch'd abroad to grace thee,
   And, as they open stand, call to embrace thee,
Why stay'st thou then my soul; O fly, fly, thither haste thee.

Here the firm structure of the verse, the bold use of paradox and novel paronomasia (*May, dismayed*), the unforced application of traditional symbolism ('arms stretch'd abroad to grace thee')—all combine to show how much a religious poet benefits from living in an age when the pulse of poetry is strong; whereas Keble's verse, like its counterparts in Victorian painting, reflects the flabbiness that issued in *fin de siècle* decadence. It is no accident that Hopkins, who moved so far away from the soft measures of such verse, again and again presents the Christ of the Cross

as the hero, the chevalier; and a profound sense of 'the
dense and driven Passion', of his compassionate suffering,
informs 'The Wreck of the Deutschland'. The drowned
nuns are in number the same as the Wounds:

> Five! the finding and sake
> And cipher of suffering Christ.
> Mark, the mark is of man's make
> And the word of it Sacrificed.
> But he scores it in scarlet himself on his own bespoken
> Before-time-taken, dearest prizèd and priced—
> Stigma, signal, cinquefoil token
> For lettering of the lamb's fleece, ruddying of the rose-flake.

Hopkins's Notebooks illustrate the old Ignatian practice
of meditation: 'videre personas, videre locum'. Amongst his
'points on Sorrow', the fifth is 'to consider how the Divinity
hides Itself . . . and how it allows the most holy humanity to
suffer so cruelly': phrases that might have come out of
Ludolf of Saxony. And it is not irrelevant to remark that the
Jesuit poet evidently accepted Duns Scotus' view that the
Incarnation was an expression of Divine Love not con-
tingent on the Sin of man.

To the very turn of the century belongs the poetry of
Alice Meynell and Francis Thompson. In her lines on the
Crucifixion, Alice Meynell comes to the furthest point of
the *mysterium* of Christ's suffering:

> Oh, man's capacity
> For spiritual sorrow, corporal pain!
> Who has explored the deepmost of that sea,
> With heavy links of a far-fathoming chain?
>
> That melancholy head
> Let down in guilty and in innocent hold,
> Yea into childish hands deliverèd,
> Leaves the sequestered floor unreached, untold.
>
> Only one has explored
> The deepmost; and He did not die of it
> Not yet, not yet He died. Man's human Lord
> Touched the extreme; it is not infinite.

But over the abyss
Of God's capacity for woe He stayed
One hesitating hour: what gulf was this?
Forsaken he went down, and was afraid.

Thompson is a Christianized Shelleyan. A phrase of
Shelley's ('heaven's wingèd hound') provides the title of his
most famous poem; and his generous study of 'that straying
spirit of light' dwells on *Prometheus Unbound*—in which
Panthea sees 'a youth/With patient looks nailed to a
crucifix', and the chained giant, though he will not speak
Christ's name, prays the Fury to

Remit the anguish of that lighted stare
Close those wan lips; let that thorn-wounded brow
Stream not with blood.

Thompson's ornate rhetoric, his empurpled sunrises and
sunsets are no longer acceptable and 'The Hound of
Heaven' is no longer recited. Yet almost all of his specifically Catholic verse retains its resonance, whilst his prose
reveals his acquaintance—due doubtless to the Meynells,
his befrienders—with the meditative and recusant literature
that has had a place earlier in these pages. The 'After-strain'
of the 'Ode to the Setting Sun' presents us once again—
after an interval of six centuries—with the stark silhouette
of Mary and the Cross against the evening sky that evoked
'Nou goth sonne under wod', the first lyric to be quoted
here. It also catches, however faintly, that note of harp
music which the Cross gave forth to Herbert's ear. Feeling
forces its way through rhetoric.

Now with wan ray that other sun of Song
 Sets in the bleakening waters of my soul:
One step, and lo! the Cross stands gaunt and long
 'Twixt me and yet bright skies, a presaged dole.

Even so, O Cross! thine is the victory.
 Thy roots are fast within our fairest fields;
Brightness may emanate in Heaven from thee,
 Here thy dread symbol only shadow yields.

Of reapèd joys thou art the heavy sheaf
    Which must be lifted, though the reaper groan;
Yea, we may cry till Heaven's great ear be deaf,
    But we must bear thee, and must bear alone.

Vain were a Simon; of the Antipodes
    Our night not borrows the superfluous day.
Yet woe to him that from his burden flees,
    Crushed in the fall of what he cast away.

Therefore, O tender Lady, Queen Mary,
    Thou gentleness that dost enmoss and drape
The Cross's rigorous austerity,
    Wipe thou the blood from wounds that needs must gape.

So, too, in 'The Veteran of Heaven' the age-old figure of *Christus miles* once more stands forth: the title alluding not to the time-expired soldier but to one practised in warfare, skilled in battle, who, as in Old English verse, returns to Heaven with victory. It derives, in fact, from the presentation in the *Golden Legend* of Christ's last great 'leap'. For the *Legend* (which here follows largely the *Glossa Ordinaria* and the *Celestial Hierarchy* of the Pscudo-Dionysius) says that 'some angels who knew not plainly [fully] the mystery of the Incarnation, Passion, and Resurrection marvelled when they saw Our Lord ascend and asked: "Who is this that cometh from Edom" . . . And He answered: "I am He that speaketh in Justice. . . ."'[23] The poet extends this interrogatory in sounding stanzas:

O Captain of the wars, whence won Ye so great scars?
    In what fight did Ye smite, and what manner was the foe?
Was it on a day of rout they compassed Thee about,
    Or gat Ye these adornings when Ye wrought their overthrow?

'Twas on a day of rout they girded Me about,
    They wounded all My brow, and they smote Me through the side:
My hand held no sword when I met their armèd horde,
    And the conqueror fell down, and the Conquered bruised his
        pride.'

What is this, unheard before, that the unarmed makes war,
    And the Slain hath the gain, and the Victor hath the rout?
What wars, then, are these, and what the enemies,
    Strange Chief, with the scars of Thy conquest trenched about?

'The Prince I drave forth held the Mount of the North,
  Girt with the guards of flame that roll round the pole.
I drave him with My wars from all his fortress-stars,
  And the sea of death divided that My march might strike its goal.'

This, to be sure, is the poetry of triumph, if not of triumphalism, rather than poetry of the Passion: illustrating the hazards of elaborating the limited martial metaphor of liturgy and Scripture. Joy in the overthrow of evil blurs with the joy of battle, as in Prudentius' *Psychomachia*, or *Paradise Lost* or—to come down to Thompson's time—*The Napoleon of Notting Hill*.

The trenches of the First World War were to prove the grave of all such rhetoric. Yet from the mud and blood of those trenches there emerged in the vision of a great poet once more the sublime paradox of *Christus miles*.

VIII

FROM ADAM BEDE *TO* ANATHEMATA

THE deepening, enlarging, and revivifying of belief is not brought about solely by saints, theologians, or philosophers; at some periods of history they contribute little to these processes. The Spirit bloweth where it listeth, the Word of God is not bound, and the century of Dante and of *Piers Plowman* is not the only one in which Christian mysteries have been given new shape and substance by writers whose catalytic power the Church has been slow to acknowledge. If the Logos can speak through parable and allegory it can also speak through fictions to which allegory gave birth and for which parable supplied a pattern and a language.

The rise of the novel is sometimes equated with the growth of secularism. It would be less misleading to say that in the modern novel the focus of meditation shifts from God to Man. It reflects, and reveals, and creates, a new kind of self-knowledge, hitherto expressed in essays (Montaigne) or autobiography (*Religio Medici*) or in a painter's self-portraitures (Rubens or Rembrandt). To portray the human condition is to portray and meditate on the enigma of human suffering, to depict characters faced with that enigma.

The Wesleyan movement had owed its success not only to its power in presenting Faith as a remedy for sin but also to its appeal to those bowed under the burden of suffering. To invoke fiction as evidence of spiritual change and experience is always hazardous. But it has long been recognized that George Eliot drew from the life (as well as from family recollections of an earlier generation); and if we would understand why the hymns of Cowper and Toplady answered to men's needs we might do worse than ponder on the prayer that Dinah Morris, in *Adam Bede*, makes for Hetty Sorrel: a prayer that takes some of its form and fervour from those same hymns. 'Jesu, thou present Saviour! Thou hast known the depths of all sorrow: thou hast entered that black darkness where God is not, and hast uttered the cry of the forsaken. Come Lord, and gather the fruits of thy travail and thy pleading: Stretch forth thy hand, thou who art mighty to save to the uttermost.'

The note struck here is heard throughout the book. The Positivist writer who privately renounced revealed religion expressed with a power that no preacher of her time possessed the sense that 'in all the anguish of the children of men infinite Love is suffering too— yea, in the fullness of knowledge it suffers, it yearns, it mourns'. Nor does she eschew biblical language: 'The true cross of the Redeemer was the sin and sorrow of the world—that was what lay heavy on his heart—and that is the Cross we shall share with him, that is the cup we must drink of with him if we would have any part in that Divine Love which is one with his sorrow.' So too her Dinah Morris shares with fourteenth-century mystics a belief in visible manifestations of Christ: 'making her hearers feel that he was among them bodily, showing the print of the nails in his hands and all the other marks of the Passion'. Seen in this context, the Methodist revival of hymnody shows a likeness to the Franciscan movement that produced so many fourteenth-century lyrics, though as the novelist noted there is something distinctive in the plangent cadences of the later time, 'a strange blend of exaltation and sadness'.

But *Adam Bede* is more than an imaginative re-creation of the Evangelical experience: it is itself an interpretation and extension into personal history of the pregnant and prophetic saying of Isaiah: 'Surely he hath borne our griefs and carried our sorrows' (Isa. 53:4). And it is the novelist who comes closest to ordinary English life and character who regrets the banishment from the English scene of those images of the Crucified that in Catholic countries were set among clustering blossoms in sunny cornfields.[1] 'Man needs a suffering God': the assertion is the more ineluctable because made by a writer who also describes with most delicate sympathy and perception worshippers and modes of worship that seem to have lost all sense of that necessity. By the same token, satiric touches in *Scenes of Clerical Life* do not diminish the effect of the passages in which Mr Tryan points to the Saviour who has drunk the cup of human suffering and Janet yearns to throw herself at the foot of the Cross, 'where the Divine sufferer would impart Divine strength'. The contrast with a parallel scene as presented— or rather, as distanced—by Virginia Woolf in *Mrs Dalloway*, seventy years later, is revealing: 'No one knew the agony, said Miss Kilman. He said, pointing to the crucifix, that God knew. But why should she have to suffer when other women, like Clarissa Dalloway, escaped. Knowledge comes through suffering, said Mr. Whittaker'—and passes out of the story.

George Eliot, then, like Cowper, apprehends the Cross as the symbol not simply of vicarious but also of compassionate suffering. St. Paul's prayer 'that I may know the fellowship of his sufferings, being made conformable to his death' (Phil. 3:10) has been, so to say, retranslated—and without resort to the exegetes beyond the author of the *Imitatio*, whence she took the image of 'the King's highway of the Cross'.

A critical élitism, for which Bloomsbury was partly responsible, has banished from modern literary history the Masefield who followed *The Everlasting Mercy* with a verse-play on *Good Friday* (1917) and a sensitive novel, *Eggs and Baker* (1936). The play—in this respect foreshadowing David Jones—makes much of the Roman context of the Crucifixion; Jesus never appears; and as often Masefield resorts to the abstracts Truth and Beauty as his touchstones. But the novel, subtitled 'The Days of Trial', supplies what the drama lacks. As George Eliot had re-created the pieties of her childhood, so Masefield in this story presents an honest baker of the eighteen-seventies whose radical fervour springs from a reading of Isaiah rather than Tom Paine. The Trial is that of two men, a thief and a half-wit, for murder. The baker sees it differently from his neighbours: 'In Jerusalem something of this sort must have gone on from midnight till midday . . . everybody eager for all the forms to be observed.' Suddenly he finds himself weeping not for the accused but for the poor beset Christ, seized in the midnight, without sleep, and manhandled, mocked, bully-ragged, cross-examined, scourged, and then condemned by some-body perplexed and trying to help, yet having, after all, to apply the code. 'Something of the Spirit of Christ is in the dock there in Rapp and Magpie,' he exclaims. 'It was that little something that Christ died to save. Somewhere in Rapp's heart is Christ's own brother, if only I were Christ enough to save it.'

The visualization here (though it would have been unimaginable and unacceptable to William Law or his followers) is in terms no different from those of medieval meditative verse, the compassion is akin to Langland's as displayed in the prayers of Robert the Robber and Repentance to him 'that art oure fader and oure brother'. Whatever our views of the theology of Atonement, the fact stands out that through the centuries all sorts and conditions of men have found in the suffering Christ their sole resort.

For so long, that is, as they have given any credence to the biblical narrative which is the ultimate source of Christian poetry. Even the *sournois* Hardy of 'Panthera', who seizes on a late Talmudic legend to show a Roman legionary witnessing the crucifixion of the son he had casually fathered on Mary, will re-create scenes of the Passion in biblical terms: in 'The Servant's Quarters', whilst Peter denies his master, we hear the clink of Christ's chain and the echo of the cuffs rained on him.

But in the 620 pages of the *Oxford Book of Twentieth-Century Verse* the only poem on the Passion is one with the dismissive title 'New Approach Needed':[2] a callow exercise intended doubtless to shock, yet blasphemous in a deeper way than a sonnet by a lesser-known poet, R. A. K. Mason, whose *Ecce Homunculus* has a better claim to our attention, if only because it betrays a bitterness that is itself part of the experience of the Cross and presents a Christ who 'boldly went to die':

> Still wore the gallant mask, still cried Divine
> Am I, lo for me is heaven overcast
> Though that inscrutable darkness gave no sign,
> Indifferent or malignant; whilst he was poured
> By even the worst of men at least sour wine.

The 'mask' of *humanitas*—so figured by the Fathers—has here been wilfully transferred to *divinitas*; and 'indifferent or

malignant' reflects the monistic philosophy that Hardy and
Housman had espoused.

Yet such verses and books of verse as these just cited are
not the only index to modern consciousness. Against them
we may set Edith Sitwell's 'Still Falls the Rain', that prayer
of the 1940 fire-raids addressed to

the Starved Man hung upon the Cross.
Christ that each day, each night, nails there, have mercy on us—
. . .
Still falls the Blood from the Starved Man's wounded Side:
He bears in His Heart all wounds . . .
Then—O Ile leape up to my God: who pulles me doune—
See, see where Christ's blood streames in the firmament:
It flows from the Brow we nailed upon the tree
Deep to the dying, to the thirsting heart
That holds the fires of the world.

Here the adaptation of Marlowe's lines belongs to the poet's
earlier manner. But the poem as a whole, like the others in
The Song of the Cold, has an unexpected gentleness and
compassion, marking what one can only describe as a
conversion. The Cross, as in the Anglo-Saxon poet's vision,
still touches the four quarters of the sky.

A younger poet, David Gascoyne, in his *Ecce Homo*, also
sees the horrifying face of the Son of Man lit up by fire-
raids; a labourer and a factory-hand on either side and the
centurions wear riding boots:

> Behind his lolling head the sky
> Glares like a fiery cataract
> Red with the murders of two thousand years
> Committed in his name and by
> Crusaders, Christian warriors
> Defending faith and property.

He who wept for Jerusalem now sees this prophecy extend
across the greatest cities of the world. Now the prayer is

> Not from a monstrance silver-wrought
> But from the tree of human pain
> Redeem our sterile misery,
> Christ of Revolution and of Poetry

—where the last line may, or may not, point forward to the so-called 'theology of liberation', which in Germany was to develop out of a theology of suffering.[3] Geoffrey Hill's meditation on the Passion in his *Tenebrae* (a two-edged title) is less committed, leaving us (and him?) uncertain where he stands and what belief he is reflecting:

> I fall between harsh grace and hurtful scorn.
> You are the crucified who crucifies,
> self-withdrawn even from your own device,
> your trim-plugged body, wreath of rakish thorn.
>
> What grips me then, or what does my soul grasp?

Four great novelists from different continents have in our own day presented the Passion as perpetually re-enacted. In *Christ Recrucified* the Cretan Kazantzakis describes a literal re-enactment: in a Greek village still under Turkish domination the choice of actors for a traditional Easter play determines that they act out their scriptural roles in ordinary life till the innocent young shepherd who was to have played Christ is sacrificed. In Patrick White's *Riders in the Chariot*, which like his *Voss* reveals a profoundly Christian view of suffering and fellow-suffering, the same sacrifice is re-enacted analogically in the Antipodes, 'where the nails of the Southern Cross eat into the sky'. The victim is a German-Jewish refugee; and the scene could be set against Graham Sutherland's Crucifixion at St. Aidan's, East Acton, where a gaunt and bloody Christ hangs on a cross that might be the gallows of a concentration camp. *Rising*, R. C. Hutchinson's last and richest novel, reaches its climax when its protagonist, Sabino, bent on destruction, is healed and saved, in body and in soul, by the man whom he has pursued, tortured, and left for dead. Even if one has not read Hutchinson's earlier novels with the scenes like that in *Johanna at Daybreak*, in which the Polish girl, stern with grief from her lover's death at German hands, abandons the German airmen she has nursed, only to find that one with bleeding hands has taken from her the key to their room—even apart from such hints of redemptive suffering, one scarcely needs the author's last notes—'The love we are concerned with is the *Christian* love . . . Sabino puts himself into the hands of the Risen Christ'—

to seize the inner meaning of the tale. A final instance:
William Faulkner, in the most mysterious of his books,
pointedly entitled *A Fable*, has a corporal-Christ who is
betrayed by one of his twelve disciples and dies for Peace
between a penitent and an unrepentant thief.[4]

The Great War did indeed seem to add a new dimension
to human suffering; it was fought, as many a soldier noted,
in a terrain of scarred wayside Calvaries. Herbert Read wrote
in 1914:

> His body is smashed
> through the belly and chest
> the head hangs lopsided
> from one nail'd hand.
> Emblem of agony
> we have smashed you!

And almost every poet of the muddy and bloody trenches
evokes Gethsemane and its sequel. 'At a Calvary near the
Ancre', wrote Wilfred Owen,

> One ever hangs where shelled roads part
>   In this war He too lost a limb,
> But his disciples hide apart
>   And now the soldiers bear with him.

Owen even saw himself, training troops, as 'teaching Christ
to lift his Cross by numbers, and how to adjust his crown'.
Robert Graves, remarking that George Moore's *The Brook
Kerith* seemed peculiarly timely at the Battle of the Somme,
recalled that when respect for organized religion died,
'reverence for Jesus as our fellow-sufferer remained'.[5]

There is, then, indubitable evidence that the more agnostic and sceptical the age, the greater is the human appeal of
the one who was 'touched by the feeling of our infirmities'.
The 'spiritual miracle' (in R. H. Hutton's phrase) of that
Cross which early Christians were so slow to accept as their
sign and symbol now proves easier of acceptance than the
lesser, physical miracle of the Resurrection. Yet this recognition of the reality of Christ's suffering is not a specifically
Christian, or even a distinctly religious perception. To see
the Cross as the epitome of the world's woe requires no

special grace. It is on the efficacy of its redemptive and vicarious sacrifice that Christian hope must rest, and though some modern Hindu and Buddhist teachers come close to an understanding of the Crucifixion only the Christian creed accepts the figure of the Cross as a fountain of life-giving blood. Amongst the foremost witnesses of the sufferings of the Great War stands a unique writer, David Jones, who came to view the whole of that experience in the light of this creed, and who set down his vision in the prose-poem *In Parenthesis* (1937). The pattern of scriptural phrase and Lenten liturgy underlying this evocation of the history of a battalion of Fusiliers at the Somme in 1916 has lately been convincingly displayed.[6] It may be instanced in the allusion to Isa. 63:1–3 (the lesson for Wednesday of Holy Week) that lurks in 'the dyed garments strung up for a sign' in a German trench; in the infantrymen, 'each bearing in his body the whole apprehension of that innocent' (as St. Paul bore about in his body the marks of the Lord Jesus), waiting 'all in a like condemnation'; and in the Latin epigraph from Lam. 2:12 (the second lesson of Good Friday) at the beginning of the account of the battle at 'the place of a skull'. The same pattern reappears in the rituals and action of Jones's *Anathemata* (1952), a long preparative for the action of Good Friday as Roman troops would have regarded it.

If these studies reach a conclusion in the work of David Jones it is not because they have been deliberately contrived so as to lead up to the poetry, painting, and design of an artist whose rare quality is only now coming to be recognized. This largely self-taught Londoner, son of a Welsh father and a Kentish mother, has knitted together ancient texts, liturgical allusions, motifs from the *Vision of a Rood*, *Piers Plowman*, the meditative writers—not to mention Malory, the *Mabinogion*, and Nonconformist hymns—as if he were constructing a kaleidoscope view of the very works that we have chronologically considered. Yet he assures us that these texts and motifs became available to him by accident and that he simply allowed himself to be guided by them. It was not a question of rearranging the old, but of reviewing the whole of Western culture in the light of Christian creed as embodied in Christian liturgy. Celtic myth, the Roman *imperium*, sea-shanties, popular song, children's games, the discipline of the camp and of the ship, all take on a new significance, whilst the technical achievements of Joyce and Eliot enable him to give Christian poetry and meditation a new shape. The Waste Land blossoms like the rose, Ulysses' keel grounds in a Welsh cove. Jones celebrates London riflemen and the legionaries of the tenth Fretensis with an equal lustre. But ultimately his work owes its force to his experience of human suffering and endurance in the holocaust that was the Great War.

David Jones wrote for the listening ear—his two masterpieces have been broadcast with notable success—and drew for the seeing eye. The drawings and paintings that best display his genius cannot be 'read' at a glance. But, as with Chagall, the only contemporary painter that he in any way resembles, there is in them more of magic than of mystery, and nothing of the occult. If they hint at mystery it is at the *mysterium crucis*. Time and again they point to the Passion. Thus the *Vexilla Regis* (1948) presents a tree that stretches like that in the Anglo-Saxon poet's vision from earth to heaven.[7] It is marked with a single great nail, and at its foot thorn and bramble cluster in a rough crown (so, in a fourth-century sarcophagus, a wreath crowns an empty cross, and in later representations the wreath of thorn encircles this *crux invicta*). To the left, on a smaller tree, nests a symbolic pelican in her piety. To the right, on a decorated trunk pegged into the ground with three pegs, stands a Roman eagle. No human figure is visible, only riderless horses that like those in Malory's last chapter 'go whither they would'. The title of the picture would scarcely be intelligible did we not know the history of the Holy Rood Tree. For a crucified figure we must turn to the frontispiece of *In Parenthesis*. A naked but helmeted soldier hangs between two torn and leafless trees on the Western Front, entangled in barbed wire and in the very posture that the painter gives to Christ in his unfinished Oblation and Immolation of the Cross;[8] the intent of this frontispiece is made clear by the tailpiece: a figure of the Lamb as it had been slain. In a later drawing the fourth stanza of *Vexilla Regis* is edged with an Anglo-Saxon line, 'Ongyrede hine þa geong hæleð' from the *Vision of a*

Rood, and the *Agios Ischyros* of the Good Friday *Improperia*. In yet another inscription (1939) we move from Cloelia Cornelia and Tristan and Essylt to the 'Pliant Puella' who in the fields of Ephrata bore the LOGOS who jousted alone, his only habergeon *humana natura*:⁹ phrasing that takes us back to *Piers Plowman*, and further back still.

The frame and informing spirit of both these books are soldierly and Roman. Now for the first time a poet presses home the credal clause 'suffered *under Pontius Pilate*', here presented as the colonial governor of a troublesome province, whose legionaries preserve the *limes* only by an inflexible and disciplined routine: a different ruler from the Pilate of the mystery plays, and with his troops drawn from all quarters of the Roman *imperium*. Throughout *Anathemata* we are aware of the centurion at the foot of the Cross— though he is never actually mentioned or presented; whilst in *The Tribune's Visitation* that other centurion (of Matt. 8:8), who said 'Domine non sum dignus', is seconded to a unit stationed in upper Britain, where his fatigues foreshadow those of Jones's fusiliers on the Somme. There is a hint here of the Kipling of *Puck of Pook's Hill*, a hint confirmed by a passage in the Preface to *Anathemata*.¹⁰ But Jones's vision—perhaps one should say rather his power of myth-making, or of fusing myths—is profounder than Kipling's. With him soldiering provides a whole language of signs, a language that remains valid for a generation that knew a later war.

His mode of creation can be appropriately illustrated by a passage in the Fifth Part of *Anathemata* intended as preparative for the final Passion sequence. A seaman speaks:

      That was hers
that laboured with him that laboured long for us at the winepress.
  When he came to town
               upon a' ass's pony:
At the lit board
and in the dark-hour garden
       before the bishop's curia and
       within the Justiciar's mote-hall
       raised to the mock-purple
    and

at the *column*, . . . cap-tin.
          On the ste'lyard on the Hill
weighed against our man-geld
          between March and April
when bough begins to yield
          and West-wood springs new.
Such was his counting-house
          whose queen was in her silent parlour
on that same hill of dolour
          about the virid month of Averil
that the poet will call cruel.

As in *Piers Plowman*, paronomasia is of the essence in *Anathemata*. For the title itself has more than one meaning, and the subtitle 'teste David cum sibylla' signals a return to metaphysical religious wit. Here we begin with a play on *labour* and a phrase from a fifteenth-century book of Meditations: 'labouring all that long time in the winepress of his blessed Passion'—a figure that we have met before.[11] Then comes the entry into Jerusalem to the tune—one might almost say—of 'Yankee Doodle'; such 'outrageous' and ironic use of popular song here serving at the same time to characterize the particular narrator.[12] There follow spare allusions to the Last Supper, Gethsemane, the arraignment before Caiaphas (here, as in the medieval plays and miniatures, pictured as a bishop) and before Pilate, and the scourging at the Column. No names are mentioned; and what the steel-yard is we know only from that Good Friday hymn, the *Vexilla Regis*, to which Jones so persistently returns and which says of the *arbor*, the Cross:

> Statera facta est corporis
> Praedam tulitque tartari

—it is made a balance whereon the weight of human sin is offset by the Divine Body; a figure that Crashaw had enlarged on, and that is occasionally represented in 'Byzantine' paintings. And so, through a phrase of medieval song ('Bitwene Mersh and Averil, when spray biginneth to springe . . .') and a nursery rhyme, we come to the *Mater Dolorosa*.

The Passion sequence to which these lines serve as prelude is titled 'Sherthursdaye and Venus Day', a deliberate juxtaposing of a classical and a medieval name ('Hit was upon a Scere Thorsday that ure Loverd aros', begins the Middle English ballad on Judas). The narrative resumes at the point where an earlier synopsis had stopped:

> He that was her son
> is now her lover
> signed with the quest-sign
> at the down-rusher's ford.
> Bough-bearer, harrower
> torrent-drinker, *restitutor*.

The meaning of 'Jordan' is 'down-rusher'. The bough is the Cross, but suggests also the Golden Bough that is carried by Aeneas; its bearer will harrow hell. With the last line, compare Psalm 110:7: 'de torrente in via bibet'.

> Her Thursday's child
> come far to drink his Thor's Day cup:

'Thursday's child has far to go'; *Thor* suggests an outraged God.

> Grown in stature
>   he frees the waters.
> (Nine nights on the windy tree?
>   Himself to himself?

The allusion is to the verse in *Hávamál* cited above.[13]

> Who made the runes would read them—
>   wounded with *our* spears.)

The *Vision of a Rood* had been spelt out in runes—originally a secret system of signs—on the Ruthwell Cross; but here we have to do with the secret language of suffering, which the Creator will experience.

Soon we catch a phrase, by now familiar, from the Good Friday versicle *Quid ultra debui facere?*:

> What more should he do
>   that he hasn't done?
>   His dispositions made
> he would at once begin the action.

With this we move into military metaphor and symbol. The
Melchizedek of Gen. 14:18, priestly antetype of Christ, here
figures as he is sculptured at Rouen, where he presents to an
Abraham garbed as a knight Crusader the sacred meat and
wine:

> a rites-offerant
> of an immutable *disciplina.*
> Rex Pacis was his name
> gentle, was his station.

The Latin title renders the Rex Salem of Gen. 14 (in the
Vulgate), for *Salem* means Peace, and once more a children's
rhyme is weighted with new meaning. For a page or two such
significances pile up.[14] But of the stages and traditional
settings of the Passion this poet will say nothing till he comes
to the 'cry from the axile stipe' ('electa digno stipite', said
Fortunatus)

> at the dry node-height
> when the dark cloud brights the trembling lime-rock.
> (All known clouds distil showers.
> Is there no water in that dark cloud
> for the parched lime-face?
> What unknown cloud then, is this?)

> As the bleat of the spent stag
> toward the river-course
> he, the *fons* head,
> pleading, *ad fontes*
> his desiderate cry:
> SITIO.

Here the fountain of living waters (John 7:38) is paradoxi-
cally identified with the lime-rock of Calvary (Matt. 27:51)
and with the deer that yearns for those waters: 'quemad-
modum desiderat cervus ad fontes aquarum' (Ps. 42:1; the
referent of the simile must not be overlooked: 'ita desiderat
anima mea ad te, deus'). And SITIO is to be heard as the
priest intones it on Good Friday, to no fewer than six notes,
GGAGFF. Yet in no sense is this note held for long. Soon
we catch the rhythm of another children's rhyme, ingeni-
ously misapplied:

> What will the naiads
> do now, poor things

(a hint here of implications like those of 'From haunted spring ... the parting Genius is with sighing sent', in Milton's Nativity Ode).

The third day-relief arrives, and brings a glimpse of Roman Palestine, with Pilate at sleep after tiffin under a mosquito net—'They sting like death at afternoon': a seemingly casual phrase that perhaps glances at a title of Hemingway's, and certainly serves to recall to us death's doings that afternoon on what the soldiery call Skull Hill.

> The mated corbie
> with his neb
> forcipate, incarnadined—
> prods at the dreaming *arbor*
> ornated *regis purpura*
> as his kind, should.

Calvary, as a battlefield, is fit place for the birds of prey that tear at the corpses in Old English heroic verse.[15]

David Jones speaks more than once of the dreaming *arbor* and the dreaming bough. The phrase carries with it all the associations attaching to the tree dreamed of by the Old English poet—yet also presents the Rood as passive, transfixed. In much the same manner later lines describe it as *mortised*, made into a *deadly* cross; *dry-stiped*, as hewn from its *stipes* or stock; *infelix*, because of its burden; *effluxed*, because moist with blood and water; yet also *ornata regis purpura* and *fulgida*—phrases from the *Vexilla Regis* still sung in Jones's time on Good Friday after the cross was kissed and returned to the altar, and as the chalice containing the host was brought back from the altar of repose. And it is with the Good Friday Mass of the Presanctified that *Anathemata* ends:

> What did he do other
> recumbent at the garnished supper?
> What did he do yet other
> riding the Axile Tree?

Christ rides the Rood in a medieval verse cited earlier in this book.[16] But the ultimate phrase is indubitably David Jones's own; suggested, clearly, by 'axle-tree', a typically English adaptation of a Norse term for the beam on which wheels

revolve; but recalling also the *eaxle-gespann* (intersection) of
the Old English *Vision*, whilst at the same time embracing
the sense of the Latin *axis*, as Shakespeare does in

> strong as the axletree
> On which heaven rides
> (*Troilus and Cressida*, i. iii. 66–7)

—for this is the Cross that stretches from earth to heaven,
the axial beam round which all things move: 'Stat crux dum
volvitur orbis'.

To annotate *Anathemata* is to risk suggesting that the
poem is weighted with erudition. Certainly Jones took gladly
what scholars could give him,[17] but his learning was patchy
and subjective, and he candidly admits that his memory was
sometimes at fault. Essentially he was an artist-craftsman,
having some affinities with Eric Gill, but as many with
Joyce. His lines are richly allusive, but the allusions are
never private, there is no application of the Divine sufferings
to the individual soul either in the Meditatives' or the
Methodists' fashion. The name of Jesus and the term 'cross'
never appear, though the LOGOS, the incarnate word,
hovers over all; before the Passion Jones presents the
Nativity. The Latin liturgy that provides so much of the pith
and sinew of the poems is a public, corporate act, and
Anathemata, for all its seeming abstruseness, is a public
poem. Ironically, this resounding affirmation of the oneness
of Christian culture by a master of the vernacular appeared
just as the said liturgy was about to be dismantled.

The legion guarding the *limes* kept its hold on David
Jones's imagination. In *The Tribune's Visitation* the tribune
gradually moves beyond the limits of his own idiom to share
the perceptions of the centurion on Skull Hill who said:
'Truly this was a just man, this was the Son of God.' And in
the fragmentary *Fatigue* we hear the tread of the Procurator
of Judaea's night-relief ('Pick 'em up in front') as they march
to provide the *speculatores* (or 'Special Branch') with tamper
and tackle, the four hooks of Danubian iron, the tall reed
from upstream reaches, the seaspurge from tidal Syrtis, the
small crock of permitted dope, and the other *impedimenta* of
military executioners. Thus the whole Roman world (and

the Romano-British world) is invoked and involved. A line
of fourteenth-century Welsh turns into 'Quis est vir qui
habet coronam?', reflecting Isaiah's 'Quis est iste qui venit
de Edom?', just as a later line puts a phrase from Aeneid II
into the setting of a Sunday-school hymn:

> *squalentem barbam*
> without the circuit wall
> of his own *patria*.

The tribune sees his men standing at noon under the
pitiless sun, 'where your scorching back-plates rivet' and
where the swarming flies pattern black

> the thirsting Yggdrasill
> *In ara crucis torridum . . .*

As in the Old English poet's *Vision*, the Tree, here named
after the ash of Norse mythology that dripped hydromel,
shares the sufferings of its parched burden. The torrid heat
makes an altar of the Cross (*ara crucis* is a phrase from an
early hymn) on which the body of Christ is baked into life-
giving bread—another figure found in medieval verse.[18]
Thus once again the Crucifixion suggests, fulfils, the promise of the Eucharist. The dawn of Good Friday breaks in 'the
red-dyed sky-drape from over Bosra way': unconscious of
the scriptural significance of his language, the Roman
sergeant points north-east towards Bosra—where a great
frontier fortress had yet to be built.

Again there is no depiction of the suffering felon, the *vir
dolorum*. There is no place for it in the military routine. Yet
in one sense, and a very profound sense, the whole of David
Jones's work is devoted to that theme. Out in the dark of No
Man's Land, entangled in the wire, Private Shenkin ('Pick
'em up Shenkin') hears the half-cries of his mates who gasp
their own *Sitio* as they call on Bella, or Ned, or God the
Father, because with him there is neither wounding nor
unwounding; on the Lamb, because he was slain; on the Son
of Man, because he could not carry the cross-beam of his
stauros; on the Son of Mary, because like Peredur he left his
mother, to go for a soldier: for 'he would be a *miles* too'.

Thus in the *Visitation*, as in Jones's reading of *The Ancient*

Mariner, we come ultimately to a sense of the whole argosy of Mankind, for whom the voyaging of the Redeemer is pleaded in the Mass.[19]

With *Anathemata* and the related pieces, we are drawn beyond consideration of literary genres, even as we are drawn beyond theological formulas. We are conscious, not of the theology of liberation, but of the liberation of theology—from academic patterns and worn stereotypes, and vain repetitions. That 'He bore our sins on his own body on the tree' becomes more than a credal affirmation. We apprehend it afresh in the light of two thousand years of human suffering. The deepening and revivifying of Christian belief is not always achieved by theologians or philosophers. It is sometimes entrusted to poets: to a Dante, a Langland, a David Jones.

NOTES

CHAPTER I.

1. The most recent edition is by Michael Swanton (1970). To the bibliography in *CBEL* i. 275 should now be added B. K. Braswell, *Medieval Studies*, xli (1978). Miss Woolf's account (*Medium Ævum*, xxvii) perhaps overemphasizes the uniqueness of certain elements whilst not taking account of docetic elements in Apocrypha.

2. Cf. the achievement of the Romanesque *Volto Santo* in presenting the Two Natures in one image in contrast to separate representations of the cross-bearing Christ in the lower register, the King of Glory in the upper. See E. H. Kantorowicz, *The King's Two Bodies* (1958), p. 61 and n. 42.

3. For the complete riddle see *Sweet's Anglo-Saxon Reader*, rev. D. Whitelock (1967), p. 172. For the Cross as the clue to Riddle 53, see F. H. Whitman, *Medium Ævum*, xlvi (1977), 1–11.

4. Reproduced in G. Schiller, *The Iconography of Christian Art* (1968, 1972), Pl. 238.

5. Cynewulf seems to have such an emblem (and perhaps also our poem) in mind when he expands the description of the *sigores tacn* in the *Acta Sancti Cyriaci* ('vidit signum crucis Christi ex lumine claro constitutum . . .') into

> geseah he frætwum beorht
> wliti wuldres treo ofer wolcna hrof
> golde ge[g]lenged; gimmas lixtan.
>
> (*Elene*, 88–90; cf. 1224–6)

With *wuldres treo*, compare *wuldres beam*, l. 217, *Vision*, l. 97.

The association of the Constantine story with the Invention of the True Cross by Helena, the basis of Evelyn Waugh's novel of that name, is effectively illustrated in the Romanesque Stavelot Triptych, now in the Pierpont Morgan Library, New York. One door of this depicts the vision (with an angel pointing to a cross in a circular firmament), the victory, and the emperor's baptism. The other shows the Invention, and the dead man being raised to life by the *lignum vitae*. The gem-decorated centre of the triptych originally concealed a fragment of the True Cross. For photographs and discussion, see *Cahiers de civilisation médiévale*, 82 (1978), 105–20. This and similar works were probably prompted by the Second Crusade (1167). Veneration of 'the blessed wood on which God was stretched' is expressed in the early Pseudo-Sibylline Oracles, viii. 217 ff.: see H. O. Taylor, *The Classical Heritage of the Middle Ages*, 4th edn. (1957), pp. 251–3.

6. D. Rock, *The Church of our Fathers*, ed. Hart and Frere (1905), i. 250, 240.

7. See *Sweet's Anglo-Saxon Reader in Prose and Verse*, rev. D. Whitelock (1967), p. 78.

8. Carleton Brown, *Religious Lyrics of the XIVC*, 2nd edn., rev. G. V. Smithers (1952), No. 40. On *Crux fidelis* see J. Szövérffy, *Traditio*, xxii (1966), 1–41.

9. Cf. the *Vitis Mystica* of St. Bernard; and see p. 165 below. Fortunatus' emphasis on brightness was doubtless a specific allusion to the splendour of the reliquary that contained a fragment of the True Cross. The brightness was later given material form in the small crosses studded with gems that were made from the eighth century onwards, like that of Desiderius now in the Museum at Brescia.

10. *Catena Aurea* on Matt. 28:2.

11. Certainly later devotional verse uses this motif liberally, as in the *Corona Beatae Marie*:

> Ploret ignis, fleat terra,
> Planget aether, aqua mera
>   Grandi cum absinthio.
> Caelum omne lamentetur
> Morte Jesu, nulla detur
>   fletui remissio.
> Ploret omnis res creata.
>
> (Dreves, *Analecta Hymnica*, XXVI)

(Let fire lament, earth weep, air shall grieve, and the pure water with strong wormwood. Let the whole heaven bewail the death of Jesus, no respite be given to weeping. Let every created thing lament.)

The Latin poet is following the prescriptions of Geoffrey de Vinsauf, who in his passage on the Passion (*Poetria Nova*, 1390 ff.) depicts Nature as suffering because its Lord suffers: a figure that he calls *conformatio*, and that Milton uses to depict the consequences of the Fall:

> Earth felt the wound, and Nature from her seat
> Sighing through all her Works gave signs of woe
> That all was lost.
>
> (*Paradise Lost*, ix. 782–4)

12. A. S. Walpole (ed.), *Early Latin Hymns* (Cambridge, 1922), No. 35.

13. See *Bulletin of the Metropolitan Museum of Art*, June 1964.

14. The native verb *stigan* (*gestah*, l. 44) became almost mandatory in this context and is applied as late as the fifteenth century to Christ mounting the ladder: 'Oure Lord was compelled to steyen up on this laddre' (unpublished manuscript of Nicholas Love, *Meditations on the Life of Christ*; cf. edn. cited in n. 26 to Ch. II, p. 239). A fifteenth-century Scots poem will invoke 'the pasche lamb that on the croce did clym' (*Devotional Pieces in Verse and Prose from MS Arundel 285 and MS Harleian 6919*, ed. J. A. W. Bennett, Scottish Text Society, 3rd ser. xxiii (Edinburgh, 1955), p. 274. Cf. *Three Middle English Sermons from the Worcester Chapter MS F.10*, ed. D. M. Grisdale (Leeds, 1939), p. 27: 'Crist ... stied up o the cros'.

15. An eleventh-century prayer said in the thirteenth century by English nuns kneeling before a crucifix incorporated elements from Fortunatus as well as from the *Passio* of St. Andrew, the five invocations being in honour of the five wounds:

'Adoramus te Christe et benedicemus tibi quia per sanctam crucem redemisti mundum. Tuam crucem adoramus, domine, tuam gloriosam recolimus passionem. Miserere nostri qui passus est pro nobis. Salve crux, sancta arbor digna, cuius robor preciosum mundi tulit talentum. Salve crux, que in corpore Christi dedicata es et ex membris eius *tanquam margaritis ornata.*

> O crux, lignum triumphale,
> mundi vera salus, vale,
> inter ligna nulla tale
> fronde, flore, germine.
> Medicina Christiana
> salva sanas, egras sana.
> Quod non valet vis humana
> sit in tuo nomine' (etc.).

(We adore thee, Christ, and bless thee because by the holy Cross thou hast redeemed the world. We adore thy Cross, O Lord, we commemorate thy glorious passion. Have mercy on us, thou who didst suffer for us. Hail, holy Cross, worthy tree, whose precious timber bore the world's ransom. Hail, O Cross dedicated to the body of Christ and adorned with his limbs as with pearls. O Cross, triumphant wood, true salvation of the world, precious among trees in leaf and flowers and fruit, medicine of Christians, save the sound and heal the sick. May what human power fails to do be done in thy name.)

See M. B. Salu (ed.), *Ancrene Wisse*, pp. 194–5, and Dom A. Wilmart, *Ephemerides Liturgicae*, xlvi (1932), 22–65. There are evidently close likenesses with exercises in two eleventh-century Roman psalters that later gave way to 'The Hours of the Cross'. For the prayers and ceremonies associated with the Veneration of the Cross in the late Anglo-Saxon period, see B. Raw, 'Prayers and Devotions in *Ancrene Wisse*', in *Chaucer and Middle English Studies in Honour of R. H. Robbins*, ed. B. Rowland (1974), p. 265 and nn. 30, 32, 55.

16. It is only in John that Christ carries his own cross, 'like a conqueror the symbol of victory', as Chrysostom says. This presentation survived in art till late in the Middle Ages: see G. McN. Rushforth, *Medieval Christian Imagery as illustrated by the painted windows of Great Malvern Priory Church* (Oxford, 1936), p. 71 and notes. But the pseudo-Bonaventuran *Meditationes* (see p. 34 below) were to popularize the different version of the incident given in the Synoptic Gospels.

The *titulus* ('Rex glorie' in the Crucifixion scene by the St. Francis Master in the National Gallery derives from Ps. 24:7.

17. The equivalence of *spectaculum* and *wæfersyne* perhaps explains why in the Paris Psalter Ps. 69:11 ('factus sum illis parabolis'), *parabolis* is rendered by *wæfersyne* rather than by *bispel*, the Anglo-Saxon term for 'proverb' found in other versions. Likewise, the version of Ps. 140:5 in the

same Psalter perhaps explains the difficult word *inwidhlemmas* (*Vision*, l. 47; usually glossed 'words of malice'): in 'absconderunt superbi laqueos mihi', *laqueos* is rendered *inwitgyren*, a compound of the same order: so *hlemmas* may have the sense of 'strokes' rather than 'wounds'. Similarly, *in lacrimis* (Ps. 80:5) is rendered in this Psalter as *deorcum tearum*, where *deorc* represents adjectives equivalent to 'bitter', 'hostile' in other versions. C. S. Lewis long ago noticed the association of pain and blackness (*The Allegory of Love* (1936), p. 44).

18. R. H. Connolly, *Latin Hymns*, p. 200.

19. *The Sunday Sermons of the Great Fathers*, ed. M. F. Toal (1958), ii. 236: a sermon for Easter Sunday, which duly cites Phil. 2.

20. Ibid. ii. 240.

21. Gen. 49:3. Cf. *Christ and Satan*, 508–9:

> þa me on beame beornas sticedon,
> garum on galgan.

(There men pierced me on the tree, with spears on the gallows.) Even if one interprets l. 62 as a metaphorical description of the grief of the Rood, not the thrust of the spear (cf. *biteran stræle*, *Beowulf*, 1746), it must be read in the light of such texts as 'sagittae tuae infixae sunt mihi' (Ps. 38:2), which for St. Augustine refers to the pains and punishment we must suffer in this life.

22. *The Sunday Sermons of the Great Fathers*, ii. 236.

23. Carleton Brown, *Religious Lyrics of the XVC* (1939), No. 111.

24. *Canterbury Tales*, B 451–62. The verses are quoted below, p. 83. The association of the Lamb with the Cross is found in an early hymn, in which Christ is described as

> ductus hora tertia
> ad passionis hostiam
> crucis ferens suspendia
> ovem reduxit perditam

(led at the third hour to the sacrifice of the Passion, enduring the hanging on the Cross he brought back the lost sheep).

Here *hostia* implies that Christ is the Lamb (Walpole, *Early Latin Hymns*, No. 99).

CHAPTER II.

1. For these and other texts cited in this chapter see D. Gray, *Themes and Images in the Medieval English Religious Lyric* (1972), Ch. 7, and his *A Selection of Religious Lyrics* (Oxford, 1975), Nos. 21 and 20. The second quatrain was noted by T. Hearne (*Collectanea*, OHS vii. 127); other versions in Bodleian MSS Digby 45, fo. 25, and Rawl. C.317, 113ᵛ (Latin and English). The first line of the first quatrain should be read as 'Now that the sun goes down'.

2. See *Speculum*, lii (1978), 426.

3. See G. McN. Rushforth, *Medieval Christian Imagery*, pp. 192–5. G. Schiller, *The Iconography of Christian Art*, Vol. ii, gives several examples of

English representations of the Crucifixion. But the English developments have not yet been fully treated.

4. See F. Wormald, *PBA* xxx (1944), 4 ff. The MSS in question are BL Harl. 2904, fo. 30, Pierpont Morgan 709, fo. 61ᵛ (both gospels), BL Arundel 60, fo. 52ᵛ (a psalter from Winchester). In the Byzantine area the two figures had appeared on enamels in the late sixth century: K. Wessel, *Byzantine Enamels* (1967), p. 44. To these Otto Pächt would add the Pembroke Gospels.

5. A notice of the first Easter play at Canterbury dates from Lanfranc's time. In setting up the Rood Lanfranc may have been acting under some Continental influence: Ealdred of York gave a cross 'of German work' to Beverley, and the Abbot of Bury had the *Volto Santo* of Lucca reproduced to scale. See M. Gibson, *Lanfranc* (1977), pp. 64 f. and P. Brieger, *Medieval Studies* (Toronto), iv. 85.

6. But the OE passage represents Christ at the Last Judgement reciting his sufferings to Man who still hangs him on the Rood of his sins. It is probably to be related to Caesarius of Arles, *De Judicio Extremo* (*PL* 39. 220; Carleton Brown, *Religious Lyrics of the XIVC*, p. 203).

7. See the *St. Albans Psalter*, ed. O. Pächt *et al.* (1954), Pls. 129, 137, 70, 114. The objection that Gilbert Crispin put into the mouth of a Jew in his Disputation between a Christian and a Jew, who argues that Christians adore images, provides evidence of representations to be found in English churches in the early 12th c.:

'Ipsum etenim deus effigiatis aliquando miserum pendentem in patibulo, cruci clavis affixum (quod ipso etiam visu horrendum est), idque adoratis; et circa crucem effigiatis semi-puerum solo nescio unde exterritum et fugientem. lunam semi-puellam lugubrem, semumque lucis suae cornu occultantem. Aliquando autem deum effigiatis sublimi solio sedentem manuque porrecta signangem; et circa eum quasi magni dignitatis prestigio aquilem et hominem [symbols of the evangelists]. Has effigies Christiani exsculpunt, fabricant et depingunt unde possunt et ubi possunt, et adorant et colunt: quod lex a deo data omnimodo fieri vetat' (cit. J. A. Robinson, *Gilbert Crispin* (1911), p. 65).

8. The turning of the back probably has specific Messianic suggestion: cf. Isa. 1:6, and see p. 13 above.

9. Cf. p. 12 above.

10. For the Anglo-French text, see H. E. Allen, *Writings ascribed to Richard Rolle* (1927), p. 362; the Latin text, a *summa* of the teaching of Hugh of St. Victor, has been edited by Helen Forshaw (British Academy, 1973): see p. 93 of that edition for the English verses. For the later English translation, see C. Horstmann, *Yorkshire Writers* (1895–6), i. 218–61; cf. W. A. Pantin, *The English Church in the Fourteenth Century* (Cambridge, 1955), pp. 222–3.

11. The view that the *Meditationes Vitae Christi* incorporated a genuine Bonaventuran work, *Meditationes de Passione Christi*, has been challenged by Petrocchi (*Convivium*, 1952, 757–78), and more recently by Sr. M. Jordan Stallings in her valuable edition of the *Meditations* (Washington, DC, 1965). Both draw attention to the influence of Pseudo-Bede, *De*

Meditatione Passionis Christi per septem diei horas libellus. For the ardent and moving verse *Laudismus de Sancta Cruce*, ascribed to Bonaventure, see F. J. E. Raby, *Christian Latin Poetry* (1927), pp. 422–4.

12. See Grace Frank, *The Medieval French Drama* (1954), Chs. xiii, xvii, and *The Northern Passion*, ed. F. A. Foster, EETS OS 145 (1912), pp. 47–125. Miss Foster prints the relevant parts of the French text (pp. 126–76). It appears to have influenced the account of the Passion in *Cursor Mundi*.

13. *The Wohunge of Ure Lauerd*, ed. M. Thompson, EETS 241 (1958), p. 33, ll. 502–7.

14. On the late 12th-c. Bury Cross (see p. 79), as in the St. Swithun's Psalter of 1170, the eyes of the BVM are shaped to emphasize her sorrow.

15. See Carleton Brown, *English Lyrics of the XIIIC* (1932), pp. 8–10, for text and partial ME version; and R. Woolf, *The English Religious Lyric in the Middle Ages* (Oxford, 1968), p. 244. For a later prose version of the *Stabat Mater*, see *Devotional Pieces in Verse and Prose*, ed. Bennett, p. 287; and for a Latin antecedent attributed to Augustine see Ludolphus de Saxonia, *Vita Jesu Christi*, t. iv (edn. of 1878), Pars Secunda, Ch. lxiv. 10.

16. H. E. Allen, *English Writings of Richard Rolle* (1931), p. 67.

17. *Religious Lyrics of the XIVC*, No. 2B. In another version Christ is described as 'My sweet lemman'—a set phrase of English love-song.

18. See *The Book of Margery Kempe*, ed. S. B. Meech, EETS OS 212 (1940), p. 291.

19. *Religious Lyrics of the XIVC*, No. 69.

20. Ibid., No. 91.

21. Ed. cit., p. 161.

22. Ed. G. Holmstedt, EETS OS 182 (1929), p. 214.

23. For a meditative work ascribed to him with a possible Anglo-Norman base, see M. Morgan, *Medium Ævum*, xxii (1953), 94–5. Such works later found favour with the Bridgettines (see p. 59 below): two of the MSS described by Miss Morgan are of Carthusian provenance.

24. See *The Holkham Bible Picture Book*, ed. W. O. Hassall (1954). The accompanying text is mainly Anglo-French; possibly it was intended for merchants or rich tradesmen.

25. Julian of Norwich, *A Book of Showings*, ed. E. Colledge and J. Walsh (Toronto, 1978), pp. 311–12, 324–5. Cf. the exposition (highly rhetorical) of the Parable of the Servant in Ch. 51: the 'kirtle' of Christ's humanity is ragged and rent by the rods and the scourges, the thorns and the nails, the drawing and the dragging; the flesh rent from the headpan dries again, clinging to the bone; there is wallowing and writhing, groaning and moaning. Julian's imagery perhaps owes something to an early version of the 'XV Oes' (see p. 136) which were sometimes attributed to St. Bridget and so likely to be known to Julian. Cf. (e.g.) in the Scots version of the Oes:

> And as a fagit that is dry
> Off mir, thow hang on rude anerly.

26. *The Mirrour of the Blessed Lyf of Jesu Christ : a translation of the Latin Work entitled 'Meditationes Vitae Christi'*, ed. L. F. Powell (Oxford, 1908), p. 256.

27. See for example, *Christi Leiden in einer Vision geschaut*, a 14th-c. text ed. F. P. Pickering (1952); the non-scriptural details probably have literary origins: cf. review by J. K. Bostock, *Medium Ævum*, xxiii (1954), 130.

28. The enumeration of the tools of torture led to the instruments of the Passion becoming a popular theme in art; they are not to be construed (as they were by E. W. Tristram) as symbols of a 'Christ of the Trades'. For their representation as heraldic arms (reflecting 15th-c. heraldic preoccupations), see Rushforth, *Medieval Christian Imagery*, pp. 171 f. For *Arma Christi* rolls in verse, see R. H. Robbins, *Modern Language Review*, xxxiv (1939), 415–21; *Neuphilologische Mitteilungen*, lxx. 98, and *Modern Philology*, lxviii. 37. Such rolls were heraldically appropriate when Christ figures as a knight.

29. See Pl. 1 in Woolf, *English Religious Lyric* and her discussion of the Five Wounds as linked with the Capital Sins (p. 225). The hero of *Sir Gawain and the Green Knight* is very much a man of his time in placing 'alle his afyaunce upon folde in the fyve woundez / That Cryst kaght on the croys' (642–3).

30. See *Devotional Pieces in Verse and Prose*, pp. xi, 240, 260. The *Vitis Mystica* (attributed to St. Bernard) likewise glosses *Sitio* as signifying 'immensitatem nobis ardentissime caritatis', but admits a literal interpretation also: 'siccatus sanguinis effusione, ossa habuit sicut cremiis arefacta'; similar phrases are found in Nicholas Love.

31. Cf. also Carleton Brown, *Religious Lyrics of the XIVC*, No. 96; and John Audelay, *Poems*, No. 7.

32. The insertion occupies ll. 1757–64 of the so-called *Northern Passion* (see n. 12 above). The passage in Lam. 1:12 was first connected with the Passion in the 9th c., and later applied by St. Bernard, *Meditatio in Passionem: Opera*, ed. Mabillon, ii. 503 (cf. i. 888).

33. And not least the sin of swearing. Thus gamesters, by their oaths,

> Oure blessed lordes body they totere,
> Hem thoghte that Jewes rente hym noght ynogh . . .
>
> (*CT* C 474–5)

Cf. *Religious Lyrics of the XIVC*, No. 95, ll. 145 ff.

34. *Gemma Ecclesiastica* (Rolls Series), i. 43. A poem in BL MS Harl. 2253 urges men to cry to 'sweet Jesus on the rood, "Cryst, thyn ore".' In the very next poem (on 'derne' (secret) love, parallel in its pattern) the lover falls at his mistress's feet, crying 'ledy, thyn ore'. *English Lyrics of the XIIIC*, Nos. 90, 91.

35. See p. 153 below.

36. It can conveniently be read in the humbler Temple Classics edition.

37. Cf. Margery Kempe's report of a Palm Sunday sermon: 'Our Lord Jesu languoreth for love'; *William of Palerne*: 'He has languored for your love a ful long while' (cit. *OED*); and Chaucer, *Merchant's Tale*, 673 (CCC MS). The version of the poem cited is that printed in the *Oxford Book of English Verse*.

38. Ludolf of Saxony describes it as a garment worn by fools, to mark

them out. Cf. Amphilochius' sermon for Easter Saturday in *The Sunday Sermons of the Great Fathers*, ii. 192.

39. Cf. Ludolf: 'de juncis spinosis et aculeatis valde angulos habentes; alii dicunt illos *juncos marinos* fuisse'. Nothing in the Gospels suggests that the crown of thorns played the part in physical torture that later writers assign to it.

40. *Moralia*, XXXIII. ix.

41. See R. M. Dawkins, *Medium Ævum*, xvii (1948), 34. For a different reading of the chirograph as a testament or charter, see Brown, *Religious Lyrics of the XIVC*, No. 16. 23: 'Vor love the chartre wrot, / the enke orn [ink ran] of hys wounde'. See also Walpole, *Early Latin Hymns*, No. 60. 15 f., No. 99. 12, and note Paulin. Aquil. vi. 14: 'chirographum/mortis cruore diluit rosifluo' (cit. Walpole), and Hoveden, *Latin Poems*, ed. Raby (Surtees Soc,), p. 150: 'scribit amoris literas'. This last image is first found in vernacular form in the early *Wohunge of Ure Lauerd* (283): *love-letter*, with secular reference, is not found before the 16th c. A 15th-c. sermon alters it to a letter giving Christ his credentials as 'ambassador': 'gaily written with divers letters: for five vowels in this letter were Christ's five wounds, and the other wounds were the consonants': *Three ME Sermons*, ed. Grisdale, p. 77.

The figure derives in part from Col. 2, in part, improbable as it may seem, from an application (found in the *Concordances* of St. Antony of Padua, ed. J. M. Neale (1867), p. 9) of Gal. 6:11: 'Ye see how large a letter I have written unto you with mine own hand.'

42. *English Lyrics of the XIIIC*, No. 69.

43. Pallor signifying that the blood was drained away. The body on the other hand is often 'wan and blo', livid, as in 'Woefully Arrayed' (see p. 58). *Blo* is a Norse adoption that fits the requirement of simple and short words for such passages.

44. *Religious Lyrics of the XIVC*, No. 77; cf. No. 47. 9.

45. See n. 8 to Ch. I.

46. *English Lyrics of the XIIIC*, No. 64. The smith of l. 2 is an apocryphal figure who in the mystery plays is bidden to make special nails for the Crucifixion. Even in a devout prayer there is room for a reference to them:

> Write how, whan the cros was forth broght
> And the nayll of iren wroght
> How thou began to chever and quake
> —Thyn hert was woo thogh thou ne spake.
> (*Religious Lyrics of the XIVC*, No. 91, 33–6)

The 'tree' was traditionally fifteen feet high.

47. *A Selection of Religious Lyrics*, No. 30.

48. *Yorkshire Writers*, ed. Horstmann, i. 235.

49. *English Writings of Richard Rolle*, p. 21.

50. *Religious Lyrics of the XIVC*, No. 82. The Worcester Sermons cited above (Ch. I, n. 14), being preached in Lent, repeatedly advert to the Passion, and show Bernardine and Bonaventuran emphases: c.g., 'The Jews took the cross and squatten it so often into the ground till it could

stand up of itself . . . the bones rattled together and all the flesh cankered' (p. 11). Mary ('says Bernard') asks to die with her son, and laments the loss of the joy she had 'when I lulled thee in thy cradle and hoclid thee on my knee' (p. 12). Christ addresses her as 'Woman', for if he had said 'Mother', her heart would have broken. 'Behold', he says, 'how I am forbuffeted and forbeaten, how all the veins and sinews in my body be all to-crais and all to-broken' (p. 47). A dialogue (in which Christ refers to John as 'my own dear brother') purports to derive from St. Bernard. But later the preacher cites the (lost) *Meditaciones* of a William of Hexham for the incident on the road to Calvary when children and people of Jerusalem cast 'podayle [muddy water] and dirt' at Christ's head, which Mary wiped away (p. 68). We have Wycliffite evidence that presentations of the sufferings in mystery plays 'moved men to compassion and devotion' and to bitter tears: see *English Wycliffite Writings*, ed. A. Hudson (1978), p. 100.

51. *Meditations on the Supper of our Lord*, ed. J. M. Cowper, EETS OS 60 (1875), ll. 691–3; 567–8; the rare verb *punge* is used by Rolle in a similar context: 'buffetynge and *pungynge* with the thornes' (*Psalter*, xxi. 5). There is nothing in style or versification to justify the attribution to Mannyng. Six other renderings, in verse or prose, were made of this section of the *Meditationes* in the fourteenth century.

52. Quotations are from Powell's edition (see n. 26), pp. 228–50. The *Mirrour* was printed twice by Caxton and no less than six times by his successors.

53. For editions of Ludolf's *Vita*, ancient and modern, see E. Salter, *Medium Ævum*, xxxiii (1964), 26 ff. About 1500 John Fewterer, Confessor-General of Syon Monastery (Bridgettine), based his *Myrrour or Glasse of Christes Passioun* loosely on Ludolf: another English version of the Passion section derives from a French translation. Carthusians were evidently largely responsible for the circulation of the *Vita*.

54. *A Selection of Religious Lyrics*, No. 28.

55. R. Woolf, *English Religious Lyric*, p. 198; cf. p. 408.

56. *A Selection of Religious Lyrics*, No. 27. An unpublished version on a flyleaf in MS Bodl. Lyell 24 begins:

> Woefully araydc
> The sonne of a mayde
> Beholde manne and se
> with tresoun betrayede
> And onne the [tre?] splayde
> For the love of the.

57. *The Bridgettine Breviary of Syon Abbey* (Henry Bradshaw Soc., 1969). Lydgate takes older motifs to extremes. In his *Pilgrimage of the Soul* he calls on 'Moon, stars and firmament' to 'weep and cry as loud as ever ye may', and Mary appeals to *Sin*: 'Is ther in the no drope of kindenes?'

58. Indicative of this vogue is the addition in a manuscript of the *Missa Quinque Vulnera* in a Hamburg Missal (1509), now in the Old Library, Magdalene College, Cambridge, though the devotion itself was already

well estabished by the time *Ancrene Wisse* came to be written. The anti-parodic *Pange Lingua Magdalenae* (*Analecta Hymnica*, L. 532: cf. *CHM* iv (1961), 41) is another sign of a shift in emphasis.

59. *Yorkshire Writers*, ii. 273, 275. So too Rolle prays, 'Grant me grace to judge myself wisely.' For him the gall offered on the Cross symbolizes 'unkind' disobedience to the Divine will: ibid. i. 92, 113, 234.

60. *Religious Lyrics of the XIVC*, No. 95. 73–80.

CHAPTER III.

(The theme of Christ the lover-knight has been discussed by several scholars, notably the late Rosemary Woolf (*Review of English Studies*, NS xiii (1962), 1–16), who gives useful references. My approach is somewhat different from hers and as far as possible I have refrained from reproducing her long quotations.)

1. Job 7:1. It is pertinent to our theme that Job's history was read as prefiguring the Passion.

2. The sculpture, on the inner west wall of Rheims (mid 13th-c.), is reproduced in Joan Evans, *Costume in Medieval France* (1952), Pl. 96. The identification has been questioned; but an earlier Mosan plaque (reproduced in *Cahiers de civilisation médiévale*, 82 (1978), Fig. 16) already shows Abraham in armour.

3. For the Latin text, see B. Hauréau, *Notices et extraits de quelques mss. latins de la Bibl. Nat.* iv (1892), 26–6. Hauréau also prints the following late 13th-c. version by a Dominican, Guy d'Évreux:

'Quaedam domicella erat, quae fuit dives et de magno genere, scilicet natura humana, vel fidelis anima, quia domina super omnem creaturam inferiorem, sed a quodam potente per violentiam et injuriam exheredata, scilicet diabolo, et ita depauperata quod non inveniebat in terra aliquod auxilium, quia purus homo satisfacere non valebat. Quod audiens filius cujusdam magni regis, scilicet filius Dei Patris, desponsavit eam, scilicet quando sumpsit carnem, et pugnavit cum illo potente, scilicet hodierna die, et restituit hereditatem, quia per passionem Christi redditur via coeli. Sed tamen in bello occisus est ex vulneribus assumptis. Sed quid fecit illa? Accepit arma et posuit in camera sua, et quotiescumque videbat ea flebat; et, dum rogaretur quod se maritaret, semper currebat ad illa arma et, cum videbat ea, tantum dolebat in corde suo quod nullo modo concedere volebat. Non enim dederat oblivioni amicum suum. Etiam sic debet homo accipere cor et recolere passionem Christi, et, si rogatur 'de marier', id est tentatur de peccato, debet recurrere ad arma amici sui, scilicet Christi, et tunc non peccaret. Sed scitis quod est de quibusdam sicut de mulieribus Lombardiae, quae in morte maritorum se lacerant et in crastino se maritant.' (iv. 26–7).

Another 13th-c. version is in BN MS 16499:

'Fuit quaedam domicella fragilis et debilis, quae magnam terram jure hereditario a patre patris sui tenebat. Quidam magnus princeps et potens impugnabat eam valde graviter et auferebat totam hereditatem suam. Ipsa autem quaesivit consilium et auxilium ab amicis suis carnalibus, et nullus erat qui auderet, vellet vel sibi posset dare auxilium contra illum principem propter fortitudinem et potentiam principis; imo quilibet intendebat custodire res proprias. Illa domicella erat in angustia et cordis tristitia, quia nemo videt damnum quin doleat; nesciebat quid facere. Tandem venit quidam juvenis baccalarius qui dixit illi: 'Domicella, si velletis esse sponsa mea, et quod essem sponsus vester, ego vobis redderem totam terram vestram quietam et pugnarem contra illum principem fideliter et fortiter.' Ipsa consentit et eum desponsavit. Ipse autem contra principem tam pugnavit ut eum devicit et terram reddidit domicellae, scilicet sponsae suae. Illa tamen pugna tam fortis et crudelis fuit quod in illa mortuus fuit ille sponsus. Ipsa autem domicella accepit arma ejus et vestes et posuit in camera propria, et quotidie respiciens ea saturabat de lacrymis. Multi alii quaerebant eam in uxorem et ipsa semper respondebat quod libenter haberet consilium et breve. Ipsa intrabat cameram, et, respiciens arma sponsi sui qui ita fideliter pugnaverat pro se et mortuus fuerat et tam dilexerat eam, statim exibat de camera cum lacrymis et dicebat eis quod amore prioris sponsi sui nullum alium acciperet. Sic respondebat omnibus. Domicella ista est quaelibet fidelis anima; terra ejus, sive hereditas est terra viventium, coeleste regnum; princeps qui aufert ei terram istam est diabolus . . .; juvenis baccalarius fuit Christus.' (Hauréau, v. 152)

Yet another variant (hitherto unnoticed) is found in the *Moralitates* of the 14th-c. Dominican Robert Holcot:

'*De Filio Dei*. Moralitas IX. Narratur quod fuit quidam miles, qui fecit proclamare hastiludia, et ipse amore cuiusdam dominae hastiludiavit. Et quia hastiludia non sunt in noticiis propriis virtutis, qui debet hastiludiare, sed in noticia illius pro quo vel qua hastiludia committuntur, iste miles signavit se circumquaque literis aureis vel amoris. Ante militem scribebatur sic: Cor meum inclinatum est ad unam puellam pro cuius amore hodie bellum defendo. Post militem scribebatur ille versus: Amorem nostrum nullus fastidiat, quia profunda sauciat [sanat] si cor tangat. A dextris militis scribebatur sic: Verus amor nunquam quiescit, semper agit et non tepescit. A sinistris scribebatur illa sententia: Ubi amor est, ibi frequens cogitatio et desiderium si non possideatur illud quod amatur. Iste miles est Filius Dei' (etc.). The *moralitas* follows. (*Praelectiones* (1586), p. 717: Adams H 682.)

See also J. A. Herbert, *Catalogue of Romances in the British Museum*, iii (1910), 55, 192.
4. Hauréau, iv. 25–6.
5. *Religious Lyrics of the XIVC*, p. 94.
6. *Chronicle of Peter Langtoft* (Rolls Series, 47), 126.
7. Cit. Woolf, *RES* NS xiii. 7.
8. Cit. Woolf, *The English Religious Lyric in the Middle Ages*, p. 51.
9. S. Wenzel, *Verses in Sermons* (Cambridge, Mass., 1979): see pp. 45, 160–2.
10. See Woolf, *English Religious Lyric*, p. 46. For Bozon's shorter poem 'Coment le fizdeu fu arme en la croyz', see D. Legge, *Anglo-Norman Literature* (1963), p. 230.

11. For this poem and its cognates see D. Gray, *A Selection of Religious Lyrics*, Nos. 43 and 61. The latter version, which begins 'In a tabernacle of a toure / As I stode musynge on the mone', includes an address of the BVM to Man and to her son. Its opening lines suggest an 'anti-parody' of a secular situation, with a Venus-figure set in a 'tabernacle' (as in the *Knight's Tale* and the *Roman de la Rose*). *Amore langueo* is to be read on the edge of Fra Bartolomeo's painting of St. Catherine of Siena.

12. The phrases are from a poem printed by Horstmann, *Yorkshire Writers*, ii. 15. The last line of the stanza runs: 'thi syde al open to luf-schewinge'. Cf. *Revelations* of Julian of Norwich: 'our lord looked into his side and said this word: 'Lo how I loved thee . . .' (Ch. 13, short text). See further p. 43 above.

13. Cf. pp. 50–1 above. The motifs recur in the Cornish *Ordinalia*; and cf. R. Morris (ed.), *Legends of the Holy Rood*, EETS OS 46 (1871), p. 195.

14. See *RES* NS xiii. 12.

15. *Religious Lyrics of the XIVC*, No. 125, p. 223.

16. *English Lyrics of the XIIIC*, p. 86.

17. Horstmann, *Yorkshire Writers*, i. 426.

18. *The Mirrour of the Blessed Lyf of Jesu Christ* (see Ch. II, n. 26), p. 223. Ludolf of Saxony (see p. 55) gives Michael's words as: 'tua est virtus, tu potes contra mortem et infernum genus liberare humanum . . .' (iv. 18).

19. Lydgate, *Minor Poems I*, ed. H. N. MacCracken, EETS ES 107 (1911), p. 251. The poem is a compendium of chivalric and Passion imagery. Cf. ibid., p. 218: 'Al this was doon, O man, for love of the! / A standard splayed, thy lord slain in that fight'.

20. *The Book of Margery Kempe*, ed. S. B. Meech, p. 148. It is possible that Lydgate had in mind a crucifix rather than a *pietà*: cf. the quotation s.v. *pity* in *OED* from a will of 1489.

21. *A Selection of Religious Lyrics*, No. 40. The application to the Passion of OT texts characterizes medieval devotional verse; in the Moral Concordances of St. Antony there are 33 such references as against 7 to the NT.

22. *Piers Plowman*, B xix. 6–14. The unusual failure of alliteration in 12b is noteworthy: one MS reads *Cristes* for *Pieres*, but this is clearly inadmissible. For the *Arma Christi* see R. H. Robbins, *Modern Language Review*, xxxiv (1939), 415–21, and other references given by J. C. Hirsh, *Medium Ævum*, xlviii (1979), 64–5. John of Grimestone's verses, 'a scheld of red, a cros of grene', are accessible in *The Oxford Book of Medieval English Verse*, No. 270. For some representations, see BL MS Royal 6 E vi, fo. 15ᵛ, and A. Caiger-Smith, *English Medieval Mural Paintings* (Oxford, 1963), p. 58.

23. *PL* 26. 160; cf. Ludolf of Saxony, *Vita Christi*, ed. cit. iv. 103–4, and the following passage in MS Pembroke College, Cambridge, 72, fo. 62ᵛ: 'Quod titulus psalmarum p. notatur in fine ne corrumpas in tribus linguis: *malchus* judeorum, *basileus* exornatum, *rex confessorum* . . . lingua commemorat perfidiam judeorum.'

24. See *Anglo-Saxon England*, Vol. 2 (Cambridge, 1973), p. 11.

25. *Medium Ævum*, xxiii (1954), 13, 11. 353–4.
26. *Religious Lyrics of the XIVC*, p. 64. 'Baner' might seem to allude to Song of Songs 2:4 ('his banner over me was love', AV); but the Vulgate reading is very different.
27. *The Apocryphal New Testament*, ed. M. R. James (1926), p. 135. As Christ had claimed power to summon twelve legions of angels, Hell speaks in the same terms.
28. Cf. the application to Christ in the alliterative *Morte Arthure* (c. 1350) of the archaic alliterative term *renk* (warrior): Arthur promises to go on a crusade 'to revenge the renke that on the rode dyede' (3217). Similarly Christ is called 'a *child* that is mild and wlonc', i.e. a splendid warrior or youth of noble birth, 'and eke of grete munde' (guardianship, authority: a term found elsewhere only in Layamon): *English Lyrics of the XIIIC*, No. 54.
   Lydgate may have known a passage in Ludolf, *Vita Christi* (iv. 21), which has a similar figure to *sheltroun*. For his *Vexilla Regis* see his *Minor Poems I*, ed. MacCracken, No. 8, and Woolf, *English Religious Lyric*, pp. 205, 209.
29. *Religious Lyrics of the XIVC*, p. 22.
30. Ibid., p. 95.
31. *Three ME sermons*, ed. D. M. Grisdale, p. 49.
32. *Religious Lyrics of the XIVC*, No. 63. It continues:

> Elles wer thi deth idiht
> Yif mi fihting ne were.
> Sithen I am comen and have the broht
> A blisful bote of bale,
> Undo thin herte, tel me thi thouht,
> Thi sennes grete an smale.

We might expect 'Undo' to begin a plea to a lady from a wounded lover-knight; instead the following words suggest a preacher urging confession.
33. For the Latin antecedents of this passage, see W. F. Bryan and G. C. Dempster, *Sources and Analogues of Chaucer's Canterbury Tales* (1958), p. 668, and *Neuph. Mitt.* lxxix (1978), 126–7. Gavin Douglas will use the same phrase (possibly alluding to Augustine, *De Civitate Dei*, xxi. 14), in upbraiding the easy-going Christian, the 'caitive wicht' who has to be reminded what 'thy King Christ in battell / sufferit for the': 'Lyis thou at eis? Thy prince at bargane [in conflict] fell.' *Liber Eneydos*, xi, Prol. 190 ff.
34. R. L. Greene, *The Early English Carols* (1977), Nos. 269, 265. The Collect for Peace (taken from the medieval primer) in the Book of Common Prayer, in the response 'For there is none other that fighteth for us, but only thou, O God', transfers the figure of Christ fighting for mansoul to the Deity who will give victory in actual war.

CHAPTER IV.

1. Cf. the legal imagery of Prol. 133–5 and xviii. 335 ff.
2. Cf. *The Sermons of Thomas Brinton*, ed. Sister M. A. Devlin, 2 vols.

(London, 1954), i. 160. This sermon was probably preached on Passion Sunday, 1374. Langland might conceivably have heard it.

3. Cf. the prayer at the blessing of the Paschal Candle.

4. Cf. *Religious Lyrics of the XIVC*, No. 48:

> The ded he tholed in his manhede
>
> . . .
>
> He rayse ogayne thurgh his godhede.

(He suffered death in his human nature, but rose again in his divine.)

5. Cf. *Ancrene Riwle*, ed. Mabel Day, EETS 225 (1952), p. 49. Panofsky could find only one example of this cry on a *titulus* of the Crucifixion.

St. Catherine of Siena was equally insistent. In the words of her 15th-c. English translator: 'When he was lifted up on high, he was not departed from the earth as by that, for with the humanity he was knit verily and coupled.' She puts the following image into the mouth of God himself: 'Beholding of my goodness that ye might not otherwise be drawn, I sent him to be raised up on the tree of the cross. Thereof I made a ghostly anvil, whereon the Son of Man should be forged' (*Orcherd of Syon*, ed. Phyllis Hodgson and G. M. Liegey, EETS 258 (1966), p. 69).

6. *Sermons of Lancelot Andrewes*, ed. G. M. Story (1967), p. 154.

7. It must be added that the 'C' version of the poem, probably written not so many years later as earlier critics assumed, presents Langland's lines in significantly different form. Whether the following changes were made by a cautious scribe, or whether Langland himself felt it necessary to clarify his meaning or improve his alliteration, one cannot say.

(i) For 'and us synful yliche' (B v. 494), C reads 'oure soule and body lyche' (viii. 129); which represents the patristic gloss on *ymaginem et similitudinem nostram.*

(ii) The verse from Genesis that includes the Vulgate phrase is replaced by a less obviously apposite quotation from John 14, which inverts the order of vv. 9 and 11 and gives the *videt* of the Sistine and Clementine texts instead of the generally accepted *vidit.*

(iii) C introduces a qualifying 'as hit semed' (viii. 130).

(iv) C replaces 'for mannes sake' (496) by 'in forme of man', and omits the negative in the following line, and the whole of 498, so that 496–7 are represented by 'On a Fryday, in forme of man feledest oure sorwe', which perhaps reflects the wording and intent of Hebrews 4:15: 'For we have not an high priest which cannot be touched with the feeling of our infirmities; but was in all points tempted like as we are, yet without sin.'

8. Langland himself more than once returns to this verse in Genesis; e.g. at B x. 367: '[God] seith "slee nought that semblable is to myn owen liknesse . . ." ', and especially at ix. 31 ff.—a passage too long to quote, but worth perusal.

9. *De Sacrosancto Trinitate* 24 (*c.* 1165). Cf. H. A. Wolfson, *The Philosophy of the Church Fathers*, 3rd edn. (Cambridge, Mass., 1970), p. 423.

10. *De Fide Orth.* III. iii (*PG* 94. 993–6a), cit. Wolfson, p. 426.

11. For ease of reading one might place parentheses after *sorwe* (498) and *captivitatem*. The *Golden Legend*, curiously enough, makes no mention of the grief of creation; though in regard to the Last Judgement it says (glossing Luke 25): 'the sun is deprived of his light, as though he wept for the dying of men' (Temple Classics edn. of Caxton's translation, i. 12; cf. 20).

12. *Sunday Sermons*, ed. Toal, ii. 192.

13. Ludolf of Saxony quotes a fine passage from Chrysostom on this (ed. cit. iv. 119) and adds much of his own, as well as the story of Dionysius' sight of the 'eclipse' at Athens. In saying '*about* midday', Langland is following Luke 23:44 ('*fere* hora sexta').

14. Dom. III in Quadragesima: *Homilies of Ælfric*, ed. J. C. Pope, EETS 259 (1967), p. 274.

15. The C text, though it obscures the sequence, enlarges on the heraldry, speaking of *cognisance*, *cote-armour*, and *pensel*.

16. In the *Pore Caitiff* (ed. C. Horstmann, *Yorkshire Writers* (1896), ii. 421) the horse *caro* is saddled with *mansuetude*; and in a poem on 'Cristes throwunge' (passion) in MS Jesus College, Oxford, 29 it is said:

> Ne hedde he none robe, of fowe ne of gray
> Ne he nedde stede, ne none palefray,
> Ac rod uppe on asse, as ich eu segge may.

(Ed. R. Morris in *An Old English Miscellany*, EETS OS 49 (1872), pp. 37–57, ll. 66–8.)

17. *Liber armorum*, in *The Boke of St. Albans*, 1486, sig. a ii.

18. F. P. Pickering, *Literature and Art in the Middle Ages* (1970), Pl. 29a; cf. *Summa Theologica*, iii, q. 46, art. 1: Christ's suffering not from the necessity of compulsion but from that of the end proposed.

19. See *Chronicle of Peter Langtoft*, ed. T. Wright, Rolls Series 47 (1868), ii. 427–71.

20. See G. D. Squibb, *The High Court of Chivalry* (1959), pp. 1–2, and Anna Baldwin, *Medium Ævum*, l (1981). See also R. Jaques, 'Langland's Christ-Knight and the Liturgy', *Rev. de l'Univ. d'Ottawa*, xxvi (1967), 146, and R. Axton, *European Drama of the Early Middle Ages* (1974), pp. 166–7.

21. Psalm 22, which prophesies the Passion, and which dictated the medieval mode of viewing it, includes the verses: '. . . *dogs* have compassed me . . . they pierced my hands and my feet. . . . I may tell all my bones' (vv. 16–17).

22. The manuscripts, except for HM, read *recreant rennyng*; perhaps a fixed phrase that poet or scribe used automatically. But KD substitutes *remyng*, 'crying'.

23. HM *renegat* is weak; the word is not evidenced before Chaucer.

24. Ludolf of Saxony (ed. cit. iv. 122 ff.); cf. references there given.

25. *PL* 94. 61.

26. Cf. the figurative use in *Sir Gawain*, l. 1856: 'Hit were a juel for the jopardé that hym jugged were': alluding to the lady's belt—perhaps with the suggestion that it would do duty for a precious stone worn as a charm.

CHAPTER V.

1. *Surcoat* is a comparatively late adoption from Old French, no example being datable before 1300: see the romance of *Sir Degaré*, 791, and cf. *Sir Gawain and the Green Knight*, 62, and *Canterbury Tales*, A 617.
2. See *Gesta Romanorum*, ed. S. J. Herrtage, EETS ES 33 (1879), p. 23. All subsequent quotations are from this edition. The nursery tale of the Black Bull of Norroway includes a corrupt version of the story, in which a gallant young knight is to marry whoever washed his bloody shirt. A stranger-damsel pleads with him:

> Seven long years I served for thee,
> The glassy hill I clomb for thee,
> The bluidy shirt I wrang for thee
> And wilt thou no wauke and turn to me?
> (Robert Chambers, *Popular Rhymes of Scotland*, 1841, p. 98)

3. 'Perch' (peg) appears in a similar context in Chaucer's *Roman de la Rose*, l. 225.
4. For this carol, see R. L. Greene, *The Early English Carols*, No. 322. I assume that the carol was adapted to the circumstances that Professor Greene describes, not written for them.
5. The verses, in MS Bodl. Eng. poet. 65, pp. iv–v (*c.* 1630?), have not hitherto been printed.
6. The incident is described by Sir John Hackett in *I Was a Stranger*, an account of his escape after Arnhem, 1944.
7. The collection was first printed as a whole in *Devotional Pieces in Verse and Prose from MS Arundel 285 and MS Harleian 6919*, ed. J. A. W. Bennett, Scottish Text Society, 3rd ser. xxiii (Edinburgh, 1955). This edition appeared too late to be considered by Helen C. White in her excellent study, *The Tudor Books of Private Devotion* (Madison, 1951); the introduction should be read in the light of that work, and amplified from it. For the Northern associations of the manuscript, see ed. cit., introd., *passim*.
8. Lydgate, *Minor Poems I*, ed. H. N. MacCracken, p. 356. For *Vide quid pro te patior*, see Carleton Brown, *Religious Lyrics of the XIVC*, No. 70 and n.
9. See Greene, *The Early English Carols* (1935 edn.), No. 165, and J. Stevens, *Music and Poetry at the Early Tudor Court* (1961), p. 373. The poem is found in the Fairfax MS, which includes four other Passion poems of comparable quality.
10. Cf. Rolle: 'hanged on the rode-tre / The bricht angels brede'; and *Piers Plowman: The Prologue and Passus I–VII*, ed. J. A. W. Bennett (Oxford, 1972), p. 185.
11. I have deliberately excluded them from the present study, partly because V. A. Kolve has given them a whole chapter (Ch. viii) in *The Play Called Corpus Christi* (1966), marking the difference from liturgical drama, in which the Crucifixion rarely occurs. For a comparison of the York and Towneley Crucifixion, see C. Davidson, *Speculum*, l (1975), 270–83. For religious plays as Dunbar saw them, see Anna J. Mill,

Medieval Plays in Scotland (1937). He is thought to have written the *Droichis Part of the Play*, an Interlude preserved in the Asloan and Bannatyne MSS.

12. They would include the custom (alluded to by Herbert) of cleansing the house on Easter Day, extinguishing the fire, and strewing rushes and sweet flowers: 'ryght soo', says Mirk, 'ye schull clanse the howse of your soule . . .' (*Festial*, ed. T. Erbe, EETS ES 96 (1905), p. 129).

13. The piece is printed in full in *The Oxford Book of Christian Verse*, ed. David Cecil, No. 181.

14. The scriptural phrases were not made mandatory in the Mass till the sixteenth century. But similar expressions had long been part of the liturgy—for example, the prayer at the Elevation prescribed in *Ancrene Wisse* includes the following: 'The house of my soul is too narrow for thee to enter. Let it be enlarged by thee. It is in ruins. Repair it . . .' (*The Ancrene Riwle*, tr. M. B. Salu, 1955, p. 13).

15. See J. A. W. Bennett, in *Philological Essays Presented to Angus McIntosh* (Edinburgh, 1981), pp. 299–308.

16. Lentulus' *Epistula* survives in MS Cambridge Univ. Lib. Dd. 3.1.6 (ed. Fabricius, *Codex Apocryph. NT* i. 301). To him is attributed the belief that Christ never smiled, though in fact John of Salisbury records it a century or more earlier: see *Policraticus*, ed. C. C. J. Webb, i. 305n.

17. See *The Anglo-Saxon Benedictine Office*, ed. J. M. Ure (Edinburgh, 1957). For the ME version of *Speculum Ecclesie*, see C. Horstmann, *Yorkshire Writers*, i. 254–8, and pp. 51–2 above. The address to the reader at the beginning of each of the Arundel Hours ('in the first complyn think with compassioun', 'Walk [wake] of thi sleip, O man, at matyn hour', etc.) is found also in the English rhymed version of the *Meditationes*—for example, 'Now crystyn creature, tak good hede / And do thyn herte for pité to blede' (at evensong); 'Se, man, a sight of gret dolour' (*Meditations*, ed. J. M. Cowper, ll. 297, 901).

18. For other verse 'Hours of the Cross', see *Religious Lyrics of the XIVC*, Nos. 55 and 34, *Religious Lyrics of the XVC*, No. 93. In No. 34, l. 28, 'His mytte, his strengthe, lotede [lay hidden] in heighe holi thout', is yet another allusion to *latens deitas* (see p. 101). Bishop Brinton allocates the episodes to the hours of the day, beginning at midnight and proceeding through *mane*, *hora prima*, *hora tertia*, *hora sexta* (the hour in which Adam stretched forth his hand to the forbidden tree, and Christ his hands on *crucis lignum*), *hora nona* (Christ expires), *hora vespertina* (the Last Supper), *hora completorii* (Christ prays for his disciples): *Sermons*, ed. Devlin, pp. 364–5. The disposition of the hours is different in (for instance) the Hours of Our Lady's Dolours in the Arundel MS (ed. cit., p. 235). For other variations, see *Medium Ævum*, xliv (1975), 273. John Audelay's rambling, panoramic verses on the Passion, though headed 'Hoc incipiunt hore passionis' (*Poems*, ed. B. J. Whiting, EETS OS 184 (1930), No. 14), are but slightly related to the Hours.

19. For Philip, see F. J. E. Raby, *Christian Latin Poetry* (1927), pp. 395–401. For his poem, see *The Oxford Book of Medieval Latin Verse*, ed. Raby (1959), No. 256. Its phrasing sometimes betrays the influence of the

hymns of Fortunatus and the *Planctus Mariae*. For a Middle English version, see *Legends of the Holy Rood*, ed. R. Morris, EETS OS 46 (1871), pp. 131, 197. See also R. Woolf, *The English Religious Lyric in the Middle Ages*, pp. 252–3; and for an Anglo-Norman version see *Romania*, xiii. 521; cf. xliii. 21.

20. 'They saw three men coming out of the sepulchre and a cross following after them, and the head of the third figure overpassed the heavens, and a voice came from heaven saying: "Hast thou preached unto them that sleep?" and an answer was heard from the cross saying "Yea".' *The Apocryphal New Testament*, ed. M. R. James, p. 93.

21. Cf. Woolf, *English Religious Lyric*, p. 226.

22. The presence of Salome and 'Mary Jacobi' at the Cross, affirmed by Kennedy at 1081–2, is asserted by Nicholas Love *et al.* The (apocryphal) appearance first to the BVM after the Resurrection (1429) had long been accepted: it is represented in the east window of Fairford Church (Glos.).

23. *A Goodly Prymer in Englyshe*, sig. 3 E4ᵛ: cit. White, *The Tudor Books of Private Devotion*, p. 97. Ch. xiii of this book, on the 'XV Oes', should also be consulted.

24. Ibid., p. 147.

CHAPTER VI.

1. Moreover the Counter-Reformation itself by a restrictive policy as regards apocryphal materials (in particular those that had gathered round saints' lives) tended to dry up certain springs of devotion that sprang from the cultus of the Crucifixion. Michelangelo found the horrific and tearful elements in Flemish religious art abhorrent.

2. For earlier texts of the 'XV Oes' see *Devotional Pieces*, ed. Bennett, pp. i–ix, and R. Tuve, *A Reading of George Herbert* (1952), p. 119n. Thomas Dekker, playwright and pamphleteer, cites St. Bernard's rendering of Christ's plea from the Cross in the 'Pithy Sentences' appended to *Five Birds of Noah's Ark* (1609).

3. Louis B. Martz, *The Poetry of Meditation* (1954), p. 19; see also the useful appendix. J. A. Symonds had earlier taken note of the Jesuit mode of spiritual exercises (in a darkened chamber): see his *History of the Renaissance in Italy*, vi. 287 ff. He remarks that Sarpi (whose orthodoxy was suspect) followed a similar practice, meditating on a crucifix and a skull and the Agony of Christ (vii. 205).

4. *The Saints' Everlasting Rest* (1656); cit. Martz, p. 171.

5. See H. R. McAdas, *The Structure of Caroline Theology* (1949), Ch. iv and p. 138. He quotes (p. 157) a passage from Horneck's *Great Law of Consideration* (1676): 'Dost thou see a crucified Jesus stretching forth his Arms to embrace thee, and dost thou feel no warmth, no heat, no zeal, no devotion?' *The Holy Rood or Christ's Crosse Containing Christ Crucified described in speaking picture* (1609) by John Davies of Hereford contained just such images.

6. Cf. D. V. Erdman, *The Illuminated Blake* (1975), p. 355. The Cross is a Druidical oak. The figure of Albion is in a composite of 'Latin' and St. Andrew's Cross positions: see D. Hirst, *Hidden Riches* (1964), pp. 53–4.

7. The reference is to Col. 2:14. See also p. 164 below.

8. Cit. Helen Gardner, *The Divine Poems of John Donne* (1978), p. liii.

9. *Devotional Pieces*, Pl. opposite p. 7.

10. What Martz says of Crashaw in this respect (*Poetry of Meditation*, p. 115) could not be bettered.

11. The opening lines voice Donne's dislike of Precisians who were scandalized by roods or crucifixes, and of legislation against such furnishings (which came to be replaced by the royal arms).

12. See J. A. W. Bennett, *RES* NS v (1954), 168–9. For Justus Lipsius (who figures in Rubens' *Four Philosophers*) and his limitations, see Pickering, *Literature and Art in the Middle Ages*. The likeness to a mast had been noted by Minucius Felix in the second century; cf. the Old English *Exodus*, l. 82, and *Famulus Christi*, ed. G. Bonner (1976), pp. 197–203. The cross in the Towneley Plays 'stands up like a mast' (ed. G. England, EETS ES 71 (1897), p. 265): cf. the figure of the ship of the Church illustrated in Pierpont Morgan MS 799: the yard bears both Christ and a sail and the 'crow's nest' carries a pelican in her piety. St. Peter is at the helm. Gibbon cites the passage in Lipsius (*Decline and Fall*, ed. Bury, ii. 299, n. 29).

13. Cited from John Fewterer's translation (early 16th c.) of Ludolf's *Vita* by E. Salter, *Medium Ævum*, xxxiii (1964), 33.

14. 'Frown' (l. 6) does not necessarily at this date denote displeasure; it could here signify perplexity, bafflement at the cruel injustice meted out to him.

15. *Religious Lyrics of the XVC*, No. 92. Miss Woolf also noted this correspondence (*English Religious Lyric*, p. 227), and cf. her remarks on the Holy Sonnets (pp. 131, 133, 396).

16. *Religious Lyrics of the XIVC*, No. 15. Friar William had met the same antitheses when translating *Gloria Laus et Honor*: e.g. 'the volk of Gywes with bowes comen ageynst the / And we wyth bedes and wyth song meketh us to the' (ibid., No. 14). The version of *Popule meus* in Grimestone's Commonplace Book (ibid., No. 72) is in four lined stanzas, less effective and calling for more elucidation. A shorter poem on *Homo vide quid pro te patior* (from a Latin text ascribed to Philip the Chancellor, d. 1236) is printed ibid., No. 77; for an Anglo-Norman version see *Romania*, xiii. 58. Cf. also *Devotional Pieces*, item 13 and p. xvi.

17. Some clues to the development of the *Improperia* are given in Brown, ed. cit., p. 247. The Reproaches appear in England in the tenth-century *Regularis Concordia* (Hardison, 131–2) and have a place in *The Northern Passion* (ed. F. A. Foster) and the *York Plays* (ed. Toulmin Smith, p. 36. 127–30). Palestrina's setting remains the most memorable (see *The Oxford Dictionary of the Christian Church*, s.v. Palestrina).

18. See R. Tuve, *A Reading of George Herbert*; the polemic pardonably directed at William Empson for his misunderstanding of 'The Sacrifice' can be detached without detriment to Miss Tuve's main thesis. It is curious that Canon Hutchinson, the learned and discriminating editor of Herbert's poems, should have ignored entirely the association with the *Improperia*.

19. The Latin passage is the ultimate source of the Dialogue between Christ and the Angels in the Chester Ascension Play, which Miss Woolf traced as far as the *Glossa Ordinaria: English Religious Lyric*, p. 200, where she notes some pictorial representations of the winepress. Cf. also the *Bulletin of the Metropolitan Museum, New York*, 1964, p. 331.

20. Cf. (i) Dame Julian, *Revelations of Divine Love*, Ch. 12: 'but yet lekyth hym better that we take full homely his blessed blode to washe us of synne: for ther is no licor that is made that he lekyth so well to give us'; (ii) *Myrrhour of Our Ladye* (1530, p. 239): '. . . with three lyquores, that is with wepynge teares, with bloody swette, and with blode'.

21. *Religious Lyrics of the XIVC*, No. 77.

22. Cit. K. Young, *The Drama of the Medieval Church* (1933), i. 548.

23. See Tuve, *A Reading of George Herbert*, Pl. VII. The two scenes are lined by the depiction of grapes in the vineyard and by captions beneath them. Cf. also the bottom panel of the 12th-c. Mosan enamel cross reproduced (e.g.) by Miss Tuve as a frontispiece. Exegetes from Augustine onwards saw in the grapes of Numbes 22 a figure of Christ and in the staves on which they were carried the Cross. They appear thus in the English *Pictor in Carmine*, repr. by M. R. James in *Archaeologia*, 94 (1951), 161.

In the (old) Roman Missal the parable of the Vineyard as given in Matt. 21 is the Gospel for the third Friday in Lent; when the Lesson is Gen. 37:5–28: the story of Joseph betrayed by his brethren, who say, 'Come let us kill him': hence Joseph figures as an antetype of Christ.

24. The *Hours* have been published by George Braziller (New York, 1966) and provide a vivid example of the late medieval treatment of the Passion sequence. Still more pertinent is the alabaster Crucifixion (*c.* 1500) now in Norwich Museum: below each of the wounds is a chalice to catch the precious blood.

25. *Religious Lyrics of the XIVC*, No. 16. 19–24. For the history of the figure, see J. M. C. Spalding, *The Medieval Charters of Christ*, and Tuve, *A Reading of George Herbert*, p. 132n. See n. 41 to Ch. II.

26. *Religious Lyrics of the XIVC*, No. 91. 29–76. A 17th-c. variation is found in Alabaster's sonnet 'Upon the Ensignes of Christes Crucifyinge' (see p. 169 below):

> O sweete and bitter monuments of paine,
> Bitter to Christ who all the paine endur'd,
> But sweete to mee, whose Death my life procur'd,
> How shall I full express, such loss, such gaine.
> My tongue shall bee my Penne, mine eyes shall raine
> Teares for my Inke, the Cross where I was cur'd
> Shall be my Booke, where having all abjur'd
> And calling heavens to record in that plaine
> Thus plainely will I write: *no sinne like mine.*
> When I have done, to thou Jesu divine
> Take up the tarte Spunge of thy Passion
> And blot it forth: then bee thy spirit the Quill,
> Thy bloode the Inke, and with compassion
> Write thus upon my soule: *thy Jesu still.*

27. *Literature and Art in the Middle Ages*, pp. 285 ff.; cf. Tuve, *A Reading of George Herbert*, Pl. XI and p. 45, and J. A. W. Bennett, *The Humane Medievalist* (1965), p. 30.

28. *Three ME Sermons*, ed. Grisdale, pp. 69–70. The passage begins with an allusion to Orpheus and Amphion.

29. Herbert doubtless knew commentaries on the Psalms such as that by Cornelius a Lapide that embodied the accepted gloss on the verses cited. The stretching was also interpreted as part of the process of parchment-making (see Woolf, *English Religious Lyric*, p. 213) or of preparing a drumskin (see Pickering, *Literature and Art in the Middle Ages*, p. 299).

30. For an excellent discussion of these epigrams see the chapter by W. Hilton Kellcher in *The Latin Poetry of English Poets*, ed. J. W. Binns (1974). But it does not touch on No. XXI, discussed above. Miss Amy Charles (*George Herbert*, 1978) thinks that the *Passio* may have been a Lenten exercise, but one given special seriousness by Herbert's grave illness in February 1622.

CHAPTER VII.

1. See *The Sonnets of William Alabaster*, ed. G. M. Story and Helen Gardner (1959).

2. For the early dissemination of the legend in England see *The Legend of the Cross*, ed. A. S. Napier, EETS OS 103 (1894). For representations in English medieval art see (e.g.) G. McN. Rushforth, *The Early Glass of Malvern Priory* (1935), and A. S. Wayment, *The Windows of King's College Chapel* (1974).

3. In the 'Hymn to Christ' Donne had written of Christ as 'th' Eternall root / Of true love'. The engraving at the head of the verses represents minutely all the instruments of the Passion—including the cock, the anvil on which the nails were forged (shown, for example, in the *Holkham Bible Picture Book*, ed. W. O. Hassall (1954), fo. 51ᵛ), and a plant of gall.

4. See p. 164. Crashaw alludes to Cupid's arrows as superseded as weapons of love by Christ's wounds in a Latin epigram (8 April 1634). L. C. Martin (ed.), *The Poems of Richard Crashaw* (1927), p. 65.

5. *Religious Lyrics of the XIVC*, p. 118. For the Latin original of this and some striking earlier images, see ibid., p. 275.

6. I adapt the rendering of Pickering, *Literature and Art in the Middle Ages*, p. 303, to whom I owe this and the following quotation. Gotfrid perhaps knew the *Vitis Mystica* of St. Bernard, in which we find the following expressions: 'Cithara tibi factus est sponsus, cruce habenti formam ligni. ... Nam nisi ligno affigeretur expansus, neutiquam verborum sonum ederet tanquam citharans' (etc.). *Opera*, ed. Mabillon, ii. 440C.

7. See p. 165 above.

8. He may also have seen a crucifix mounted on a crossbow, as on that shown in Pickering, op. cit., Pl. 30b, which resembles one now in the Fitzwilliam Museum, Cambridge. I am not so sure as Pickering is that

Mathias Grünewald meant to suggest the bow-figure in his great painting of the Crucifixion.

9. For an account of them see K. J. Larsen in *The Latin Poetry of English Poets*, ed. J. W. Binns (1974), Ch. IV. Ronald Knox described Crashaw's Latin verse as 'Martial Christianised'.

10. *Poems*, p. 57.

11. *Poems*, p. 23.

12. Reprinted in *Wayside Poems of the Seventeenth Century*, ed. E. Blunden and B. Mellor (Hong Kong, 1963), p. 70.

13. By Veronica Delany (Oxford, 1978). The poem cited (*Crucifixus pro nobis*) is accessible in *The Oxford Book of Christian Verse*, ed. David Cecil, No. 179. For an allusion to Crashaw in one of Thimelby's poems, and other information about him, see *N&Q*, 1966, p. 256.

14. Ed. cit., p. 54. Cary's drawing prefixed to this poem shows a rayed Crucifixion with blood pouring into a chalice. Sister Delany suggests that this may derive from Rollenhagen's *Delectorum Emblematum Centuria Secunda* (1611), which George Wither had used. But the likeness is not close and the motif is common: cf. p. 226 above.

15. *Centuries of Meditation*, i. 86–7.

16. Cressy was chaplain to Lady Falkland and served Catherine of Braganza. His edition represents the last flicker of medieval spirituality.

17. It is one of the adornments of Belinda, in *The Rape of the Lock* :

> On her white breast a glittering cross she wore
> Which Jews might kiss, and infidels adore:

a discreet allusion to the Catholicism of the Ferrar family; the custom of kissing the cross on Good Friday (on which day the Catholic liturgy prescribes special prayers for the conversion of the Jews) gives the lines a special piquancy. It seems unlikely that non-Catholics wore crosses as ornaments at that date. Pepys, who owned a fine crucifix (*Diary*, 20 July 1666), had in 1674 (the year of the Popish Plot) been forced to deny that he had ever possessed such an image.

18. *Correspondence*, ed. R. W. Chapman, 13 Jan. 1759.

19. The influence of the liturgy for Holy Week in its late medieval and Renaissance musical settings must have been profound, but is immeasurable. For a brief survey of the subject, see Percy Scholes, *The Oxford Companion to Music*, s.v. Passion Music.

20. C. Brigg, Preface to *A Serious Call*, edn. of 1899, p. xxxiv.

21. See Austin Warren, *Richard Crashaw* (Louisiana, 1939), Pl. opposite p. 170. The passage from *Stimulus Amoris* is quoted, and translated, by Eric Auerbach, *Literary Language and its Public* (English edn., 1965) in the Excursus: *Gloria Passionis*, which is pertinent to the present study.

22. See R. Tuve, *A Reading of George Herbert*, Pls. II and IIIa, XIIIb. The *Biblia Pauperum* would more accurately be called, as Henry Guppy suggested, the *Biblia Predicatorum*. It was certainly not a 'poor man's Bible'.

23. *The Golden Legend*, trans. Caxton, Temple Classics edn., i. 113. For Christ's 'leaps', see R. E. Kaske, *Medium Ævum*, xxix (1960), 22.

CHAPTER VIII.

1. So for Samuel Butler, the most unorthodox of Victorians, in *Alps and Sanctuaries*, the Passion images that were objects of pilgrimage in the Alps symbolize the difference between the life he admired there and the arid or propagandist Protestantism against which he had revolted. D. H. Lawrence (*Twilight in Italy*, pp. 7–24) registers a similar if more complex response.

2. Unless we count Frank Prince's 'Soldiers Bathing', with its reading of Pollaiuolo's bloody battle-scene as a commentary on the Crucifixion:

> the picture burns
> With indignation and pity and despair by turns,
> Because it is the obverse of that scene
> Where Christ hangs murdered, stripped, upon the Cross, I mean,
> That is the explanation of its rage.

As a Catholic poet Prince can add:

> We too have our bitterness and pity
> And even we must know, what nobody has understood,
> That some great love is over all we do . . .

It is signalled in the evening sky by a 'streak of red that might have issued from Christ's breast'.

3. Notably in Jurgen Moltmann's *The Crucified God*, with its emphasis on the 'scandal' of the Cross and its reading of the *suprema verba* as a sign of Christ's profound abandonment by God. Von Hügel's remark that the theology of suffering is full of pitfalls for the high-minded (*Essays and Addresses*, ii, 1962) applies particularly to this Luthero-Catholic apologetic, though Moltmann does not commit the fault of viewing the Crucifixion as a martyrdom.

4. It would be easy to pursue this theme in the works of a more popular if more obviously Catholic novelist, Mr Graham Greene, though the words in which he suggests it often come *ex ore infidelium*: 'the search for suffering and the remembrance of suffering are the only means we have to put ourselves in touch with the whole human condition. With suffering we become part of the Christian myth' (Colin, in *A Burnt-Out Case*, p. 151): a comment that illuminates a passage in a slighter, earlier work: in *Stamboul Train* Dr Czinner, returning to Belgrade to die for his cause, catches sight of a silver cross: 'and for a moment flattened himself against the wall of a steep street to let the armoured men, the spears and the horses pass, and the tired tortured man' (p. 113, Penguin edn.). Similar perceptions can be found in such unlikely sources as Nathaniel West's *Miss Lonelyhearts* ('It is only through suffering that you can know Him': p. 51, Penguin edn.) and W. D. Howells's *A Hazard of New Fortunes*: 'We can't throw aside that old doctrine of the Atonement yet: the life of Christ, it wasn't only in healing the sick and going about to do good; it was suffering for the sins of others. That's as great a mystery as the mystery of death. Why should there be such a principle in the world? But it's been felt, more or less dumbly, blindly recognised ever since

Calvary. . . .' In James Agee's *A Death in the Family* it is the *suprema verba* of Calvary that convey comfort to the grieving widow (p. 107, Quartet edn.).

A recent French film version by Eric Rohmer of *Le Roman de Perceval* is said to introduce a striking symbolic re-enactment of the Passion: 'A brutally concise Latin text is sung as Christ, played by the actor who has been Perceval, undergoes arrest, interrogation, flagellation, humiliation and crucifixion, with a final thrust of the side-piercing lance' (*Cambridge Review*, 1980, p. 89).

5. Yet Moore's novel, which links Christ with the Essenes, gives no account of the Passion: like Lawrence he tells the Resurrection as simply recovery from the extremes of pain. I owe the quotation from Graves to Paul Fussell, *The Great War and Modern Memory* (Oxford, 1975), p. 119. Owen's sentences are from a letter to Osbert Sitwell, which pursues the analogy to the nailing of the feet and the cry of *Sitio*: see Sitwell's *Noble Essences*, p. 120. Paul Fussell is perhaps a shade too eager to classify such images as 'sentimental', just as his assessment of David Jones's Arthurian 'pastiche' misses the ironies and the bitterness.

A somewhat contrived painting by (Lady) Elizabeth Butler, entitled *Eyes Right* and showing a group of soldiers, followed by an ambulance wagon, passing a wayside Calvary, was widely reproduced in 1916: see *Country Life*, 1978, p. 155.

In *Mr Britling Sees It Through*, published in the same year, an agnostic civilian, distraught by the horrors of the War, likewise turns to 'a poor mocked and wounded God, nailed on a cross of matter' (p. 406; cf. p. 304); Wells was never to come closer to an understanding of Christianity.

6. T. Dilworth, *The Liturgical Parenthesis of David Jones*, Golgonooza Press, Ipswich (1979). Two allusions of a different kind require explanation at this date: 'the long trail awinds at 4.55 prompt' (*In Parenthesis*, p. 130) glances at a popular song; and 'men walk in red white and blue' (p. 186) refers to the colour of convalescent uniforms in military hospitals.

7. The picture is reproduced in *Agenda*, 49. The tree has some thematic resemblance to the Cross in the Psalter of Yoland de Soissons, a hybrid of artefact and twelve-branched, richly foliated tree with a Pelican at the top. According to the Old French version of the tale of Seth, the Earthly Paradise contains one tree in which a pelican nests, another in which God's son weeps for man. A miniature of the Crucifixion in the Psalter of Robert de Lisle shows a pelican in her piety sitting above the Cross (BL MS Arundel 83).

8. Siegfried Sassoon had seen the same resemblance, as had Whitman and G. M. Johnston, a soldier poet of the Boer War: see Jon Stallworthy in *Review of English Studies*, NS 31 (1980), 232.

9. *Agenda*, David Jones second issue (n.d.), Pl. 23. Ephrata is the ancient name for Bethlehem: Gen. 35:16, 19; 48:7.

10. Kipling's instinctive feeling for the *limes* was of the same order as David Jones's: he divined that the XXXth legion had been stationed on the Roman Wall thirty years before archaeologists confirmed his guess.

11. See p. 75 above. The book cited is *Meditations in the Time of the Mass*, a manual by Longforde.

12. The shock effects of phrases from secular song are not altogether different from those achieved by some medieval preachers: see, for example, Greene, *The Early English Carols* (1977 edn.), p. l.

13. p. 57. An earlier reference in 'had I the job of mortising the beams . . . I'ld take m'time and set that aspen transom square to the *Rootless Tree*' is surely (*pace* René Hague) to the Shetland carol cited above, ibid.

14. David Jones himself supplies a page of notes: but they are not exhaustive and some modern readers may fail to catch the echo of a once-well-known hymn in 'Before the fleeting hills / in changing order stood', or, later, the debt owed to Dunbar's 'Nativity' (l. 2) in 'all known clouds distil showers', a weighted allusion to his rendering of Isa. 45:8, *nubes pluant justum*, part of an Advent versicle. Dunbar's macaronic use of Latin verses anticipates Jones's.

15. Cf. Jones, *The Sleeping Lord*, p. 86.

16. See p. 56.

17. For example, he owed his knowledge of the Ruthwell Cross to the illustration of it in R. H. Hodgkin's *History of the Anglo-Saxons* (1935).

18. See p. 57.

19. See the Introduction to *The Ancient Mariner* (Rampant Lions Press, 1972), which adverts repeatedly to the Passion and the Eucharist, the supreme act of thanksgiving.

INDEX

Edinburgh University Main Library

Title: Poetry of the Passion : studies in twelve centuries of English verse /
Due: 16/12/2015 21:59:00 GMT

Total items: 1
23/09/2015   12:12

Please return books to the library from which they were borrowed.